MORE FROM OUR OWN
CORRESPONDENT

MORE FROM OUR OWN CORRESPONDENT

Edited by Tony Grant

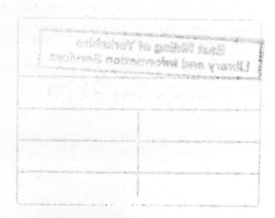

**LARGE
PRINT**

First published 2008
by
Profile Books
This Large Print edition published 2008
by
BBC Audiobooks Ltd
by arrangement with
Profile Books Ltd

UK Hardcover ISBN 978 1 408 41491 0
UK Softcover ISBN 978 1 408 41492 7

British Library Cataloguing in Publication Data available

Printed and bound in Great Britain by
CPI Antony Rowe, Chippenham, Wiltshire

CONTENTS

Correspondents   357

Introduction

Tony Grant

When *From Our Own Correspondent* started its regular broadcasts, in 1955, the BBC employed only a handful of foreign correspondents—and they didn't get out a great deal. In those days, the Corporation relied on international news agencies for coverage of foreign affairs and the small band of correspondents felt underused. FOOC, as we call it, was created specifically to give them more to do, it was to be a forum in which they could provide context and background to some of the stories in the news.

Today, the correspondent may possibly have a gripe or two, but being under-employed is not one of them. As BBC outlets multiply and staff numbers contract, the correspondent covering a major story can expect to make scores of broadcasts in a day with bulletins to be serviced, two-way interviews to be done, radio and television packages to be constructed and web-pages to be filled.

At the same time, budgets are under scrutiny as never before and a closer than ever eye is being kept on the news-gatherers' spending. In this climate, it's not surprising that many correspondents say FOOC is their favourite programme. It's a chance to forget productivity for a bit and to describe how it feels covering momentous events in often exotic locations. And when they're rarely asked to fill more than a minute or so of airtime, they welcome the opportunity FOOC gives them to sit down and write at some length, perhaps 800-words, a five-minute broadcast, about the story, the characters in it and the surroundings in which it is developing. While the other outlets rarely have the space to explore fully the context to a story, in FOOC the correspondent can explain the part history has played in shaping events. History is a feature of most of the dispatches aired on FOOC and it is the thread which pulls together all of the chapters in this book

Producing *From Our Own Correspondent* these last dozen years has been like a magic carpet ride. You arrive at the office at the start of each week not knowing which parts of the world you'll be taken to in the days to come, and what stories you'll be told. And working with the correspondents has been a richly rewarding experience; I admire hugely their professionalism, skill and their courage and would like to thank all those who've contributed to the programme over the years. Thanks too to my colleagues at FOOC: Andrea Protheroe, whose work on these pages has been invaluable, and Sarah McDermott. I would also like to express my gratitude to Malcolm Downing in the BBC's Foreign News department and to Christian Archer and his colleagues who work in News Traffic and are the first point of contact for the correspondents in the field.

As the correspondents' world changes along with the world around them, *From Our Own Correspondent* remains largely unchanged. In the fifty plus years that it's been on the air, the presentation style may have altered a bit, our office has moved from one BBC building to another and members of the FOOC team have come and gone but the formula for the programme remains the same: it still has no interviews, sound effects or mood music. It remains a simple collection of radio essays written by correspondents eager to tell you about events unfolding in their part of the world. I'm not sure how many other BBC programmes will be around to celebrate their one hundredth birthdays, but it's a fair bet FOOC will still be on air then, still celebrating the arts of writing and story-telling.

1

Blood on the Streets

Monica Whitlock

Hundreds of people were reported killed when security forces opened fire on a crowd of protestors in the Uzbek city of Andijan. The violence followed a court hearing in which local people were accused of plotting against the government. (19 May 2005)

They stood quietly, in their best clothes. Men on the right, their shoes polished, their hair combed. They barely spoke. They did not even smoke. Just a neat, double file stretching down the edge of the road. Then came benches, set out for the elders and the women, rows and rows of women in long headscarves and dresses in pale colours. There were babies and children, all in their best, in hair-ribbons and ties.

They had come to show that they could not bear any more. They needed justice for their relatives, twenty-three young men on trial, charged with belonging to a radical Islamic group bent on overthrowing the government. 'My son owns a café,' said one mother. 'He went to work one day and he didn't come back. He was a good boy, a good Muslim, I don't understand why they have taken him.'

Day after day, they came back. They stood in the rain, they stood in the snow. Spring came and they stood in the hot sun. More people joined in—

1

the ordinary, respectable residents of Andijan. They came, not just for these young men, but from years of sorrow, tolerated in silent patience. People whose businesses had been wrecked by extortionate tax, people who could no longer afford to eat properly. Most of all, people whose children had gone to jail, accused of plotting Islamic revolution in a state that brooks no opposition. 'My son, when they put him in prison, they taped a plastic bag over his head till he confessed,' said one mother.

One middle-aged man, Bahram, had two sons on trial and he had served five years himself. He invited us home. 'They beat us all the time. They shaved my head with a razor until the blood ran. They hung me up by the arms and poured icy water over me. Then they made us put our hands in dirty toilets and they didn't let us wash. I am telling you things I have never told anyone, I have never told my children. But I am telling you now because the time has come, we have to speak, we have to tell the world.'

And the demonstration grew, quietly, carefully. Boys brought tea and mineral water. Ladies baked cakes and handed them round. They cooked a lunch of rice and meat. And each day, as the court closed, they quietly walked home. They even swept the road behind them. On the ninetieth day 3,000 people politely, quietly, joined the line. 'We are here just because we want to lead normal lives like normal people,' said one. It was amazing. Was the tide really turning? Were the ordinary folk of Andijan proving stronger than the state?

On the ninety-first day the security forces moved in and that night a group of men, probably from the line, stole some guns and opened the prison, shooting the guards. They drove to the main square in Andijan and took over the mayor's office. Hundreds then thousands of people joined them, shouting: 'Freedom! Freedom!' Astonishing. Drawn by the commotion came thousands of others. People on their bikes stopped to look, stayed to hear some speeches. Bazaar traders came. Kids. It began to look as though, perhaps, the day had come. After all, what could the government do against such a huge crowd? President Karimov flew to Andijan in the small hours.

The president did not come to the square. He stayed, invisible, in Andijan. Then came the test. A soldier shot one young man, the cue for the crowd to run away. But they didn't, they ran towards the soldiers. And so it was over. Only later the story emerged from those who survived. They saw troops open fire straight into the square, spraying machine guns to and fro. It went on for three hours. Some people stayed put and read the last rites. Most broke for cover, racing down the streets, the soldiers at their backs. They ran into the narrow lanes of the old quarter and the soldiers ran them down. One family said later that their son went out to buy bread and was shot in the head. He hadn't even known there was a demonstration happening. Next day, residents were washing blood from the streets more than a mile from the square. Some people made it out of the city and they walked through the night to the border with Kyrgyzstan. Soldiers, they say, ambushed them as they tried to swim the river. 'I went to the square with my mum,' a boy told us,

3

weeping. 'I went for justice.' He was fifteen.

The government would say this story is a pack of lies. They say Islamic fundamentalists were trying to topple the government and the army fired only after hours of negotiations broke down. They say, too, there never was a demonstration in Andijan.

Change comes not when some group of radicals seizes power—that's just a shift at the top. It comes when Mr and Mrs Ordinary take a stand. When the cake-shop owner and the teacher and the barrow boy come together and say they are not afraid any more.

2

Monks Protest

Andrew Harding

Buddhist monks were marching in cities across Burma, calling for an end to the country's military dictatorship. (22 September 2007)

Rangoon is looking shabbier than usual these days. It's a damp, stagnant city trapped in a snaking curve of the Irawaddy river. Ancient buses rattle past gloomy warehouses and bright pagodas. Grand colonial buildings green with moss back on to dark courtyards reeking of sewage and decay. The generals who rule Burma moved out of the city last year, having built themselves a brand-new and spectacularly pointless capital nine hours' drive to the north. Thousands of frustrated civil servants were forced to follow them, almost overnight. Since then, the authorities seem to have stopped paying for Rangoon's upkeep. And the trees now loom low over the avenues, patting the heads of passing cars.

Today, somewhere in this city of nearly five million people, a Burmese woman called Nilar Thein is on the run. She's thirty-five years old, with a broad, open face, dark shoulder-length hair and a reputation for extreme stubbornness. She's been hiding for a month now, moving every couple of days to a new house, hunted by a huge force of security officials, policemen in plain clothes, informers and hired thugs. Nilar is number five on a long list of 'terrorists'—the generals' term for almost anyone who dares to challenge them.

They've already arrested her husband, Jimmy, and more than a hundred other pro-democracy activists. No one knows where they're being held or what will happen to them. The authorities stopped allowing the Red Cross to visit their jails and more than a thousand political prisoners a couple of years ago.

Nilar and Jimmy lived in a small second-floor apartment in the north of Rangoon. Not far away is the house where Burma's democracy icon Aung San Suu Kyi is still being kept under house arrest. Their apartment is now guarded by plain-clothed policemen. Two at the door. Two outside. Two across the road. They're waiting to see if Nilar will come back for something rather precious, her five-month-old daughter, Nay Kyi, or Sunshine. Nilar took the child with her at first. But Sunshine's cries were in danger of giving them both away. Now Jimmy's elderly mother is looking after her. One night recently, Nilar sneaked back close enough to hear the baby crying through an open window. 'They're using her as bait,' she said. 'I should be breast-feeding her. But I can't give in.' She has, a friend told me admiringly, an indomitable spirit.

Nilar and Jimmy are members of what's known as the 88 Student Generation, a reference to the last major uprising against the military here back in 1988. They've both spent time in jail already. Nilar nine years; Jimmy sixteen. They both thought hard about whether to have a child at all, given their particular lifestyles.

And now Rangoon is swirling with rumours that Jimmy's dead. Tortured and killed in prison. The rumours are very probably not true. Maybe they've been spread deliberately, to get Nilar to give up.

More likely they're just a product of the silence that festers here, in the absence of any independent news. The newspapers in Rangoon are all tightly controlled. No pictures of monks demonstrating this week. Instead there are photos of the generals giving lavish gifts to monasteries. Inside are venomous editorials—styled, it seems, on the North Korean model, lashing out at traitors within and devious foreign enemies. I read the papers over breakfast, then stepped out of the hotel wrapped in a cloud of paranoia. Surely the authorities have spotted the foreign journalist. Why is that man watching me from the café over the road? Did this taxi driver just happen to be driving past at the right time?

There is good reason to be wary. On the phone, diplomats and activists here talk carefully; no names, no details. Rangoon slang. In the past few weeks, hundreds of mobile phones have been cut off by the authorities. The police write down the number plates of cars on certain roads. Informers watch every street corner. E-mail is restricted. Yahoo and Gmail accounts are often blocked. Well, half blocked. For all the security and the fear, this is not a competently run country. And it's not China. Hotels and Internet cafés use dozens of proxy servers to bypass the government's crude attempts to police the Internet. And that's why footage of the latest protests here, of thugs beating up demonstrators, of hundreds of monks marching through Rangoon, is leaking out to the world.

The protests seem to have caught everyone by surprise. Certainly, almost no one expected them to gain such momentum. They were triggered by the government's unannounced overnight decision to slash fuel subsidies. Isolated in their new capital, the generals either didn't know or didn't care what impact this would have. But suddenly millions of people couldn't afford the bus home, or to school.

It's easy to miss the poverty here if you pop in as a tourist. The decay in Rangoon can seem quaint and rather exotic. But Burma is in real trouble. Over a third of children under five are malnourished. There are places along the Irawaddy where hunger is so acute that, a foreign aid worker told me, if this were Ethiopia we'd be calling it an emergency. But the generals are busy signing oil deals with China, buying weapons from Russia, building golf courses for themselves and selling hydro-electric power to Thailand, despite 90 per cent of families here having no electricity. And yet this was, and should be, a wealthy country. So what's gone wrong?

One rainy night I slipped out of the hotel and went to meet someone who knows the local economy inside out. We sat and talked in the back room of a bar. It took a while to work out what I could call him, or her, on the radio. The protests have made people ultra-careful right now—one foot out of line and they're convinced they'll just vanish into prison—so we finally settled on the necessarily vague title of a 'well-informed observer'.

'Officially,' the observer explained, 'Burma's economy is growing by a spectacular 12 per cent a year. But that's nonsense. The story goes that the country's senior general, Than Shwe, was chairing a cabinet meeting and simply announced that we need double-digit growth. And so a figure was conveniently plucked out of thin air on the spot.'

'This is,' the observer was starting to get worked up, 'the world's most inept government. It takes a lot of stupidity to run a rich country into the ground. The generals are good at cutting ribbons and opening dams. But they're barely educated, and incapable of taking advice. When they go abroad to meet their foreign counterparts at summits, they simply get bored, they can't actually follow the discussions of finance ministers with PhDs.'

'As for ordinary people, there's severe, silent suffering here,' the observer said. 'And when the generals doubled the price of fuel, people who live on twenty-five pence a day, families who eat one meal a day—well, they just fell off the edge of a cliff.'

The next morning, I watched a small boy racing through puddles to join a crowd scrambling for free handouts of rice. Gaunt men wolfed the food down where they stood. We were on the drab outskirts of Rangoon—a rainstorm had just swept across the Irawaddy; umbrellas sprouted like mushrooms on the muddy streets. The rice was leftovers from a nearby monastery. The monks had been round the neighbourhood with their own black alms bowls an hour earlier, collecting donations of food from local shopkeepers.

I went into the monastery, one of half a dozen clustered round a tall, golden pagoda. A row of brown, orange and maroon robes hung in neat lines from the wooden balconies upstairs. In the dormitory, the young monks were talking about the demonstrations. One flexed his muscles with a grin. 'We're ready to fight,' he said. The others nodded their shaved heads solemnly. One monk described an elaborate organisational structure linking monasteries around the country; plotting and planning. This week, hundreds of monks have already marched through Rangoon, some holding their begging bowls upside down. The meaning is clear: they are rejecting donations from the military. It is the equivalent of excommunicating them. One group released a statement calling the generals 'great thieves'.

So, how will the thieves react to this extraordinarily public humiliation? Will they crack down like in '88, or sit back and wait for fear to do its job?

There are 400,000 monks in Burma, and so far most have not taken to the streets. Sitting quietly in his monastery, an older monk explained to me: 'We are born afraid here and the army will never run out of bullets.'

9

Something has changed this week in Burma. Perhaps something profound. But there's a lot of wishful thinking going on too. It's so tempting to imagine a velvet revolution. Nilar Thein and Jimmy reunited with their baby daughter. Aung San Suu Kyi walking calmly out of imprisonment, her uncompromising stance finally vindicated after years of isolation. But the odds are still not good. The generals have their own version of reality; their surreal capital, their shiny new constitution. Their plans for carefully supervised elections later in the year. Somewhere in the backstreets of Rangoon, Nilar Thein is sitting alone and alert, waiting for the wrong sort of knock at the door. Hope is keeping her going. But in Burma, hope hurts.

3

Emergency Rule

Chris Morris

The Pakistani leader General Pervez Musharraf was under pressure to end the state of emergency he had imposed and to free thousands of opposition figures who had been detained. The Pakistani military meanwhile was involved in heavy fighting with pro-Taliban militants in the north-west of the country. Islamic militancy was one of the reasons General Musharraf gave for imposing the state of emergency. (17 November 2007)

I have images in my mind of all the main players in Pakistan's political drama as events have ebbed and flowed through the past two weeks. Benazir Bhutto, framed picture-perfect behind coils of barbed wire. Pervez Musharraf, wiping sweat from his brow and sounding combative. Imran Khan, gulping down a chicken burger before disappearing into the night, while he was still evading arrest. And lawyers, students, journalists, demonstrating on the streets, chanting in unison, the soundtrack of the state of emergency.

But beyond that there are the tens of millions of Pakistanis for whom emergency rule means nothing. Life goes on, shops open and close, the kids go to school. And there is a deep sense of disillusion with the entire ruling class, whether in or out of uniform. 'They play their games,' said a man in the chemist shop, his eyes glued to the TV screen, 'and we watch the cricket.' Sadly, Pakistan's finest were slipping to another disappointing defeat across the border in India—but the implication was pretty clear: generals and prime ministers may come and go, so too democracy and military rule, but nothing much will change.

And on the surface, that feels like a reasonable assumption, born of bitter experience. But one thing is different this time, a fact which Pakistan's moderate majority acknowledges with some discomfort. The threat from Islamist militancy, from people taking up arms against the state, is greater than ever before. It can be difficult to judge how serious the situation is; it's important to guard against over-dramatisation. But it is serious.

In Waziristan and Pakistan's other rugged tribal areas close to the Afghan border, peace deals with militants have collapsed. There is no civil administration. The writ of the state no longer runs there—it never really did. And some nasty people, local and foreign, are running riot. Of even greater concern is the Swat valley in the North-West Frontier Province. A place of high mountains, green meadows and dark blue lakes, it has Pakistan's only ski centre and likes to describe itself as paradise on earth.

But paradise has, for the moment, been lost. The Swat valley echoes to the sound of artillery fire and helicopter gunships. A series of towns and villages have fallen into insurgent hands, and the army is scrambling to win them back. Security officials have been beheaded; shops selling western music and Indian films have been set on fire; and schools for girls shut down. As Uzbek and Waziri militants mix with disgruntled locals, the insurgency could spread to other vulnerable areas. For now, Taliban-style Islamic law has been declared in places where everyone from the elite to ordinary families used to go on holiday. And that's got them spooked. It is a bumpy winding road to Swat, but the valley is only 150 miles from Islamabad. So there is a war on, and if you talk to Western and Pakistani security analysts here, many of them will tell you that in the last few months Pakistan has been losing. The winners have been forces linked to al-Qaeda and the Taliban.

If nothing is done to reverse that trend, they will have more room to manoeuvre, more space in which to operate and, in the long term, greater freedom to run training camps and plan attacks around the world. It is a grim prognosis, but one on which everyone seems to agree.

General Musharraf cites the threat from militancy as the main reason he imposed emergency rule. 'Is democracy more important than the country?' he asked rhetorically this week. 'If the country is becoming a failed state, which is more important? Obviously,' he concluded, answering his own question, 'save the government, save the nation.'

You can also hear Benazir Bhutto warning that 'the Taliban are getting nearer and nearer'. She vows to use 'empowerment, employment and education' to stop parts of Pakistan becoming the focal point of international terrorist plots which, she says, 'threaten us all'. But that's where she and the general part company. Elections under emergency rule, his current plan, won't produce a legitimate democratic mandate. And that's making a lot of people very worried.

Pakistan's politicians, of course, haven't exactly covered themselves in glory in the past. But one retired general I spoke to was adamant that real democracy has to be restored. 'I can't understand why Pervez doesn't see that,' he said, referring to the president who used to be his junior. He scratched his head with something approaching impatience. 'Musharraf means well, but he thinks he's the only one who can save us.' As he turned to leave, he stopped and took my hand. 'The army shouldn't forget,' he said. 'We have to have the support of the people to take strong action against extremism. Otherwise they'll think this is a war we're fighting for the Americans rather than for the people of Pakistan. It would be a disaster. We wouldn't win.' And that is why, beyond the sound and fury of the moment, events in Pakistan affect us all, wherever in the world we are.

4

A Railway Town

Artyom Liss

*The Soviets made special arrangements for the cities
they built in the more inhospitable corners of their
empire. Workers who braved the extreme cold in
Siberia were rewarded with bumper pay packets.
Special trains shipped in supplies of fruit and
vegetables from the orchards and fields of the sunny
south; there were paid-for holidays on the balmy
shores of the Black Sea. But with the demise of the
Soviet Union and the subsidies, some of those
communities became little more than ghost towns.
(3 May 2007)*

My train left Blagoveschensk, one of just a handful
of cities in the Russian Far East, at six o'clock in
the evening. By 6.15, all signs of human habitation
had gone. I was alone in my four-berth
compartment and the only thing I could see
through the window was the vast and empty
Siberian taiga. Every three hours or so, we stopped
in a tiny village. But there were no passengers on
the platforms, only guards in jaded uniforms and
old ladies selling fruit and vegetables.

This was a sixteen-hour journey crossing one of
Russia's eighty-nine regions; the size of Germany
but with a population of only 900,000.

My destination was Tynda, a model Soviet town built in the last decades of Communist rule. As our train slowed down somewhere in the outskirts, a huge building emerged from a seemingly virgin forest. Tynda railway station is covered in marble and granite and it's immense. Thirty years ago, thousands of young people came here, into the middle of the taiga, to build a railway. It was one of the Soviet Union's biggest projects: the Baikal-Amur line. Thousands of miles of track were laid on marshes and permafrost.

In the Soviet era, this project was the subject of numerous propaganda exercises dreamed up by Moscow. Back then, newspapers were full of reports about twenty-year-olds who put up with freezing cold in the winter and with swarms of mosquitoes in the summer; they lived in railway carriages, in tents, even in petrol tanks, and all because their country desperately needed the railway.

Now, most of these people are gone. In the 1980s, 80,000 people lived in Tynda. Only 30,000 remain. They haven't seen much change here. There are still red stars on lamp posts, and in the middle of Tynda's main road stands a huge bronze statue of a hammer and sickle. But the high-rise apartment blocks which line this road are now half-empty; and at the end of the street, a dairy farm and a bread factory stand in ruins. No work's been done here for years. Even at the railway station, everything is quiet. The cargoes the old Soviet government hoped would help to boost the economy in this part of the Far East failed to materialise and now, in the new, capitalist Russia, the station's quieter than ever.

A few minutes away, there's a neighbourhood which locals call 'The New Tynda'. In fact, it's the oldest part of the town. Here, people still live in converted railway carriages as they did thirty years ago.

Outside number 23, a scabby dog stands guard. It's too old even to bark at me; it just growls and bares its teeth in warning to stay away. This is the home of Yevgeni, one of Tynda's veterans. He was only five when his parents brought him here in 1973. They had always planned to leave the city as soon as the railway was finished. But they are still here. Yevgeni trained as an engineer. But the only job he can find now is as a security guard. For that he gets the equivalent of about £100 a month.

The road to Yevgeni's home isn't paved. There is no running water; no heating; no plumbing. 'I'd love to leave,' he tells me. 'But even if I find somebody stupid enough to buy this carriage, I won't get more than 250,000 roubles for it.' That's about £5,000. 'In any proper city,' he went on, 'that would probably buy me about five square metres of living space. I'd love to get out of Tynda—but I don't think I ever will.'

But while Yevgeni and thousands of people like him are dreaming about leaving Tynda, there are thousands queuing up to get in. They are not Russians. They're North Koreans. Just outside the town, there's a big wooden fence with barbed wire running along the top of it. If you peep in, you see neat rows of barrack blocks and a square with a big monument covered in Korean hieroglyphs. This is where the loggers live. There are now 1,500 North Korean lumberjacks in Tynda. None of them would give me his name, but all of them admitted

16

that they're in Tynda for the money. One lumberjack told me he would do anything not to return home at the end of his three-year posting.

He'll have to go, though. The authorities ensure nobody stays on in Russia. And so in Tynda, once a model Soviet town but now a place which has lost all sense of direction, there are thousands who want to leave but can't. And side by side with them, neighbours from abroad who are desperate to stay but who will have to go.

5

The Passionate Gardener

Chris Bowlby

In turbulent times, gardens can become places of privacy and retreat, even independence amidst totalitarianism. One belonged to a man who campaigned against the Nazis, lived through Communism and then German reunification.
(3 March 2007)

The garden centre and nursery in Zwickau where he worked, neat rows of greenhouses and piles of tools and pots, is still there, while the rest of this small town in Saxony has been swept through by the winds of German reunification. Blown away are most of the monuments of Communist rule. In front of the greenhouses is a garishly coloured Trabant car on a plinth, a mocking memorial to the crude contraptions that used to be made in a factory next door. What's left of that factory is now making parts for Volkswagens. Over the road, where the East German People's Army was based with its smoke-belching and deafening Russian tanks, is now a slick Land Rover showroom.

Herbert—he was my wife's grandfather, who died recently—was pleased that his garden centre had survived all this change, an island of green amid the advertising hoardings, a sign of the continuity of nature among the disarray of human change. The green spaces he created were not, however, simply retreats from the world, far from it. For Herbert the passionate gardener had also become a Communist in his teens. 'Bread and shoes politics', as he once described it to me, a response to the families in the depression with neither shoes to wear nor bread to eat. And when the Nazis took power in the 1930s, he waged from his potting sheds his own courageous resistance, until the Gestapo came trampling in and forced him to dig up the typewriter, buried in a flower bed, on which he'd been writing anti-Nazi leaflets. He was sent to prison, threatened with execution. But this indomitable handyman, desperate for freedom and the outdoor life he adored, had a metal file smuggled into prison inside a cake, and sawed away at the window bars of his cell in the night until he could escape and walk across the mountains to Czechoslovakia and Poland to eventual wartime exile in Britain.

It was a green but not altogether pleasant land he'd reached. He was detained initially in Britain as an enemy alien and sent on hazardous voyages to Australia and Canada, where he was able to gather information about local flowers and plants.

Finally, he was brought back and allowed to tend the English gardens he so admired. Among the papers he left behind after his death are grateful letters from a naval officer in Cambridgeshire and a golf club secretary in Cheshire, testifying to his dedication and green fingers. But after the war it was the red of Communism that drew him back to his home, where, he hoped, he could help a socially just, peaceful East Germany blossom out of the ruins left by the Nazis.

But back in his nursery he watched the tank drivers over the road assert themselves and the society, dominated by its Soviet occupiers, wither into bureaucratic dullness. Denied much chance to travel, he did his best to create gardens full of shapes and fragrances to remind him of other worlds. On his bookshelves, I remember finding volumes on the great English landscape gardener Capability Brown arranged next to tomes on Marxist-Leninist horticulture which he'd show me with a mischievous grin. He always enjoyed drenching arid ideology in copious sarcasm.

After retirement he created another extraordinary garden in the allotments near the block of flats where he lived. This kind of allotment, the *Schrebergarten* with its vegetables and fruit trees, flowers and summer house, is a great tradition all over Germany and was an oasis of colour and individuality amid the monotony of much Communist life. Herbert seemed most rooted there; master of his surroundings, at one with the seasonal cycles and good gardening order that formed a far more attractive regime than the political ones he'd known.

And then Communism came to a sudden end in

East Germany and he experienced, late in life, a final bewildering change. The Soviet occupiers left, but ghostly presences returned. We were sitting once in his home in 1990 when we heard loud banging from the flat above. Herbert went to see what was happening and returned pale and speechless. His neighbour had used his balcony, the sort of balcony Herbert filled with plants, to erect a huge German nationalist flag. He'd last seen such flags amid the chaos of the collapsing Weimar Republic as the Nazis took power, and now they threatened to loom over his old age as the political far right revived. His allotment became, I think, more important than ever, a garden in which finally to try to forget the Gestapo.

He's at peace now in a town cemetery enclosing all the history of his life. There are zones for victims of wartime bombing, for slave labourers killed under the Nazis, for Soviet soldiers and East German heroes of socialism. Herbert himself is in a communal grave, strewn with all kinds of flowers left as relatives come and go. Above, fine stands of trees offer exactly the kind of natural canopy he loved, Nature's reassuring framework for a life cultivated proudly among the storms and dramas of twentieth-century Germany.

6

A Bubble of Fear

Tim Whewell

The Russian republic of Kabardino-Balkaria, not far from the Black Sea, proved a challenging destination for the visiting correspondent. (20 November 2004)

There's a mournful turtle in a well-known children's cartoon. I've been racking my brains to remember his name, but for the life of me I can't. Anyway, that's who our minder reminded me of. He was a bony bureaucrat in a brown suit and ridiculously bulgy cap, as last sported by Soviet workers on propaganda posters *circa* 1978. His face was long, his tie even longer and his thin lips were permanently downturned. I'm not surprised. Because in a region—the Caucasus—where the guest is supposed to be king, I was a guest of a most unwelcome nature. And it was Nikolai's bad luck to be my host. Nikolai was the deputy minister of press of Kabardino-Balkaria. You probably won't have heard of it and there's no reason why you should. It's one of the chain of impossibly named Russian republics strung out along the southern foothills of the Caucasus mountains, each a tiny self-contained bubble of ambitions, rivalries, hatreds and feuds.

Kabardino-Balkaria is also a self-contained bubble of fear. And that's partly why I was going: to investigate reports that in the wake of the

Beslan tragedy, just a few miles down the road, many ordinary Muslims and political dissidents were being persecuted in the name of the fight against terrorism.

My fear began to increase as soon as Nikolai made contact. He started phoning me on my mobile even before I crossed the border. Could I tell him the registration number of my taxi so he could drive out and meet it? He needed to accompany me from the minute I entered the capital. And that was only the start. I couldn't, how could he put this more gently, I couldn't stay at the hotel I'd booked because I was his guest and there was a particular place where guests of the government always stayed. For their own safety. He'd organised a whole programme for me—breakfast, meeting with the writers' union in the morning, lunch, a children's exhibition on the theme of peace in the afternoon, dinner and so on. I didn't need to carry my bag of tapes and notes around with me. It would be quite safe in my room. And I would be quite safe. Provided I never left his side.

I got the message. I could hardly fail to, since I knew that all the other journalists who'd been to Kabardino-Balkaria recently and had not been guests of the government had not been safe. Some had had their rooms raided and their notebooks torn up. One was attacked by an unknown assailant, another detained for several hours by the secret police. All were followed wherever they went. Worse, far worse, the local journalist who'd helped them had been dragged away by spooks and had her fingertips burnt with a cigarette, to help her remember not to wash the republic's dirty linen in public.

'Oh, Nikolai, tell us a joke,' demanded his boss, the press minister herself, as she raised yet another glass at a banquet we were obliged to attend. She was called Lyubov Moroz—the first name means love and the last, frost—and with her big peroxide hair and glinting teeth just a shade or two darker, she had a certain Stalinist blowsiness that with a few more vodkas I could have warmed to.

But I was scared, with that knot in my stomach which gradually turns into a permanent dull ache. I had to slip away, escape into the danger zone, to meet the woman with the burnt fingers and find out what it was my hosts in the government didn't want me to know. I had my own taxi waiting. But Nikolai was after me. And it was almost a moment of triumph when we made a sudden U-turn and he sailed on by, his face as outraged as a mournful turtle's can be.

We met our brave contact in a dark cubicle in a café on the edge of town, but when we got back to the hotel there were policemen with Kalashnikovs waiting. 'The minister,' said the receptionist, 'has been phoning constantly. She's very worried about your safety.' But of course, the real problem is the safety of the people we met. It's shocking to find that in today's Russia there can be fiefdoms like Kabardino-Balkaria that run by the rules of twenty or thirty years ago.

A day later I was out of the bubble and back into the comparatively normal atmosphere of the next republic, North Ossetia. I'd dipped my toe into fear and removed it, with a delicious feeling of freedom as the last border checks were behind me. But Fatima with the burnt fingers has to stay. She

23

treats fear as an occupational hazard. And Nikolai the minder has to stay too, condemned now to face the consequences of being such a bad host.

7

The Foreign Enemy

Frances Harrison

There was growing anti-British feeling in Iran; the media was full of spy stories and people were being urged to have nothing to do with foreigners.
(21 June 2007)

Deep down, a surprising number of Iranians believe in the conspiracy theory about the British. That there is a British hand behind everything that happens in this country. America may be the Great Satan, but Britain is the smaller, more devious devil. It makes no difference if it's someone who supports or opposes Iran's Islamic system: both blame Britain. During the last election a British colleague went around asking people who they thought would win, only to find Iranians looking at him strangely and saying, 'Surely you know the answer, you're British.' Now some Iranians accuse Britain of trying to topple the regime by supporting insurgents and separatists and, well, by having diplomatic parties.

Islamic students gathered outside the British Embassy to protest at what they called the historical betrayal of Iran by the British

24

government. It was timed to coincide with the biggest diplomatic reception of the year at the embassy, the Queen's birthday party to which 1,500 people had been invited. Already some of the Iranian guests had been telephoned and warned not to attend and hardline newspapers ran a campaign against the party saying it broke the taboo on contact with foreigners.

Someone with a loudspeaker addressed us, saying 'BBC and Reuters, don't sleep, open your ears, open your eyes and report what is happening here.' It was rather uncomfortable being the BBC representative at an event where anyone who had contact with Britain was denounced as a dirty traitor willing to eat the birthday cake of the Queen of Lies.

We went to buy water because it was extremely hot—40 degrees Celsius. The shopkeeper asked what all the fuss was about. When we told him, he said: 'What nonsense, why are they attacking the British Embassy when they themselves have been put up to it by the British?' The conspiracy theory again.

An unwitting florist tried to deliver flowers to the embassy and was quickly intercepted. In seconds the arrangement was pulled to pieces. Later we heard the delivery man ended up in hospital.

There were clashes with the police as students from the *basij* or Islamic vigilante force tried to prevent any guests entering. Shiny diplomatic cars beat a hasty retreat down the road. Puzzled-looking guests tried to approach on foot. The traffic got worse and many people gave up trying to attend the party and went home. The riot police beat the students back down the street, surrounded a group of women protestors and pushed them with their riot shields and hit them with batons. To see male policemen beating women in all-enveloping black chadors was shocking, and all because of a party. That was when the security forces started confiscating cameramen's tapes and warning them to go. They did not want to be seen on TV beating their own people to defend the British.

The whole event took a more sinister turn as guests were videoed and photographed on the way in and out of the party. Some were arrested when leaving; one woman said plain-clothes agents had tried to drag her husband out of the car. The embassy spent two hours ferrying their guests out of the compound in diplomatic cars in order to ensure they weren't arrested while going home. This was a first for the Tehran diplomatic cocktail circuit.

But what does all this mean? In the view of the radicals now in power in Iran, those who have contact with the British are dirty Iranians. Imagine what it is like to be half-Iranian and half-British in this atmosphere. One of the slogans the demonstrators shouted was: 'Lackeys of the English—shame on you.' How does that make my colleagues who work for the BBC feel? Already the relatives of one of my staff members had told him the food in his home was not halal, or Islamically sanctioned, because it was bought with money that came from foreigners. The space is shrinking for those who want to bridge the two worlds of the West and Iran. Iranians who want to reach out to the outside world now run the risk of

26

being called traitors and foreign agents.

Already three Iranian-American academics who believed in building bridges between Iranian and US experts abroad have been jailed on suspicion of spying. The intelligence minister warned Iranians not to attend conferences abroad for fear of being used by foreigners. Several Iranian journalists and activists who've gone on training courses abroad have been interrogated and even arrested on their return—to the point that it's now too dangerous to hold such events.

When the reformists were in power, they spoke of dialogue among civilisations, of democracy and the rule of law. But the radicals around President Ahmadinejad constantly speak of the enemy and they do it so much that it's seeping into people's consciousness. Personally I am fed up with being cast in the role of the enemy just because I am a foreigner.

8

Time to Go

Pascale Harter

The bickering over who should lead the fifty-three-nation African Union was settled with the announcement that it was to be Congo-Brazzaville, with the country's president, Denis Sassou-Nguesso, taking the chair. (28 January 2006)

Everyone has heard of Sudan; few have heard of

Congo-Brazzaville. And if you have, there is a good chance you're thinking of the wrong place. Nestled in central Africa, Congo has always been overshadowed by its neighbour: once Zaire, now renamed, somewhat optimistically, the Democratic Republic of Congo. It's a bigger country with bigger diamond mines, bigger wars and even bigger dictators. It can be confusing, even for correspondents! As I prepared to leave for Congo-Brazzaville, a journalist from the *Guardian* asked me: 'Didn't that used to be called Zimbabwe?' Just like his country, President Denis Sassou-Nguesso is largely unknown to the outside world. I strongly suspect it is this, rather than his human-rights record, which has resulted in him nabbing the top job in African diplomacy.

I had been in Congo for several months when I first met him, face to face, or rather face to knee as it turned out. The meeting was not without some trepidation on my part. I'd already been thrown out of one press conference for not looking smart enough and I was keen to make a success of this one. In addition to being a frighteningly snappy dresser himself, the president was rumoured to be shy but utterly ruthless when angered.

I was just congratulating myself on the front-row position I'd managed to acquire for the president's speech when a scrum of journalists closed in around me. With bodies wielding cameras, microphones and tape recorders bearing down upon me, I was soon sinking. President Denis Sassou-Nguesso began his speech. It was in the local language of Lingala, in which I could order a litre of beer but could not follow the ins and outs of a peace agreement with Congo's rebels. So I settled in to study the great man up close. I noticed he was taller than I'd expected. Or at least he appeared to be from where I was now crouched.

After ten minutes I was getting cramp in one leg. After twenty minutes it was becoming unsavoury being squashed at the bottom of a rugby scrum of middle-aged journos in 35-degree heat, and I had cramp in both legs. Eventually I became, only dimly, aware of a pause in the president's speech. He was now looking down at me with one eyebrow raised. My arms had begun to wilt under the weight of the microphone and I realised with horror that I was resting against his knees.

'Who is that girl?' the information minister later told me the president had asked. 'She is very brave,' he apparently commented. Perhaps he considered me brave for resting against the knees of a man whose private army is said to have driven around town parading the severed heads of its victims aloft on car aerials.

I certainly felt embarrassed, but rarely did I feel brave in President Denis Sassou-Nguesso's Congo. Mostly I was afraid. I was afraid of being thrown out for writing about the violence which was still going on in the country's Pool region. This rebel stronghold had been sealed off by the government and was being used as a playground for the armed forces and ragtag militias to attack the population at will. But in the end it was not my reports of army offensives in the Pool which caused my expulsion from Congo.

That came later when, after reporting an outbreak of the deadly Ebola virus in the north, I myself became a suspected Ebola case. As I languished under armed guard in a military hospital, for President Sassou I became a diplomatic disaster. If the president expelled me to Britain I could infect everyone on the plane and start an epidemic in London. Never mind bird flu, Denis Sassou-Nguesso would go down in history as the man who exported to the West a disease both easily transmitted and almost certain to result in death within seven days.

In the end, as my symptoms subsided, it became clear I only had malaria, dengue fever and hepatitis and a third country agreed to accept me. As I stood on the tarmac of Brazzaville airport at 3 a.m., waiting for the hospital plane, a familiar figure pulled up in a sleek black car. It was the information minister with a message, and a gift from the president. 'These are for you,' he told me, handing me a pair of pyjamas with Denis Sassou-Nguesso's face emblazoned upon them in a Congolese pattern. 'And the president told me to tell you that he's not angry with you, Pascale, but he does think it's time you were going.'

9

Barrow, Bucket and Bag

Sue Lloyd-Roberts

Zimbabwe's economic crisis was deepening by the day. Its people were finding it harder and harder just to get by. (8 September 2007)

For a country which is in a state of economic

collapse, there is a surprising amount of movement in Zimbabwe today. Drive through the darkened streets of Harare at night, for there is no electricity, and you see hundreds of people walking purposefully at two and three o'clock in the morning. They are the few who need to get to work: only one in five of the adult population still has a job. They take up their positions on street corners waiting for a passing car or pick-up truck. There is no petrol and regular bus services are already a distant memory. 'I sometimes wait four or five hours to get to work,' one office worker says, 'but even the bosses don't complain. Everyone in Zimbabwe understands that life is difficult.'

A couple of hours later, as dawn breaks over the capital, the remainder of the population, the mothers and the unemployed, start forming long, silent queues that wind around entire blocks of the city. There's a rumour that bread could be arriving in the city today. Five hours later, people are still waiting. Policemen arrive, apparently helpfully supervising the queue and giving a surreal air of normality to the city scene. 'They just pretend,' says one man in the queue with five children back at home to feed. 'They get the first news if a lorry is on its way with bread, sugar or mealie meal and they jump to the top of the queue and loot the food.'

Once one of the richest countries in Africa, Zimbabwe has become a barrow, bucket and bag economy. You see people walking for miles, wheeling barrows, buckets on their heads and plastic bags in hand. Like the 'bag ladies' in the former Soviet Union, always ready just in case something turns up. But it seldom does. People are starving. The evidence is in the hospitals, where tiny, wizened babies lie dying in their cots while their mothers look on helplessly. A mother cradles a child who is losing her hair and her skin, a sign of the most advanced stage of kwashiorkor, a form of malnutrition normally associated with famine. It's certainly the first time I have seen this in twenty years of reporting on the developing world. 'Zimbabwe once offered a model for public health in Africa,' a doctor complains. 'It's now becoming a textbook case of medical horror.'

Many children arrive with grandmothers. Grandmother- or child-headed families are a growing social phenomenon in Zimbabwe today, the result of the AIDS epidemic or because, if parents still have the energy and the means, they have fled abroad to look for food and to send back money.

Buses loaded with people and luggage wait for days around the petrol stations on the roads leading out of the country. When fuel eventually arrives, they lurch off, swaying precariously with the weight of passengers, on the five-hour journey to the border with South Africa. Zimbabwean immigration officials don't bother them and on the South African side they can be paid off with bribes. For those who don't have the money and who have to duck through the bush, there's greater risk. Gangs wait on either side of the river for the groups of desperate refugees. 'They had guns and knives,' one girl tells me. 'There were fifteen boys and five girls in our group. They killed one boy when he refused to give them his shoes. They raped all the girls.'

Still, they arrive in South Africa at the rate of thousands a week. The many victims of political persecution will never go back while President Mugabe is alive. Others just come for a few weeks to make enough money to take home. I met two teachers—Liliana told me she worked as a domestic cleaner while Patience told me she worked as a prostitute. 'What else can I do?' she says. 'My husband is dead and I have three children back home to feed.'

It's a situation that suits the governments on both sides. Among the refugees there are doctors, engineers, agricultural experts, just the kind of people who are needed by South Africa's growing economy. Zimbabweans have long since given up hope that the South African leader, Thabo Mbeki, will put pressure on his old friend Robert Mugabe to reform. And as for Robert Mugabe? 'This makes him a very, very happy dictator,' an opposition politician in Harare tells me. 'He gets rid of his opponents and they in turn send back money to their families in Zimbabwe and that keeps things ticking over.'

Anyone expecting a swift conclusion to Zimbabwe's agony will be disappointed. Thanks to the ingenuity and tolerance of people still in the country and the remittances sent back by those who have left, Zimbabwe's death throes could last a long time yet.

10

Gordon of Africa

Mark Mardell

Gordon Brown, before becoming British prime minister, was the chancellor of the exchequer. On a visit to Africa he signed a deal with Tanzania which would see London take care of 10 per cent of that country's international debts. (15 January 2005)

The shops don't look like they should stay upright at all. Odd angled bits of tree are forced into unnatural union with what appears to be parts of a corroding mangle, to form something a bit like a shack, but with none of the easy elegance and precision that word implies. 'This is Africa's largest shanty town, right?' I ask the treasury official. 'Slum, Africa's largest slum,' she replies forcefully.

This tour is deliberately unvarnished. When you go abroad with the prime minister, the plane, specially chartered, is never less than immaculately turned out. But Gordon Brown, hardly ever before spotted out of a suit, is jacketless, tie-less; Gordon unplugged. Rumpled, crumpled and he looks like he's slept in his clothes. That's probably because he's slept in his clothes on an overnight commercial flight. No time to waste here. It's not yet dawn in Britain as we march through the shanty—sorry—slum town.

Gordon and his treasury team have the excited and, at the start, somewhat apprehensive air of classical scholars suddenly transported back to ancient Rome. This is the stuff they've read about, they've written about, but it really exists—you can touch it and smell it.

One of the thrills of travelling alongside the prime minister is the motorcade. Lights flash, sirens scream, as police force lesser mortals to screech to a halt and drum their fingers as you hurtle serenely past. But, of course, however much he might like to be, Gordon Brown is not prime minister, and travelling abroad with him is more the Treasury's Adventure Tour rather than Downing Street's Package Deal.

On the next leg, the policeman at the dusty crossroads halts a man on a bicycle which seems to defy all known scientific laws, because it carries a tottering tower of green crates filled with empty bottles that don't fall over. Our motorcade, well, several minibuses marked VIP and Press, as appropriate, takes another left turning, taking us deeper into Tanzania's rural hinterland. Men and women stop working in the fields and lean on their hoes to get a good look at the unaccustomed traffic. A little girl playing in a giant tyre waves, and when we wave back, ducks down giggling. Even a goat stops chewing and stares vacantly at our progress. For the chancellor has made it clear he doesn't want to be dragged around shiny, new projects in the capitals but wants to smell, to breathe, the real Africa.

The village we are visiting seems to have few men, slightly more women and absolutely hordes of children: gorgeous, polite, laughing children, in bright white shirts that have been washed nearly to death. The girls in bright indigo skirts, the boys in

35

khaki shorts, both heaving mattocks that are somewhat longer than themselves.

The whole trip, in a way, is about children, and Gordon Brown does try to engage these small representatives of the future despite his total lack of easy small talk. 'How do you do? Very pleased to meet you,' he says formally to a bewildered Swahili-speaking seven-year-old. Emerging from examining the sparse inside of a mud hut, he asks the question he asks all children he encounters: 'Anyone here want to be a doctor? Anyone here want to be a teacher?'

'Anyone here want to be a prime minister?' I chip in, but disappointingly Gordon's hand doesn't shoot up. I sense the chancellor is a man who knows he must unbend, unfurl the personality that inspires such fierce destructive love in some political friends; but it's a process he seems to find rather vulgar and embarrassing.

In one briefing he's asked: Does having a son of his own now make a difference to the way he views the plight of Africa's children? His hands knot together convulsively, a few seconds pass before he answers briefly: 'Yes, of course.' Perhaps he just finds all this personal stuff a bit off-putting. Not that he's incapable of sound-bites: he says he's now seen 'grinding, relentless poverty' and so has 'had a glimpse into the aching soul of millions'.

The trouble for his vision may be that what we've seen is just normal, workaday, routine poverty that nags dully. In this village, gulping back some mineral water, I realise that a middle-aged woman is eyeing my nearly empty plastic bottle. A security officer has given his empty one to the local matriarch, and when I hand mine over to this woman, she hoots with delight, laughing, showing the label to all her admiring friends. No tragedy this, but it's humbling—a slamming home of the great gap between us. For about half a minute the thought crosses my mind of emptying the pounds in my pocket, that's licence-payers' pounds of course, not mine mind you, into more deserving hands.

The chancellor, similarly, is asking the West to make a collective, dramatic gesture. I wonder whether much of the world will regard it as a slightly daft notion which will pass, given thirty seconds' thought.

But the chancellor, even in tropical gear, attempting to chat to uncomprehending African children and awkwardly sharing his feelings, is not what you'd call a flighty man. In fact he's doggedly persistent, and world leaders may expect many a lecture now from Gordon of Africa.

11

The Senator from Nimba County

Bill Law

After years of bitter civil war in the West African state of Liberia, some semblance of peace and democracy had emerged. The country had set up a truth and reconciliation commission, modelled on the one in South Africa, and former warlords were embracing the political system. One of them was Prince Johnson, who had been involved in the torture and

37

assassination of the country's former president,
Samuel Doe. (4 November 2006)

We had just parked up outside the Capitol building in downtown Monrovia. It was another sweltering afternoon and it felt like hard rain was just a moment away. 'I'd like to see this man,' said our driver, James, 'do you mind if I come with you?' We didn't mind at all. James had been guiding us heroically through the decaying and potholed streets of this war-battered capital city for a couple of days now. Usually he'd wait patiently in his ageing Nissan while we went about our business. But I could understand his interest in the senior senator from Nimba County. Prince Johnson is better known as the man who presided over the torture and assassination of the then Liberian president Samuel Doe in September 1990.

Even by the standards of the time it was a particularly brutal slaying. Before he was killed, Doe was mutilated, his ears sliced off. Prince Johnson supervised the proceedings sitting in a chair while one of his soldiers fanned him. The whole affair was videotaped and bootleg copies, I was told, are still doing the rounds in the markets of Monrovia.

The lights were out in the Capitol building so we had to feel our way down darkened corridors to Prince Johnson's office. An aide, built like a tank and just about as menacing, gestured me to a chair to wait for his boss. James hunched up in a corner. I picked idly at bits of weed that had caught on the cuff of my trousers, dropping them on the floor. Suddenly the tank barked: 'What are you doing? You are littering. Stop now!' I weighed up a cheeky

38

response, something about the teeming mess and chaos that is Monrovia, and thought better of it. Then the senator from Nimba County swept in. A big man wearing a traditional African robe, a man used to giving orders and being obeyed. It was his forces coming from the north, from Nimba, which had routed Doe's soldiers back in 1990, driving them out of a region where they had committed numerous atrocities.

These days Prince Johnson says he has found God. 'I am a pastor, a Christian. God is in control. I have no fear.' He doesn't want to talk about the killing of Samuel Doe. 'Old news, dead news,' he says, one big hand slicing down emphatically to make the point. 'The people are tired of fighting. Change must be done through the ballot box. No more bullets.'

But he does want to talk about the army. It was disbanded as part of the peace accord that three years ago finally brought an end to a brutal fourteen years of civil war. Under the deal, ex-soldiers were to be honourably discharged and paid off. They've been demobbed, but many of them haven't got the money and they are not happy. In his role as head of the Senate Committee on National Security, Prince Johnson has positioned himself as their champion. 'It's a very dangerous situation,' he says, 'that's why I have told the senate to address the issue.' According to him, these ex-soldiers have easy access to arms. As in the past, they are prepared to fight for whoever will pay their wages. So is he telling the president Ellen Johnson-Sirleaf of his concerns? He sighs: 'She needs help, she is getting bad advice. My advice is being ignored.'

39

Prince Johnson fell out with Johnson-Sirleaf's party prior to last year's election. So he ran as an independent in Nimba County. He didn't get around to campaigning until ten days before the vote. When he did, his message was eloquent, if not Christ-like in its simplicity. 'I said: "People of Nimba, don't forget yesterday. God used me as an instrument to save you. So choose between those who ran away and I, Prince Johnson, who gave my life for you."' They got the message and he romped home with a huge majority.

And since he had raised that prickly question again, I asked him if he was responsible for Doe's murder or was it the case that he had lost control of his soldiers? At that he bristled: 'I was in perfect control. The commanding officer takes responsibility for what his unit does. Anything happened to Doe, I was responsible.' It was then the large aide abruptly fired another broadside. The interview was over: the senator had another pressing engagement. I had one more question, though. Did he have presidential ambitions? Prince Johnson paused. 'I cannot rule it out,' he said, 'but let me tell you, I always ask God to help me live one day at a time.'

Then the senior senator from Nimba County ushered me out. In the forecourt, James coaxed the Nissan into life. As we slid out of the parking lot blinking in the harsh afternoon light, he scrunched down in his seat. 'That man,' he said, 'is a hard man. What he says, he means. I was shaking the whole time you were talking to him.'

12

The School at Chocolate City

Elizabeth Blunt

During the years of civil war in Liberia in the 1990s, newspapers closed down and radio stations went off the air. Soon the only news Liberians had of what was going on in their own country came from the BBC, and from its West Africa correspondent at the time, Elizabeth Blunt. She rapidly became something of a national figure, so famous that she even had a primary school named after her. (1 September 2005)

The first time I saw my school, the rain was coming down in torrents. We'd inched our way through Monrovia's port area, past UN checkpoints, zigzagging round the potholes. Eventually we turned off to the right at Chocolate City junction. I had been warned the road was 'sandy'. That must have been in the dry season. Now it was liquid mud. We lurched and splashed our way down the road. Finally there it was, a neatly painted signboard: Elizabeth Blunt School; and underneath, its motto: 'Education, the soundest investment'. But the little block of classrooms was shuttered and empty: it was the school holidays. A woman appeared at the next-door house.

'Good morning,' I said. 'My name's Elizabeth Blunt.'

'Yes, yes,' she said. 'This Elizabeth Blunt. Elizabeth Blunt School.'

'No,' I said. 'It's me. I'm Elizabeth Blunt.'

The first word I'd had of this school came shortly after I finished reporting from West Africa in 1991 in a letter saying some people were planning to start a school and did I mind if they called it by my name. I replied that I would be honoured, and waited for more news. But what had seemed like an end to the fighting was only a brief pause, and the school owner, the teachers and the pupils were scattered by the fighting. It was only in 1998 that the school got going again and only at the beginning of last year that a letter finally came with a photo and the address in Chocolate City.

Once we'd sorted out the confusion, the woman introduced herself as Esther, the proprietor's wife and school cook, and arranged for me to come back and meet her husband and the staff. Two days later the sun was shining and all the staff and a crowd of children had turned out to meet me. I saw the seven little classrooms; concrete walls, mud floors and just a few sticks of furniture. The children had to bring their own stools, I was told, or else the teachers piled up bamboo stems and the children perched on top. Most of the classrooms had new tin roofs, thanks to kind colleagues who visited the school earlier. But the end two still leaked and so did the kitchen, a little bamboo and tarpaulin shack where Esther cooks lunch for more than 200 children a day. The food, bulgar wheat and beans, comes from the UN school feeding programme and there are greens from her own garden, but the UN are threatening to stop the rations unless the school upgrades its kitchen. The Red Cross gave them a few tables, UNICEF a kit

42

of chalks and pencils and notebooks. But like so much in Africa, this little school defies financial gravity. The figures don't even begin to add up, yet it's still there and teaching.

Liberians are proud of being Africa's oldest independent republic, but most of their governments have been spectacularly useless, so they've got a robust tradition of getting together and doing things for themselves. The school's founder, James Mamulu, was working abroad when war broke out in Liberia in 1990, and he came home to get his family out, only to be trapped himself by the fighting. All the schools were closed, so when things quietened down a bit he started a little do-it-yourself school for his own children and grandchildren and the children of his neighbours in Chocolate City. A few months later the war came back and they were right in the line of fire; the Mamulus fled so quickly they didn't even have time to bury a dead relative's body before they went. They went to Lofa County, near the Guinea border, but the war followed them there too. It was only in 1998 they were able to come home.

There was still no school for the children and most people had no jobs. Given the choice between teaching for no pay, or doing nothing at all, local teachers rallied round and the school began to take shape again. Now it teaches around 250 students, including a few former child soldiers, children from the local displaced people's camp and a forty-three-year-old woman, who joined the second-grade class to learn to read and write. Some can afford to pay school fees; most can't. The school is registered and recognised by the

43

Ministry of Education and the children have begun to take public examinations.

My morning in Chocolate City was a great delight. Although it's grown the school still has a family feel and, despite the difficulties, its staff are serious. As for the children, when I produced a big bag of lollies they came forward politely one by one, the smallest at the front, then whooped with glee when they discovered the lolly sticks were also whistles. The Elizabeth Blunt School is a credit to all of them and I'm proud to share its name.

13

A Modern Aesop's Fable

Hamilton Wende

'The eagle has landed' is one of those phrases which everyone knows, even if they've forgotten they were words spoken by the first man on the moon, Neil Armstrong. They may also have occurred to our correspondent when he was rudely awoken while trying to catch up on some sleep in Zambia.
(24 March 2007)

The crash was terrifyingly loud. I was sitting upright naked in bed in my hotel room when a spray of glass shards shot across the room covering the bed and floor. It left me utterly disorientated. My mind raced back to the war zones I had covered. Explosions or gunfire that I had experienced in Baghdad, Congo or the townships in South Africa all came flooding back to me.

But this was a quiet Sunday morning in downtown Lusaka, the capital of Zambia, a country that has never known war, and it just didn't make any kind of sense. My hands were shaking slightly and my head spinning as I threw back the covers and scrambled out of bed. Lying on the carpet below the shattered window was an eagle. It was, well, spread-eagled on its back amid the shards of broken glass.

For a moment I stood there, transfixed, staring at this bizarre phenomenon. The great sandy-coloured bird looked almost human in its semi-conscious distress. Its large wings were fully extended almost to the length of my own arms, its feet opening and shutting uncontrollably, its eyes fluttering half-open. There was something hauntingly beautiful in the deep brown colour of its eyes, in the curve of its sharp talons and in its long, scythe-like beak that would tear the flesh of my face and arms to shreds in panicked incomprehension if I picked it up.

I didn't know what to do next. I knew I had to act before it regained full consciousness. First I ran into the bathroom and wrapped a towel around my waist, partly to protect my dignity and partly to protect everything else.

I then tried to open the door, which led on to a balcony, so the bird would have an escape route. But the door kept slamming shut, on an automatic spring, so somehow I managed to wedge it open with a plastic waste-paper basket. All the while the eagle was beginning to wake up and stare at me with increasingly bright and, it seemed to me anyway, angry eyes as if it blamed me for its

45

predicament. Finally, I slipped on a pair of sandals and grabbed another towel. In a sliding, and certainly indecorous, series of panicky movements, I rushed across the sea of broken glass and wrapped a towel around the eagle.

I held it in my hands for a few moments, aware of the strange paradox of vulnerability and power contained in its warm, surprisingly light body. Its head was held straight on its shoulders. It was clearly coming to. I threw it gently out through the remains of the window. It stretched its wings and flew unharmed into a nearby tree.

As I got dressed I found myself wondering what extraordinary circumstance had brought an eagle to crash through my window. There seemed something both wonderful and vaguely disturbing about it.

My Zambian colleague was visibly distressed when I told him. 'It's a bad omen,' he said. 'Most people here believe that something terrible will happen to you now.' I didn't want to believe him, but secretly I was uncomfortable. Eagles and omens have been part of both African and Western mythology since earliest times and we cannot shake off our primal psychological feelings that easily.

The front-desk manager was both fascinated and appalled. 'I must make an immediate physical inspection,' he said, and soon my room was filled with hotel staff staring open-mouthed at the litter of broken glass and feathers. The story spread quickly through the hotel, becoming a kind of Aesop's fable for the age of air-conditioning.

'We have found the bird,' the security manager told me at breakfast. I was escorted to a room beneath the kitchen where, with a dramatic flourish, he pulled a dead pigeon out of a drawer.

'No,' I told him. 'It was an eagle. A big eagle.' I spread my arms out to make my point.

'I told you so,' a young security guard said triumphantly to his boss. 'It was chasing that little bird. The pigeon hit the window first and then the eagle crashed through the glass.'

The case had been solved.

But there was still the lingering omen to be cleared up. They gave me a new room, and all the next day the staff looked at me curiously. 'No birds this morning?' one of the elevator technicians asked.

Finally, the young security guard came to me in the lobby. 'You must not be worried,' he said, 'about the meaning of what happened. It is a good sign. That pigeon was seeking your protection. It means you are a man who has kindness.'

Of course, I hadn't the heart to point out the irony that it was the pigeon which died, and the eagle which was saved.

14

The Last Storyteller

Richard Hamilton

After more than a thousand years, the art of storytelling was under threat in the Moroccan city of Marrakech; fewer and fewer men were telling the stories which had been handed down from

47

Legend has it that the muezzin, the man who called the faithful to prayer at the top of the main mosque in Marrakech, had to be blind. It was thought that a sighted man might gaze down from the Koutoubia, as it's called, into the sultan's palace below and see his harem. But a sighted man would also see the wild teeming maelstrom of Marrakech's main square, or Jemaa el-Fna. He would see fire-eaters and fortune-tellers, acrobats and snake charmers. For all human life is here: if you walk into the square you will be besieged by men with monkeys and women trying to squeeze henna on to your hands. And then there's the noise: the square is a cacophony of drums, reed pipes and songs performed by musicians from sub-Saharan Africa.

But if you can find a quiet corner in the square you might just come across the city's hidden gems. They may not be the most obvious entertainers and they are certainly not the loudest, but if you can seek out a storyteller, or a *halaka*, you are in for a treat and an old one at that. Because storytelling in Morocco is as old as the hills, as ancient as the Atlas mountains.

I found Moulay Mohammed, a bearded man with a few missing teeth, sitting in the square in his grey *jellaba* surrounded by a circle of onlookers. He is seventy-one and has been a storyteller for forty-five years. He used to come as a boy and listen to the old men in the square tell their stories, and he was so entranced by them that he became one himself. He says he knows most of the Old Testament and all of *A Thousand and One Nights*.

According to legend, to prevent her murderous husband King Shahryar from killing her, the Persian queen Scheherazade told a story every night for a thousand and one nights. Moulay Mohammed is like a modern-day Scheherazade: he tells tales of sultans, thieves, wise men and fools; he speaks of mystics, genies, viziers and belly dancers.

Moulay Mohammed told me it's not just what he says that counts but how he says it. And even if you don't understand a word of what he says, it's still fascinating to listen to a *halaka*. You can sense the drama of the story and feel its suspense. His words are precious and they seem to hang in the air.

Today more than 40 per cent of all Moroccans are illiterate, so the oral tradition is vital. Of course storytelling is a form of entertainment, but it's much more than that. Like the parables of the New Testament, the stories are ways of conveying ideas, values and philosophies. But all this is under threat. While there used to be twenty or so *halakis* in Marrakech, there are now only about half a dozen and they are all old men. After more than a millennium, the art of the *halaka* is on the wane. Young Moroccans would rather watch TV soap operas than listen to a storyteller, much less become one themselves.

However, the United Nations cultural organisation UNESCO has intervened to try to save the stories as part of the world's oral heritage. It's even recording some of them on the Internet, so modern technology may yet come to the rescue of these wondrous tales.

I asked Moulay Mohammed if he would pass his skills on. 'If someone wants to come and learn from me they can, but it's not easy,' he said. 'It takes years to remember these stories.' And was he worried that his craft might one day die out? 'Ah, only God knows the answer to that. Today there are storytellers. That is all I know.'

Another old man was sitting in the crowd hanging on Moulay Mohammed's every word. Did he think the storytellers would still be here tomorrow? 'Moulay Mohammed is one of the best in Marrakech and we like him very much,' he said. 'But if he disappeared, a lot of his yarns would disappear too.'

And what, I wondered, did Moulay Mohammed make of television? 'Television?' he laughed. 'Why, it is something out of this world. This is real life here in the square. It is much better to sit in the square in the sun, as you are doing now, than in some dark room with a television!'

And sitting in the Jemaa el-Fna under an azure sky, I thought Moulay Mohammed was probably right. Looking up at the pink rooftops of Marrakech, the peaks of the Atlas mountains and the fabulous Koutoubia mosque, it was hard to imagine a place where I would rather be.

There may not be a blind muezzin any more in the minaret of the Koutoubia, but the story of the men who could not look down on the sultan's harem strikes a familiar chord now. The Moroccan government has just blocked the Internet device Google Earth so that people cannot look from above into the grounds of the king's sumptuous royal palaces. Perhaps in a thousand years people will be telling a story about that.

15

Leaving for Good

John Laurenson

Tens of thousands of Africans were taking their lives into their hands, trying to cross the Mediterranean to Europe on whatever vessels they could find. Many never made it. (30 June 2007)

It's dusk and a train full of rock rumbles and clanks through from the mines on its way to the port at Casablanca. A sound the people of Khouribga hear every hour, every day and night. Right now, children will be listening to that train as they lie in bed. Doctors and bankers who stop off at a park outside town after work for a beer out of sight of their disapproving fathers will be pausing in their conversation. And some will hear that train knowing that tonight they too will be leaving. For good.

Khouribga, 'Phosphate City', is also a capital of illegal migration—that desperate lunge for a better life that they call in Arabic the *hrig*. Around town, the working-age men I meet dream of getting out. Hamid is twenty but he's already given up hope of ever finding work here. Last year he went down south to Laayoune. He and four others stowed away in a cargo vessel that carries sand to Las Palmas in the Canary Islands.

'We got caught that time, but I'll try again,' he says. And what sort of work will you do when you get to the other side? *'Trabajo!'* he says, the first word he's said to me in a European language. 'Work! I don't know, manual labour . . . whatever.' He flexes his muscles and laughs. *'Trabajo, lavoro, travail, arbeit.'* Hamid's all ready for the European Union.

Ahmed, like how many others, would have gone by now if he'd had the money for the people smugglers. He's a mason. Earns the equivalent of £20 a week. To get to Europe you have to pay £650, he says. I ask him what his family thinks of the idea of his leaving. He's only twenty-one. 'My father's dead,' he says. 'My mother and my little brothers need me to emigrate. It's the only way they can get a better life.' Ahmed shrugs when I ask about the dangers. But there are few families around here who haven't lost at least one son to the *hrig*.

Fatima-Zarah has the melodious voice of her twenty-two years but already looks old. Her husband and fifty-five others from her village were drowned off the coast of Italy when their inflatable motorboat capsized and sank. She is widowed and ruined. The people smugglers were put in jail. But she never got the money back.

It was to warn people about the dangers and disappointments of the *hrig* that Khouribga Migration Radio was set up last year with a star presenter called Paco. He got his Spanish nickname from his first trip to Europe. It was the name of the coastguard who fished him out of the Straits of Gibraltar. His boat had sunk; he was drowning. The Spaniard saved his life, then sent him home. Back in Morocco, Paco, a former street vendor, joined the Association of Families of the

52

Victims of Illegal Immigration, AFVIC by its French acronym, and became an inspiration for the young people of Khouribga and beyond.

I was looking forward to meeting him. But when I arrive at the red villa that serves as AFVIC headquarters, he's gone. He went to Europe on a tourist visa. It expired weeks ago. And he's still not come home. The star of the struggle against the *hrig* has done what he's spent the past years telling other Moroccans not to do: migrate illegally to Europe. For AFVIC's president Khalil Jemmah, Paco's departure is the last straw.

'We've failed,' he says. 'There's so much stacked against us, we didn't have a chance. Pick tomatoes all day in Morocco and you get two pounds. In Spain you get twenty. And those that make it in Europe come home for summer with a car and presents and get fussed over by all the family. The others feel worthless,' he says, 'which feeds the suicidal side of the *hrig.*' Khalil Jemmah recalls one man who said, after a group of immigrants had drowned in the Straits, that he would rather have drowned with them than die a little bit each day under the pitying eyes of his parents.

It's the same desperate story from the migrant's widow, Fatima-Zarah. Her parents-in-law threw her and the children out of the house after her husband died, said she'd profited enough from them while he was alive, while he was young and strong. So she came to town looking for cleaning work. She exhausts herself for a pound or two a day, she says, which is all her two children, two brothers, her mother and herself have to live on.

'And,' she says, 'when my children ask why they can't have something their friends have, or why

53

their friends are well-dressed and their clothes are torn, I wish a thousand times that I were dead, drowned at sea like my husband, rather than have to live this life.'

16

The Long Walk Home

Adam Mynott

A peace deal brought to an end twenty-two years of civil war in southern Sudan. People from the region who had been displaced by the fighting wanted to rebuild their lives, and headed home to do so. For thousands, this meant an epic walk through dense jungle. (11 May 2005)

The pilot of our light aircraft studied his chart and his Global Positioning computer. 'We're close,' he said, and there, a mile ahead, like a red scar in the green undergrowth, was the earth airstrip. We dropped in to Tambura, a one-street town in southern Sudan, close to the borders with Uganda and the Central African Republic. All around us was dense jungle. The annual summer rains have started and mosquitoes rise in dark squadrons from the swamps.

I have one overriding irrational fear, an atavistic aversion to these attack helicopters of the insect world. A friend who works in southern Sudan for the charity UNICEF had chuckled when he heard where we were going: 'Oh, watch out for the

54

cerebral malaria,' he said. I had grinned weakly and hurriedly packed an extra tube of repellent and another long-sleeved shirt.

The 6,000 people heading home through the jungle are now more than thirty days into their extraordinary odyssey. Once the peace deal between the Sudan People's Liberation Movement and the government of Sudan was signed, the people of Raga began to make plans to go home. The road between Tambura and Raga, along which they fled in chaos four years ago, was heavily mined, so the only option open to them was to cut, by hand, a new road straight through the forest. Travelling by car, we took two days to catch up with them.

I had assumed that malaria would pose the greatest risk to the travellers. I hadn't accounted for the tsetse fly. To one who breaks into a clammy sweat at the thought of mosquitoes, the tsetse fly had acquired near-mythological status in my imagination. Thousands of generations of evolution have equipped the tsetse fly with masterful stealth, and even though it's the size of a large bluebottle, if not quite so fat, it is able to land with such delicacy you can't even feel it alight on your skin, as it prepares to drive its probe through the epidermis into the bloodstream.

Michael is seventy years old. He is blind and weak from his exertions. Sleeping sickness is endemic here and he has the parasites in his system. For some of the journey he's ridden on the back of one of the three or four trucks which are helping to move the most vulnerable. But for many days he has walked, led by his six-year-old granddaughter Mary. He is too frail to carry

55

anything. His wife and two daughters have all the family's possessions: blankets, pots, pans, plastic sheeting, knives, spoons, food and three stools perched on their heads. Michael's sons and grandson are a few miles ahead of the main group. They are part of a gang of about seventy-five to a hundred who are building bridges over the rivers which cross their route home.

Without any civil engineering training they hack down huge trees and lash them together to form pontoons, with a technical expertise that is enviable. These bridges have to withstand not just the tread of 6,000 pairs of feet but also the weight of the six-ton trucks. Ahead lie four more big rivers and a number of smaller streams.

The people of Raga are somewhere between half and three-quarters of their way through their incredible journey. More than thirty have died on the road and at the last count fourteen babies had been born. It will take another month at least before they reach their home town.

Leaving them to it, we headed back to Tambura, moved by what we had seen and reminded again of the power of the human spirit on this continent. Yes, inevitably, on the way back a tsetse fly made it past my elaborate defence system and, through a thick cotton shirt, bit me. Blood test booked early next week.

17

The Last Hitchhiker

Kevin Connolly

What had happened to the hitchhikers one used to see embarking on transcontinental journeys? Had the practice simply become too dangerous or had the advent of cheap flights made hitching redundant? Our correspondent set out from the French port of Calais determined to dip his toes in the warm waters of the Bosphorus. (20 April 2003)

There is no dustjacket on a radio broadcast to let you know what to expect inside, so let me begin with a word of warning. This is a rather unusual piece of travel writing inasmuch as I have no idea how far I am about to get, or what route I will take to get there. For this is a kind of elegy to the lost, innocent world of the hitchhiker. We might be about to embark together on a magical journey that will take us from northern France to the shores of the Bosphorus, the Black Sea and beyond, carried along by the goodwill and generosity of our fellow Europeans. Equally, you might be in for one of the most detailed descriptions of Calais ever written. The project is simply to travel to the French side of the Channel, starting point for most of our first adventures in Europe, and see how far it is possible to travel these days by hitchhiking.

I wrote this preamble because I had a nagging

suspicion that I wouldn't feel quite so lyrical about the whole business once I'd actually put it to the test. But there was a time before the birth of the low-cost airline when hitching seemed both romantic and practical, making your journey cheap but alive with the possibility of adventure.

As a child in Worcestershire I even used to hitch to school occasionally, a cool thing to do, it seemed to me, although in truth I was almost always picked up either by a teacher or by parents driving other pupils to school.

When I lived in the *Alice in Wonderland* economies of Communist Eastern Europe too, hitchhiking played a role and served a purpose. In Moscow, drivers were always desperate to earn a few dollars, so I have been taken to the Opera House on a Soviet tank transporter and driven to work in an ambulance with two patients sitting in the back. I hope and assume they were non-urgent cases.

In the old Romania you might find yourself being driven into Bucharest from the airport by an eye surgeon using his precious car to earn a little extra money, saving you the bus fare from the airport when perhaps he should have been saving someone's sight.

But in Western Europe it was never really about money, and our rising prosperity is only one of the many reasons why hitchhiking has slowly died out. Even in the Doris Days of the 1960s we feared abduction, paedophilia, serial-killing and violence by strangers, but these days we seem obsessed by our fears in a way we weren't back then.

And we are more protective now of the little bubble of private space we inhabit. We like to drive along alone with a favourite CD or radio station providing the soundtrack to our lives. Or at least we prefer that to picking up some total stranger who might bore us to tears, and then hack us to death.

Now, if you drove off a ferry or hovercraft in the port of Calais some time in the early afternoon of 2 January and drove past a lonely figure with a forlorn thumb stuck out at the roadside, then I think you should turn your radio off. Immediately. Any modest informing or entertaining that might come along in the next few minutes is not intended for you.

You might even remember the day. There was a grating wind, as cold as an ex-wife. The sky was a harsh grey and white, like a television screen when the picture goes. I was the lonely figure by the roadside, swaddled in so many layers of Gore-tex and fleece that if I'd fallen over I'd have rolled helplessly back down the ramp and on to the ferry again. I couldn't tell you now how many people I had expected to stop and offer me a lift, but after the first two ferry-loads had gone past without a single motorist so much as slowing down, I began to get a pretty good idea.

OK, I hadn't really thought that a blonde supermodel in a sports convertible was going to sweep me off into the dark heart of the continent, but equally, it hadn't really occurred to me that absolutely nobody would stop. I should have written a longer preamble while I could still feel my fingers.

In a moment of wild pre-trip optimism about how far I might be about to travel, I had bought a cheap second-hand Turkish phrase book. It is a masterpiece of unintentional humour, full of incredulous moaning: 'How much is that meal? How long until our bus comes?' But it was beginning to look as though it might have been a bit of a waste of money.

Every time a ferry or a hovercraft stopped, a fresh wave of cars crept ashore, wound through the terminal and swept straight past me. In every front seat, people were fixing their hair, scolding their children, tuning their radios, phoning their friends, and in one or two cases, swigging their beers. What they were not doing was giving me a lift, or indeed a second glance.

The sense of rejection and isolation was incredible. I had allowed perhaps a fortnight for my journey, but at this rate I would be in therapy for years. Every time the silence surged back after a wave of traffic had receded, I found myself glancing around furtively to make sure that no one else had started cadging a lift in competition with me. In this respect at least, hitchhiking turned out to be rather like sex when I was a teenager. It certainly wasn't happening to me, but I was troubled by a nagging fear that it might have been happening to somebody else.

I needn't have worried. The area was as quiet as one of those television thrillers about the aftermath of a nuclear attack. I might have been the last person left alive, let alone the last hitchhiker.

What a relief. Failing at this myself was bad enough. Watching someone else succeed at it would have been unbearable. After a while, a figure in uniform emerged from the maze of wire fences, concrete barriers and toll booths of the ferry terminal and trudged silently towards me. When we were beside each other, two lonely figures silhouetted against the darkening sky, he spoke. 'Hitchhiking, eh?' By now, my lips were so numb from the cold that they had a curiously remote feeling, as though they were someone else's. So I just nodded. 'I thought so. The others were wondering. It's been a while since we saw anyone in January, you know . . .' He tailed off and headed back to his friends, having obviously thought better of telling me exactly how long it was since he'd seen anyone hitchhiking successfully.

The French authorities use a life-size two-dimensional wooden figure with outstretched arms to warn motorists of roadworks ahead, and by now I'd begun to look like one of those, only without the fixed smile. I had embarked on my journey with all sorts of good intentions about personal safety. My mind filled with stories off the Internet about drivers who stop to offer lifts and turn out to be naked from the waist down, about robbery, homosexual rape and murder. Those resolutions had lasted exactly two hours. After that, if you'd pulled over in a hearse with the theme from *Psycho* playing on the hi-fi and an axe dripping blood on the front passenger seat to offer me a lift through a mouth-slit cut in a black balaclava, I'd have got in without a second thought. Well, I might have checked to make sure the heater was working.

Then, quite suddenly, my luck changed. A battered white van pulled up beside me and the driver, a young man in blue overalls, asked where I was going. 'South,' I said, swiftly hoisting my backpack up into the cab before he changed his mind. The van smelled strongly of seafood, but not

61

in a fresh way; rather as though it might have been used to conduct fish funerals. Still, I settled in and began to explain what I was doing and why.

'I wouldn't get too excited,' he said apologetically. 'I only live about two kilometres from here, and I'm going home. You just looked so cold.'

In the end he agreed to drive me out to a decent position on the edge of the motorway, even though it meant getting home late for dinner. It didn't quite feel like hitchhiking in the grand manner, but my scruples were deep frozen by now and I waved my Samaritan off, promising to portray him as a hero in my story. Which I hope I have.

When I started hitching again, I felt an irrational surge of confidence. After all, I had managed to secure a lift, even though it had been more a favour granted out of pity than a sharing of adventure on the road. I had broken my duck. I could practically see the shores of the Bosphorus.

Hitching by the side of the motorway, of course, turned out to be far worse. Motorists driving off the ferry had simply ignored me, driving past as though I was some sort of sophisticated three-dimensional roadworks warning. But drivers on the autoroute were different. They sped past with an air of malicious relish. Some, well many actually, even affected to believe that I was raising my thumb as I stood freezing by the roadside in the gathering darkness as a chirpy indication that everything was OK with me. One or two humorously raised their own thumbs in an answering salute as they hurtled past. Yes, it seemed everything was just dandy inside their centrally heated cabs too.

If you're ever tempted to make this gesture to a hitchhiker in the belief that they, we, might find it amusing, then allow me in my public service role to enlighten you. We don't. In fact if any of the offending motorists had suffered a puncture within walking distance of my lonely vantage point I would have beaten them to death with their tyre irons. That, I reflected, was progress of a sort, though, since it proved my point that hitchhiking was capable of producing profound social changes. Three hours previously I'd been worried about the dangers of falling into the clutches of a psychopath. Now I was turning into one. Then finally a flatbed truck swerved round me on to the hard shoulder and pulled up with a series of violent, erratic braking manoeuvres. I hesitated. It was just far away enough that it might have stopped for some reason which was nothing to do with me. The driver might even have been amusing himself by luring me up the hard shoulder with my heavy rucksack in order to drive off just as I reached the cab. But no. When I reached the door and opened it, Michel, the amiable Guadeloupean at the wheel, told me he was happy to take me as far as Lille, which is perhaps sixty miles from Calais. His dog, a burly mongrel with a big dash of Rottweiler, glared at me malevolently as he was pushed off the passenger seat to make way for me.

I had agreed a security system with my son Christopher back in Ireland under which I would send him a text message with the registration number of any vehicle which picked me up. It would not, we agreed, do much to deter any possible attack, but it might help the post-mortem to run a little more smoothly, and might speed up the murder investigation.

The system worked pretty well in the end, but I decided not to send the number of Michel's truck. As far as I was concerned, he'd prevented me from dying of exposure. If he decided to murder me I wouldn't have felt it was right to help the authorities track him down.

After about thirty miles of chasing the beam from our headlights into the freezing darkness I began to drift off to sleep, lulled by the pulsing bass of the rap music and a hint of cannabis smoke in the cab. I was jerked awake when the dog stirring on the floor at my feet suddenly pulled himself up, gripped my left leg in his front paws and began grimly humping against it. I tried discreetly easing him off with my right foot, but he was incredibly strong and had presumably been goaded into a sexual frenzy by the rap lyrics.

We drove along with Michel and I mostly silent and his dog slurping and rutting away against my leg, while I tried to dislodge it without drawing too much attention to what was going on. There's plenty of advice on the Internet for hitchhikers on avoiding unwanted advances, but that's not much use when the offender is a dog.

I got out at a motorway junction on the edge of Lille reflecting on how far short of my targets I'd fallen. Only two lifts and if I had used public transport I could have covered the distance it had taken me all day to travel in about forty minutes. And it would have cost less than £10. I had not been able to take Europe's temperature on such issues as the euro and the crisis in the Middle East. Indeed it looked as though I would spend much of the evening removing an unpleasant-looking drool stain off the leg of my trousers. At least I hoped it was just drool. I was moving through Europe at the speed of one of the crusades, and my rucksack in which I carried all my possessions on my back was unbelievably heavy. No wonder you never see an overweight snail.

I checked in to a cheap hotel in the middle of Lille and found that from the window I could see the broken neon sign of a Turkish kebab restaurant winking forlornly on and off. It wasn't much of a view, but it looked like it was going to be the closest I was going to get to the Bosphorus.

18

The Most Dangerous Road in the World

Mark Whittaker

Everyone has a candidate for the title 'the worst road in the world'. Our correspondent is in no doubt the winner is to be found in Bolivia. He went for a drive along what's been called the most dangerous road in the world—and lived to tell the tale.
(11 November 2006)

It seems perverse that one of the main roads out of one of the highest cities on earth should actually climb as it leaves town. But climb it does, to just short of a lung-sapping three miles above sea level, where even the internal combustion engine is forced to toil and splutter. Then it pauses for a while on the snow-flecked crest of the Andes before pitching, like a giant white-knuckle ride, into the abyss.

The road from Bolivia's main city, La Paz, to a region known as the Yungas, was built by Paraguayan prisoners of war back in the 1930s. Many of them perished in the effort. Now it's mainly Bolivians who die on the road in their thousands. In 1995, the Inter-American Development Bank christened it 'the most dangerous road in the world'. And, as you start your descent, and your driver whispers a prayer, you begin to see why.

The bird's-eye view is on the left, where the earth itself seems to open up. A gigantic vertical crack appears. Way below, more than a half mile beneath your window, you can see, cradled between canyon walls, a silver thread: the Coroico river rushing to join the Amazon. On the other side there's a sheer rock wall rising to the heavens. There's no margin of error: the road itself is barely three metres wide. That's if you can call it a road. After the initial stretch to the top of the mountain it's just dirt track. And yet, incredibly, it's a major route for trucks and buses.

Drivers stop to pour libations of beer into the earth to beseech the goddess Pachamama for safe passage. Then, chewing coca leaves to keep themselves awake, they're off at breakneck speeds in vehicles which shouldn't be on any road, let alone this one.

Perched on hairpin bends over dizzying precipices, crosses and stone cairns mark the places where travellers' prayers went unheeded when, for someone, the road ended. But even these stark warnings are all too often ignored. As first one, and then a second, impatient motorist overtook our car on the ravine side of the road, my own driver, who hardly ever spoke a word and only then in his native Aymara, intoned loudly, eerily and in perfect English: 'You will die!' It's not a rash prediction to make. Every year it's estimated two or three hundred people die on a stretch of road less than fifty miles long. In one year alone, twenty-five vehicles plunged off the road and into the ravine. That's one every two weeks.

It's the end of the dry season in Bolivia. Soon the rains will come, cascading down the walls of the chasm. Huge waterfalls will drench the road, turning its surface to slime. Then will come those heart-stopping moments when wheels skid and brakes fail to grip. There are stories told of truckers too tired, or too afraid, to continue, who pull over for the night, hoping to see out an Andean storm. But they've parked too close to the edge. And as they sleep in their cabs, the road is washed away around them. This is not a place to drop off.

But for now the road is a ribbon of dust. Every vehicle passing along it churns up a sandstorm in its wake. Choking, blinding clouds obscure the way ahead. Around one hairpin, a cloud of debris was beginning to clear. As it did, I could see people milling around in the road: passengers from one of the overloaded and often decrepit buses which run the gauntlet of this road. It seemed at first that they'd got off to stretch their legs, while their driver argued with that of another vehicle coming in the opposite direction about who should give way—reversing is not something you undertake lightly on a cliff edge!

It transpired instead that the bus driver was dying. Blinded by the dust, he'd run into the back of a truck. The bus's steering column had gone through him, severing his legs. There was nothing anyone could do. Mobile phones don't work here. In any case, who would you call? There are no emergency services. And no way of getting help through, even if there was any to be found. The bus driver bled to death. We edged past the crumpled bus and headed on. Further down the road we passed a spot where a set of fresh tyre tracks headed out into the void. They told their own story.

The good news is that there is now an alternative, a bypass intended to replace the old road. But people seem still drawn to the road with the vertiginous drop and still offer up their prayers, and take their lives in their hands, on the most dangerous road in the world.

19

The Golden Railway

Malcolm Billings

In the early years of the last century, many of the pilgrims travelling to the annual haj in Mecca came and went on the so-called Hejaz railway. It carried them from Damascus in Syria down through the Arabian desert to Medina in what is now Saudi Arabia. Today, some parts of the line are still in use while others have disappeared beneath the desert sands. (14 January 2006)

My first encounter with the Hejaz railway was in clouds of steam along with a pungent smell of hot grease at Kadem station in Damascus. A veteran steam locomotive built in 1914 chuffed past hauling a goods train towards the Jordan border. From the driver's cab, two soot-streaked faces leaned out to see the iron road ahead. It was like stepping back a century in railway history. But I had to remind myself that this wasn't history—this was now!

The engineer in charge of the hundred-year-old maintenance sheds, two huge stone buildings full of rolling stock and engines, pointed to the oldest locomotive in service, built in Germany in 1898. 'Just one of eleven steam locomotives in service,' he told me with obvious pride. 'If the sixty-year-old diesels break down,' he added, 'we use steam for the passenger services as well as for goods trains.'

I walked through a graveyard of abandoned rolling stock and a number of locomotives that were gently falling apart in sidings overgrown with grass and shrubs. And what I was looking at were the original carriages and engines that made up the first pilgrim trains in 1908. One carriage was armour-plated. It had rifle slits in the sides from which guards on the train could ward off attacks from Bedouin tribesmen on the train's four-day journey through the desert to Medina in what is now Saudi Arabia.

In southern Jordan it's a very different railway. Robbed of its rails and sleepers, the embankment stands proud of the desert, like some sort of natural sculpture that has always been there. The

69

embankment makes a good road until it stops abruptly at a yawning gap where a bridge was washed away by a flash flood perhaps decades ago.

On the Saudi stretch of the line there are steam engines that were abandoned after the end of the First World War. One was in Medain Saleh, a big station along the line in Saudi. The locomotive, stripped of every movable part by the Bedouin, was still in its engine shed waiting for maintenance that should have been done eighty or ninety years ago.

The last station in Jordan before the Saudi border is Mudawwara. Peeping out from behind the pillars in front of the ticket office were eight little children—seven girls and one boy, who, in the absence of his father, was the spokesman. He recited all the names of his siblings and told me through an interpreter that they had lived in the station for ten years and that very few people like us stopped to ask about the railway. I couldn't find any stations on a branch line in southern Jordan, closer to Amman. The Ottomans had sided with Germany in the First World War, so the supply of good quality British coal they had used in the locomotives from mines in Wales had been cut off. At one stage, fuel was so scarce that the engines were being fed furniture and floorboards just to keep them running. As the railway had to burn wood instead of coal, they built this twenty-five-mile-long branch line into a forest near the crusader castle of Shobak to collect it.

A local farmer confirmed that we were at the forest of Hisheh or what was left of it. 'Over there'—the farmer pointed to higher ground some distance away—'you can see tree stumps left by the Ottoman troops.' Then the Jordanian farmer accused my interpreter and me of treasure hunting. 'We couldn't even find the railway, let alone any treasure,' I protested. But the farmer insisted that we open the boot of the car to see if we had spades, shovels and any other incriminating kit.

Puzzled, I later consulted an archaeologist in Amman who put his head in his hands and said: 'Treasure hunting is destroying long sections of the railway.' Ueli Bellwader explained that the holes all around the stations we saw in the desert were not First World War bomb craters but deep holes dug by treasure hunters. 'It may sound crazy,' he said, 'but people really do believe that the retreating Ottoman soldiers buried gold around the stations. In their frenzy to find it,' he said, 'they have mechanical earth-moving equipment that is demolishing buildings and stretches of the embankment.'

And the hunt for the treasure has spawned another profitable sideline for shops in faraway Istanbul. Maps of the railway sell for serious money, along with a guarantee that the cross on the map is definitely the place to dig for an Ottoman pot of gold.

20

Adventures in Flight

Allan Little

Another landmark in aviation was reached with the unveiling of the giant Airbus A380, the largest civilian aircraft ever built. (20 January 2005)

In 1935, J. B. Priestley took a bus from London to Southampton down what is now the A33 and was dazzled by the experience and the ingenuity of humankind it revealed. He could not believe the speed of it. Villages flashed past in the twinkling of an eye. 'Thirty-five miles per hour,' he marvelled. 'I cannot imagine why anyone would ever want or need to travel faster.'

Seventy years later, I am standing in a hangar in Toulouse marvelling a little myself at the ingenuity of humankind while staring vertically upwards at the underbelly of a machine that is capable of transporting people at twenty times Priestley's optimum speed and, what's more, 800 people at the same time. The new Airbus A380 is a double-decker passenger aircraft that makes the Boeing 747 jumbo jet look puny.

At its unveiling, Airbus put on a floor show that could have opened the Olympic Games. The symbolism was all futuristic and high tech. It was designed to sell an idea: that this is an aviation revolution, that the A380 is the future, that Boeing's old jumbo is all washed up. In not much more than a year from now, the new giant of the sky will be shuttling daily between Singapore and London and between Paris and New York.

I don't much like flying. I have always found the laws of aerodynamics implausible. There was once a survey in the English-speaking world into how scientific advancement had eroded popular superstition, and it found that science and superstition had reached an accommodation with each other. I like the respondent in Ireland who, when asked whether he believed in fairies, replied: 'I do not. But they're there.' This is how I feel about the jet plane. 'Do you believe it will get off the ground?' 'I do not. But it will.'

My faith in jet planes is bolstered by experience. Last year, the British government released a list of eight airlines around the world that were currently banned from British airspace because of concerns about the safety of their aircraft. When I read the list I found that I had travelled blithely on six of them, most of these in Africa. Once, on Air Tajikistan—not, incidentally, one of the eight—the stewards were so surprised to see a foreigner that they upgraded me to first class, where the in-flight meal was a box of groceries: half a pound of cheese, a loaf of bread, a jar of pickled gherkins, a bottle of vodka and the biggest sliced sausage you've ever seen.

In Angola, I once had the rare and questionable privilege of being invited to visit the then rebel leader Jonas Savimbi, now deceased, whose secret hideout was deep in the bush. When I got to the little airstrip I was surprised to learn that the plane that would take me was already waiting. At first glance, I had mistaken it for a garden shed. I swear

73

it was made of wood. It was all sharp right angles and sloping roofs. I could not conceive that it would get off the ground. But it did. Somehow it did. Do I believe in fairies? I do not. But they're there.

On the flight, I found myself sitting beside a correspondent from the Russian news agency TASS. Have you been asked to sign one of these, he asked, and handed me a form. In English, Portuguese and Russian it was a disclaimer: 'UNITA [Savimbi's guerrilla movement] takes no responsibility for the lives of those who travel on this aircraft.' I felt a little pang of longing for the sweet solicitousness of a stewardess showing me how to inflate my lifejacket in the unlikely event of an emergency.

I was once in a tired old helicopter in Afghanistan. It was overloaded with television equipment. It scraped its ancient posterior over the peaks and ridges of an inconveniently located mountain range. That innocuous phrase—the event of an emergency—now seemed something far from unlikely. The helicopter was one of those that, in order to climb, had to accelerate forwards. So there was method in the apparent madness of the pilot, who, when the vertical grey stone face of a mountain hove into view, simply headed straight for it. On this occasion, I found myself sitting beside the correspondent of ARD German television. He looked up at the chopper's single motor straining above our heads. 'You know,' he yelled into my ear, 'if we should crash, if you survive the impact with the ground, the engine comes down and crushes you.' And this as the pilot was seeking to avoid collision with another

74

mountainside by accelerating straight towards it.

The UN airmen who used to run aid flights into Sarajevo during the siege used to stamp our passports 'Maybe Airlines'. Thank you, Maybe Airlines, thank you, UNITA, for your garden shed with wings, for making me remember what Airbus and Boeing and human ingenuity makes us forget: that flying for human beings is really quite implausible and that it is not very long since thirty-five miles an hour down what is now the A33 seemed something to marvel at.

21

A Parrot Amnesty

Will Ross

An African Grey parrot amnesty was introduced in Uganda. Although an endangered species, several hundred of the birds were being kept as pets. Under the terms of the amnesty their owners were being told they should register those parrots or face the law.
(5 February 2005)

For the first time ever, I find myself whistling to try to get a response from my interviewees. But Kappie and Chick are not up for a chat—maybe because this is such a big day in the lives of these two African Grey parrots. Their owner, Tony Ogen, has brought them in a small cage to the offices of the Uganda Wildlife Authority to be registered and licensed during the three-month parrot amnesty.

Tony approaches the desk clutching a wad of Ugandan shillings. It's at this point that the accountant behind the desk gets a little suspicious as Tony begins: 'Yes, I did have three parrots. But, sir, you will remember the letter I sent you explaining what happened?' Tony then rustles through his papers looking for a copy of the letter. 'As is indicated in the letter, while I was cleaning out their cage, one of the parrots flew away. So my three parrots have now become two and they, sir, are the two parrots standing before you. I therefore wish to purchase just the two permits.' The accountant raises his eyebrows as if to say: 'Pull the other leg', but realising this was going to be a hard one to prove, he takes Tony's word for it and gladly accepts the cash.

Inside the office, a senior member of the Uganda Wildlife Authority team is talking tough: 'If the parrot owners do not heed our warning and register their birds, we may have to take the ultimate action—seizure. And it's up to five years in prison for the owners.'

'But just how are you going to find these permitless parrots?' I ask.

'We have a crack wildlife intelligence unit and in any case we know where these parrots are,' he warned, sounding more and more like a tough-talking cop as each minute passed.

I had visions of heavily armed helmeted men wandering around the plusher neighbourhoods of Uganda's capital, scaling walls, peering through windows, breaking down doors and yelling: 'Hello Polly.'

After Tony had handed over his shillings, he

thought it was all over. But no. The Uganda Wildlife Authority had laid on a vet and she wanted to give Tony's parrots the full medical. On snapped the rubber gloves as she approached Kappie and Chick's cage, which was locked, and as is often the case in Africa, the man with the key was not around.

While we're waiting, Tony tells me all about the chats he has with his parrots when he's lonely. I then remember a musician I interviewed several years ago in Tanzania. He kept a parrot in a cage in the living room by the front door but he was beginning to regret it. You see, this musician used to stay out late drinking and would then sneak back into the house in the middle of the night trying not to wake his wife and children. But invariably he'd return from the drinking sessions to a squawked 'Where the hell have you been?' as he tried to tiptoe past the cage. In the daytime he had extremely limited success trying to teach his parrot to whisper.

When the key to the cage finally turned up, there were a few nervous moments as Tony gave instructions on how to get one of the parrots out of the cage. 'That's it, hold it by the neck,' he advised as it made the loudest squawk so far. 'But don't kill it,' added an onlooking official from the Wildlife Authority.

Having passed the medical, which was followed by some advice on how to stop the parrots pulling out their own feathers and tips such as: 'Try red pepper, they'll talk much more', I followed Tony home. The parrots readjusted as he lay the cage down flat in the back of his saloon car and whispered over his shoulder: 'Have a nice journey' before driving off.

The Uganda Wildlife Authority is against the keeping of parrots as pets but knows that there are hundreds in cages across the capital that have been captured in Ugandan woodland or sneaked across the Congolese border, along with other precious commodities. But it has decided to work with the parrot owners to make sure the birds will be well looked after, and there are plans for a breeding programme in captivity. Like many parrots in Kampala, Kappie and Chick have a pretty good view. Tony has built a large cage next to a communal tennis court. And he says they're not bad on the line calls: 'Out. 30-15. 30 all. Your advantage,' they trill.

As I prepare to leave Kappie and Chick, I spend a few more minutes pointing my microphone at the cage and whistling, determined to get a response. Eventually there are a couple of squawks followed by a whistle. But I have no idea if that was a polite greeting or more like a 'Get the microphone away from my beak, you nosy, wingless idiot.'

22

Four-legged Library

James Ingham

The hills were alive with the sight of people reading—at least they were in Venezuela where a university was running a hugely successful programme using mules to take books into remote mountain communities to

Chiquito and Cenizo greet me with a bit of a snort and a flick of the tail. Mules are too tough to bother being sweet. They do a hard job which no other animal or human invention can do as well. But these mules are rather unique. They're known as *bibliomulas*, or book mules, and they're helping to spread the benefits of reading to people who are isolated from much of the world around them. My trek started from the Valley of Momboy in Trujillo, one of Venezuela's three Andean states. These are the foothills of the Andes, but they're high enough, especially when you're walking.

The idea of loading mules with books and taking them into the mountain villages was started by the University of Momboy, a small institution that prides itself on its community-based initiatives, doing far more than universities in Venezuela are required by law to do. Accompanying us was local guide Ruan, who knows a thing or two about mules. He was their boss, cajoling them carefully as they started up the hill at a slow but steady, no-nonsense plod. The deeply rutted, dry and dusty path snaked its way up. The sun beat on the back of my neck. We were all breathless, apart from Ruan.

A break came when it was my turn to ride a mule. I enjoyed a great view of the valley but held on tight as Chiquito veered close to the edge. Hot and slightly bothered after two hours, we reached Calembe, the first village on this path.

Anyone who wasn't out working the fields, tending the celery that's the main crop here, was waiting for our arrival. The twenty-three children at the little school were very excited. '*Bibilomuuuulas*!' they shouted as the bags of books were unstrapped. They dived in eagerly, keen to grab the best titles, and within minutes were being read to by Christina and Juana, two of the project leaders.

'Spreading the joy of reading is our main aim,' Christina Vieras told me. 'But it's more than that. We're helping educate people about other important things like the environment. All the children are planting trees. Anything to improve the quality of life and connect these communities.'

As the project grows, it's using the latest technology. Somehow there's already a limited mobile phone signal here, so the organisers are taking advantage of that and equipping the mules with laptops and projectors. The book mules are becoming cyber mules and cine mules. 'We want to install wireless modems under the banana plants so the villagers can use the Internet,' says Robert Ramirez, the co-ordinator of the university's Network of Enterprising Rural Schools. 'Imagine if people in the poor towns in the valley can e-mail saying how many tomatoes they'll need next week, or how much celery. The farmers can reply telling them how much they can produce. It's blending localisation and globalisation.'

The book-mule team played noisy games with the children, listened to them read and lunched with the adults, discussing over a hearty soup and corn bread how the community can develop the scheme. One idea was using the mules to transport medicines, which can be so hard to get hold of here. Everyone I spoke to, both adults and children, was full of enthusiasm. 'It's great,' said twelve-year-old José Castillo. 'I love reading books and we get told some really nice stories.' Looking up from reading her book about Harry the cat and his trip to the vet, Gesenae Guerdo told me she loved reading too. 'We share a lot of these books,' she said. Javier Sulveran, a young, bright man in his twenties, tells me that the village is very supportive of the project. 'The children are really motivated to read and we are too. A lot of the adults are reading more. It's great that they come up here,' he says.

The university has acquired a new mule. They're going to keep it in Calembe under the care of the locals, something Javier really approved of. The mule will be able to get further into the mountains and spread the word to more villages that up to now have remained too remote.

With fond farewells, we left Calembe behind. It was clear I was leaving a place with a strong sense of community. This four-legged mobile library is not just keeping this place alive but making it thrive.

23

The Mounted Police

Hugh O'Shaughnessy

Police on horseback are a common sight. But in parts of Brazil, the police have adopted a helper of a different sort. It needs no attention from mechanics, is well suited to difficult terrain and is a willing and

The mounted police look splendid on their animals. Calm, dignified and, yes, friendly, they glance down indulgently on us visitors to the international fair in Belém. Belém, whose name is the Portuguese form of Bethlehem, is the capital of the Brazilian state of Pará and it lies near the mouth of the Amazon.

But, if anything, the police animals look even calmer, more dignified and friendlier than their riders, a real credit to the force. Altogether a fine body of men and beasts, you'd say. Sadly it's not often that full marks can be given to the guardians of the peace in Brazil. Under the military dictatorship which seized power in 1964, the police were often guilty of the greatest torture and cruelty. Their senior officers generally escaped punishment because the Brazilian regime was fallaciously presented as the 'good guys' in the Cold War. For a long time Brazil's constabularies never even reached the minimum qualification for any police force, namely, that it caught more criminals than it employed.

The dictatorship is, thank goodness, long over. There's still a taint of police excess in many spots in this enormous country, but these men, benignly guarding us on their mounts on the banks of the Amazon, are something other. Perhaps it's because they are carried not on excitable horses but on placid buffalo.

The buffaloes' muscled flanks shine. Their horns, which have a span of a metre and a half, hang down impressively for all the world like the drop handlebars of a giant's bicycle. And they've all got names: Xodo, which means 'My Treasure' in Portuguese, and Carolina, for instance, are patiently yoked together to a wooden cart. There a constable stands proudly grasping a ceremonial lance from which the force's pennant stirs lazily in the damp night air.

The buffalo can go into action with their vehicles and they're regularly called out on duty with the fire service, always ready to trot off to help douse a blaze in some thatched hut or drag a car out of the Amazonian mud.

In fact they don't usually parade here in Belém at all; they're stationed across the river in the mud of Marajó, an island the size of Switzerland in the Amazon delta. Marajó lies where the world's greatest river, 4,000 miles long, empties into the Atlantic. The Amazon is twelve times greater in volume than the Mississippi at New Orleans, and more water flows by Marajó every day than the Thames carries past the Houses of Parliament in London in a whole year.

Buffalo were introduced from Africa in the 1930s to produce milk for mozzarella cheese, meat and hides. And they bred successfully. They also took to the swampy terrain better than mere horses, whose hooves rotted disastrously in the wet. The hooves of the buffalo are more like steel than like the horn of other quadrupeds and are splayed out more widely. That enables them to work with dignity and aplomb in conditions which would have crippled horses. They've also got another recommendation that's particularly useful on Marajó, a land noted for the prevalence of its snakes such as boas and rattlesnakes. Unlike the delicate, humped zebu cattle, the buffalo are amazingly thick-skinned. 'Any snake which tried to sink its fangs into a buffalo would certainly come off second best. It would be in urgent need of a dentist,' says my friend Dutra, a teacher in one of the Belém universities.

So, a few decades ago, the authorities decided to call the buffalo in for police and fire service duty: a score or more of them are today quartered in Soure, the main town on Marajó. Their riders have clearly got good relations with them, guiding them gently on their way with reins attached to a ring in their nose. This gives the beasts something of a pained look, their great eyes cast upward in that spirit of long suffering often to be glimpsed in Italian Renaissance paintings of early Christian martyrs. But they never, it seems, lose their phlegmatic outlook on life. The other day at the show in Belém, the police were happy to pose the children of visitors on the buffalo saddles for the parents to take photographs. The constables handled the youngsters with gentleness and patience, qualities which they surely picked up from the buffalo. These traits are not, it must be said, usually associated with Brazilian police, mounted or on foot, uniformed or in plain clothes.

Riding the broad-backed buffalo is a demanding art, my Brazilian friends told me. 'It's a bit like riding a camel and it places no little strain on your upper thighs, if you're not used to it,' one recounted.

For my part, I've been powerfully affected by my recent encounter in Belém. I'll appreciate my mozzarella even more when I eat it, and I'll certainly never order a buffalo steak in any Brazilian restaurant or any other restaurant for that matter. After all, it could have come from Xodo, or Carolina, or one of their offspring, and that would never do.

24

The Last of the Jewish Gauchos

Daniel Schweimler

The gaucho is to Argentina what the cowboy is to the United States. He's the rugged, hard-working cattle driver who tamed the wide open plains of the Argentine pampas, camping out under the stars and cooking the finest cuts of beef over an open fire on the point of his knife. But in this overwhelmingly Roman Catholic country, how did Jewish gauchos appear on the scene? (10 February 2007)

You could put Arminio Seiferheld on the front cover of a calendar depicting the Argentine countryside. Piercing blue eyes look out of a brown weather-beaten sixty-something-year-old face. He wears *bombachas*—the baggy, hard-wearing trousers used by gauchos, the Argentine cowboys. And he sips the bitter *mate* tea drunk in these parts through a *bombilla*, or metal straw, out of a wooden gourd clasped in his hand. Arminio is one of the last of a disappearing breed, the Jewish gaucho. As we drive down a dirt road near his farm in the northern province of Santa Fe, he stops to talk to an elderly farm-worker in a combination of Spanish and Yiddish, an unusual mixture so far

85

from the Jewish communities of Buenos Aires and Rosario. 'He's not Jewish,' explains Arminio, as the farm-worker and his ragged, wiry dogs continue on their way. 'But he worked for my father at a time when most of the farmers around here were Jewish and spoke Yiddish.'

We pull up outside Arminio's house on The State of Israel Street in the heart of Moises Ville, a town of about 2,000 inhabitants. It's a short walk from the town's central plaza—at first glance, exactly like most in rural Argentina, with the statue of José de San Martin, the liberator from Spanish colonial rule, in the middle. But this plaza is different. On one side is the Kadima theatre, the sign written amid the ornate stonework in Spanish and Hebrew. Painted over but still clearly visible on the façade of the bank are the words 'Banco Comercial Israelita', the Commercial Bank of Israel, and the well-tended flowerbeds form a star of David.

When tens of thousands of Jews fled the pogroms in Eastern Europe at the end of the nineteenth and beginning of the twentieth centuries, they mostly sought refuge in the cities: New York, London, Paris and Buenos Aires. But one small group of Polish Jews arrived in Argentina with the ambition of recreating a biblical dream and working the land. They were sold, at greatly inflated prices, large tracts of barely fertile land in the inhospitable north. That was their first problem. Their second major disadvantage was that they'd been urban dwellers and knew little about the ways of the countryside. Very soon, after the community had been ravaged by disease and poor harvests, the remaining pioneers were reduced to living in disused railway carriages, surviving from scraps thrown from passing trains.

The wealthy Jewish philanthropist Baron Maurice de Hirsch heard of their plight and decided to fund the establishment of several Jewish communities in Argentina. The first was Moises Ville, founded in 1890. The early days were tough. Few spoke the language and not all were welcome in this predominantly Roman Catholic country. Records tell of one Jewish woman burnt to death in her house, another resident chopped up and burnt for 200 pesos and some bags of flour. But they overcame their difficulties to build a flourishing community boasting four synagogues, Argentina's first Jewish cemetery, the Kadima theatre, a Hebrew school and a thriving public library.

Arminio's father arrived with the second wave of Jewish immigrants to Argentina, those escaping Nazi Germany. He swapped three bicycles for three cows and began his life as a cattle farmer, an Argentine Jewish gaucho. Arminio has continued the tradition, but his four children, like so many young rural Argentines, both Jewish and non-Jewish, have moved to the cities. One son lives in Israel and all speak fluent Hebrew. His daughter, Patricia, who was visiting from the city of Rosario, where she teaches Hebrew, said: 'When I first went to Jerusalem, I felt at home. They couldn't believe that I came from a small town called Moises Ville that was a cradle for Jewish immigration here in Argentina.' Now only about 10 per cent of the population of Moises Ville are Jewish. However, the signs of integration after those difficult early days are apparent, with non-Jewish girls attending Israeli folk-dancing classes and the town's only bakery making and selling apple strudel, *kamish* and *cholla* breads alongside the more traditional Argentine breads and pastries.

Argentina, which has the biggest Jewish community in Latin America, has suffered anti-Semitism, which is again on the rise. But it is also a country of immigrants, with Italians, Spaniards, Russians and Germans, Catholics, Protestants, Muslims and Jews battling together to overcome harsh terrain to help build a nation.

At the end of a long day on the farm, Arminio rushes home to shower and change to officiate at the only synagogue that still functions in Moises Ville. The Jewish congregation, like most in the other rural Jewish towns in Argentina, is small and elderly and doesn't warrant its own rabbi. The future is uncertain, but for now at least the Hebrew prayers and traditions brought from Eastern Europe over a hundred years ago still mix with the sound of crickets on a starlit night on the Argentine pampas.

25

Talking to Ghosts

Hugh Sykes

Sixty years on from the Dunkirk evacuation which saved British and French troops from annihilation by the German army and air force, some of the Little

Ships that helped with the rescue returned to Dunkirk on a pilgrimage. Meanwhile, the search for some accuracy amid the myths of Dunkirk was continuing. (8 June 2000)

The Little Ships did not rescue the British Expeditionary Force from Dunkirk in 1940; they helped in the rescue of more than 350,000 soldiers. Naval vessels took most of the men out of Dunkirk harbour. But the story of the Little Ships is not diminished by that fact and exaggeration might undermine the impressive truth, that they did rescue more than 90,000 troops, mostly by operating a shuttle service from the beaches to larger ships, and then taking dozens of men back across the Channel themselves.

The troops taken to England in Operation Dynamo were not all British. About a third were French. And the Little Ships were not skippered by crusty old sea-dog owners intrepidly sailing the English Channel to save the British army. Most of them were commandeered and crewed by the Royal Navy, or by fully trained reservists. In any case, many of the owners were already fighting in France. And these Little Ships were mostly smart white-painted riverboats built for gentlemen, who would have not necessarily made ideal helmsmen under fire and/or dive-bombing by Stukas. There is an unverifiable story of one gentleman in a suit and bowler hat who arrived at his dock to find the navy taking his pride and joy away to war. He climbed on board and said: 'Wherever she goes, I go.' And so he did.

And Dunkirk was not a 'miracle'. Apart from the fact that this would imply a very selective variety of divine intervention which then ceased for five years, the calm sea of the English Channel was only one factor in the Dunkirk great escape. Fearing counter-attack, and not realising how many of the British and French were trapped in the Dunkirk pocket, Adolf Hitler had halted the German advance from the south towards the Channel ports, stopping when he'd split the Allies in half and had reached the coast at Le Crotoy near Boulogne.

And, only days before the evacuation, the cryptographers at Bletchley Park had cracked the Enigma code that was being used by the Luftwaffe, so the British were listening in to German air-force radio traffic: over the Dunkirk beaches, in nine days, 176 German planes were shot down by the RAF. The troops' escape was also partly enabled by strong rearguard action in Belgium, keeping the feared SS at bay.

In the sunshine in Dunkirk last Sunday morning, William Blackwell was walking along in the beret and blazer and medals of the Dunkirk veterans, inspecting the Little Ships tied up three abreast on the Quai Hollandais. He was part of that rearguard, a gunner with the 57th Anti-Tank Regiment. On Sunday, he was on his way to the main town square for the final official parade of the Dunkirk Veterans' Association. Before marching away into history to the beat of a drum, the old men stood proudly to attention under the plane trees, trombones gleamed in the sunlight as the band played 'Colonel Bogey', two small boys waved Union Jacks and a young girl on rollerblades skimmed along the pavement behind the onlooking crowd.

At the wide-open first-floor window of a café, two old soldiers sat with a French family watching and listening. When 'Colonel Bogey' came to an end, I turned to one of the men and asked: 'Now, what's that one called?'

' 'ollocks,' he replied. And then he added: 'I can't pronounce me Bs.'

Once you know the naughty version, it's hard to get it out of your head:

Hitler has only got one ball,
Goering has two but very small,
Himmler has something similar,
But poor old Goebbels
Has no balls at all.

There was laughter round the square as the band embellished the tune with long raspberries. But the old faces were mostly solemn, and wistful for lost friends. Albert Barnes, known as 'Joe' because he used to have a moustache like Joseph Stalin's, was almost certainly the youngest person off the Dunkirk beaches in 1940. He was fourteen years old, a cabinboy on a River Thames tugboat which brought drinking water from England. In those days, it was normal for a lad that age to leave school and get a job. And when his tug was ordered to France, he went with it. What did his parents think? They didn't know. He was often away for three days anyway. When he didn't come home, his mother went to the company office to ask where her son was.

'It's all right, madam, he's away on government business.'

He was away for two weeks. Back in England, he walked up to his front door and his mother said: 'Where have you been?'

'France.'

'France. Oh my God, you've never been to Dunkirk.'

'Yes, that's the place. Dunkirk. I remember the name now.'

Albert had been to war and seen death at the age of fourteen. He remembers bodies, and parts of bodies, floating in the sea. And the funnels of sunken ships sticking out of the water, and Dunkirk on fire on the skyline. William Blackwell, in the rearguard, is now eighty-five. He pointed at Albert and said to me: 'You might see him walking along talking to himself. But he's not talking to himself. He's fourteen years old again, and it's 1940, and he's talking to ghosts.'

26

A Living News Story

Kevin Connolly

The number of surviving veterans from the 1944 D-Day landings in France was dwindling every year. Fewer than ever took part in the annual commemoration ceremonies and it seemed important to take note of the stories they had to tell. (5 June 2004)

The polish on the medals is as bright as ever, the march past to 'It's a Long Way to Tipperary' just as jaunty, but you cannot help noticing that every year the ranks of the D-Day veterans in Normandy look a little thinner, as their numbers slowly dwindle. The Second World War is gradually becoming a different kind of history: less and less a tale we hear from the men and women who saw and did it all, more and more a story found in textbooks or on headstones in the neat graveyards of North Africa and northern France. There will come a time, of course, when the last living links with the Second World War will be those of us who merely met the veterans, rather than the veterans themselves.

It set me thinking about how far back into the past a single meeting can take us. For me it is 200 years, if you allow me to count someone having met someone who met someone who saw something extraordinary. Twenty years ago as a young newspaper reporter, I was sent off to interview a woman on the eve of her hundredth birthday. It is the kind of job you get as an office junior because no one higher up the newsroom food chain wants the task of interviewing someone who may turn out to be hard of hearing as their last job on a Friday afternoon. I was only meant to collect enough information for a picture caption but ended up spending hours in the old lady's company. In fact I had the rare experience for a young man of clearly outstaying my welcome with someone who was ninety-nine and living alone.

She told me that as a young girl in Berkshire she had helped to ring the peal of church bells that announced the relief of Mafeking in the Boer War. And when she saw that I was impressed, she recounted being brought, again as a very young child, to meet a man who seemed to her incredibly old. She was told that as a little boy he had seen the injured of Waterloo being brought by barge along the canals at the end of the field near her village. I had gone out to do the most routine of interviews, and ended up just two steps away from the great struggle against Napoleon.

Ever since then I have been fascinated by how far back into the past it is possible to go with just one or two living links. Many years after that first encounter, I was in France to interview Jeanne Calment, who was at the time, famously, the oldest living human. I was hugely encouraged by the cuttings from various tabloid newspapers which had sent reporters to meet her over the course of the previous year. Jeanne, it seemed, was not above a little flirting, or even leaning forward roguishly and putting her hand on the knee of a visiting journalist to emphasise her point. She was, I think, 122 at the time.

Maybe it is just me, but I did not bring out the coquettish side in Mme Calment's nature. The care workers who basked in the reflected attentions of the world's media on their famous client more or less carried her into the chair opposite mine. One of them leaned forward and shouted: 'Jeanne, you're sitting down now', in a voice you would expect from the captain of a whaling ship going round Cape Horn, and that was the signal for us to begin.

It was not a meeting of minds. I put my first question and then there was a pause as the care worker put her lips to the side of Mme Calment's head and bawled the gist of it into her ear. But, slowly, and rather haltingly, a fascinating story emerged. It could hardly fail to. This was a woman who, after all, was thirty-nine years old when the

First World War broke out and was already collecting her pension at the start of the Second World War.

She had met Vincent Van Gogh when they both lived in Arles—'rude and smelly' he was, apparently—and she had visited Paris when they were starting to dig the foundations for the Eiffel Tower. She had, in short, lived through so many news stories herself that she'd finally become one.

The most interesting aspect of her life, incidentally, has nothing to do with my point at the moment, but here it is anyway. When she was already very old, a sharp local lawyer tempted her into a curious deal whereby he would buy her house and hand over the money immediately, but allow her to live in it until she died. She of course outlived him by nearly twenty years and local legend had it that the deal almost ruined him.

And so there you have my two longest reaches into the past—unless you count the day I was given a glass of cognac bottled in 1804, before either the Battle of Trafalgar or the invention of Stephenson's Rocket.

Now, of course, there are video and sound archives that will give stories a sort of life many years after the last D-Day soldier has gone. But there is a different kind of life to the stories we hear at first hand which can still make us thrill to the danger and urgency of the past. So, as long as their stories continue to be told and retold by those of us who are listening now, the history that the D-Day veterans made will remain alive even after the last of them loses the one battle we all lose in the end.

27

Life and Death in Davos

Misha Glenny

*The Swiss resort of Davos hosts the World Economic
Forum each winter. But for one correspondent at
least, the town wasn't just a place for talking about
finance. (24 January 2004)*

I used to attend the World Economic Forum in
Davos on a regular basis. The organisers of this
grand meeting would invite me to talk about the
drama unfolding in the Balkans as Yugoslavia fell
apart. This was, of course, at a time when the
agglomerated power of the global movers and
shakers attending the Forum could do nothing
about restoring equilibrium to the battered
Balkans. Now, when these people really could
contribute to the redevelopment of the region, the
organisers no longer deem the subject sexy enough
to warrant issuing me with an invitation.

No sour grapes, I can assure you; perhaps the
mildest whiff of nostalgia as I read through their
press releases about all the exciting things under
discussion there this year amid the briskly chilled
temperatures and powdery slopes of this peculiar
Alpine retreat. I'm especially fascinated by one
issue: the ageing of the European population, one
of the greatest political and economic disasters-in-
waiting about which we are doing very little.

And if we continue to remain indifferent to this

problem, an ever-greater percentage of Europe's population will be old, economically unproductive, an immense drain on resources particularly in the sphere of public health, and dying—but only very slowly. Indeed, large parts of Europe will begin to resemble the great sanatorium of gently putrefying flesh which was the very soul and identity of Davos itself for almost a hundred years before tuberculosis, the greatest of all killers in the nineteenth century, was marginalised as a disease.

After a young doctor discovered in the 1860s that Davos's air and the absence of dust mites slowed the progress of the illness, TB victims from all over Europe and beyond, especially the rich ones, flocked to Davos in the desperate search for a cure. Robert Louis Stevenson wrote *Kidnapped* there, while Arthur Conan Doyle was inspired to map out the final struggle between Holmes and Moriarty at the Reichenbach Falls eighty miles away when accompanying his infirm wife to a Davos sanatorium. They were followed by Thomas Mann, whose monumental work *The Magic Mountain* was conceived and set there. Taking place on the eve of the greatest carnage of all, the First World War, Mann's novel is an astonishing reflection on life but above all on the grindingly inevitable approach of death. All those in Davos were obsessed with failing constitutions and their inevitable demise, even those who, like Mann's hero Hans Castorp, arrived perfectly healthy. In Davos, one's own mortality echoes around the mountains.

I never realised when I first travelled there that the village would compel me too to explore its eerie relationship with life and death. As my father was convalescing from a heart attack in 1990, he confessed that his father, whom he had only seen twice in his life, lay buried somewhere in Davos, having died there of TB in 1947, and that he suffered a deep sense of guilt for never having visited the grave. My brother Paddy and I took up this vicarious challenge, driving across Europe through huge snowdrifts and over forbidding mountain passes before we finally reached Davos in search of that grave. By now, we were also trying to grapple with the bizarre coincidence that our mother had shared with us. It seems that our maternal great-grandfather, a director of the Lister Institute in the 1920s, played a key role in the development of a TB vaccine and had frequently convalesced from lung conditions himself in Davos, that our maternal grandparents had met there and that my mother was possibly conceived in the place.

When we reached the chaos of white darkness, in Mann's memorable metaphoric description, our need to find the grave of our grandfather, Air Commodore A.W.F. Glenny, had assumed almost supernatural dimensions, as though the family's existence depended upon it. Paddy and I arrived at the cemetery on a bleak winter afternoon. Our spirits dissolved. The paths and other landmarks were indistinguishable from the headstones. Everything was sunk deep at the bottom of the crystallised ocean of snow where we had come to fish for a single dead soul. We waded waist-deep towards the western end where the grave must lie. We then stumbled upon one of those experiences so absurd and unlikely that one is almost embarrassed in the retelling. From among the

98

hundreds of graves, the tip of a single headstone poked through as if its resident corpse still had something urgent to say to the living before finally agreeing to join its submerged compatriots. We thought we might as well start there as anywhere, but after just a few handfuls of snow were cleared the name Arthur Willoughby Falls Glenny became visible. Before we were able to relate the events of this strange journey to our father, he was dead.

'Moments there are,' wrote Thomas Mann, 'when out of death and the rebellion of the flesh, there came to thee as thou tookest stock of thyself, a dream of love. Out of this universal feast of death, out of this extremity of fever kindling the rain-washed evening sky to a fiery glow, may it be that love one day shall mount?'

28

The Last Baby Boom

Nick Thorpe

Population levels across most of the developed world were declining and nowhere more so than in Eastern Europe. This was a region where people were living longer, the young were leaving for better paid jobs elsewhere and relatively poor countries were wondering how they would cope. (4 August 2007)

An unexpected bundle arrives in Slovakia every day, with a postmark from the 1970s. The former Czechoslovak leader Gustav Husak keeps sending gifts. During his regime, cheap flats, long maternity leave and, for want of a politer word, sheer boredom produced a baby boom. And his major boom is reproducing a minor baby boom today.

The girls conceived in the tall panel houses of the Petrzalka suburb of Bratislava or beneath the weeping willows along the shores of the Danube have reached the age of peak fertility. Slovakia is suddenly the only country in Eastern Europe where births outnumber deaths. 'Yes, it is an achievement,' beams Dr Robert Paldia, deputy head of obstetrics at the Cyril and Methodius hospital, embedded deep among the high-rise towers of Petrzalka. As populations plunge throughout the region, the plucky Slovaks are proudly producing offspring. In an incubator in the intensive-care ward on the third floor, Anna Krisztina inspects her new surroundings. She is only half an hour old, born by Caesarean, and I see her even before her mother does.

Boris Vano from the Slovak Demographic Research Centre is less impressed by the numbers. In 1974, 100,000 babies were born in Slovakia; now barely 50,000 a year, he laments. And when the boom girls have each had their baby, two if we're lucky, he foresees Slovakia slipping back into the same, shrinking population straits as the rest of Eastern Europe.

In the 1970s, his counterpart in Prague Jan Hartl explains, couples married on average after only three months of acquaintance. The girl was twenty-two and usually pregnant. Those marriages may not have survived, but their copious young are now delaying conception until their early thirties. They have access to an arsenal of contraceptives their parents could not have dreamt of. Under Communism, abortion was the most commonly available method. Gustav Husak's gift might have been even more substantial. The unintended children of yesterday could have had intended children today.

Another irony of Communist rule in Eastern Europe was that the crushing of popular resistance under the tank tracks often ended in the maternity ward. In Hungary after the failed 1956 revolution, in Czechoslovakia after the Prague Spring in 1968 and in Poland after martial law in 1981, the birth rate rose spectacularly. It was as if the youth, frustrated in their desire for greater political freedom, took consolation in their desire for one another.

In Warsaw, families minister Joanna Kluzik Rostkowska is watching the calendar. The final baby-boom generation of the Communist years, the class of 1983, is just beginning to think of procreation. Her conservative government is looking for ways to encourage them. 'Our research proves that Polish women still want to have babies,' she explains. But they also want to carry on working. So she has drawn up a package of measures, including increased maternity and paternity leave, tax breaks for businesses, flexibility for the self-employed and enabling workplaces to establish kindergartens and nurseries, in the hope that her compatriots can be persuaded back into bed. It's a model which appears to have succeeded in France, where the population is increasing by a quarter of a million a year.

Elsewhere in Warsaw, demographer Krystyna Iglicka says it can't be done in Poland. She has studied the French statistics in detail and says the only women having lots of children in France today are immigrants: 'And we don't let our immigrants stay long enough.' Poland has a growing labour shortage, as its young and skilled workers flood west, to countries like Britain and Ireland. And the latest research shows they plan to stay longer than they originally thought; the Polish babies of the future may be born in Dublin and Darlington.

At the other end of the demographic scale, Jan Hartl in Prague mourns the disappearance of the profession of grandparent. In the 1970s, you became a grandparent at forty-five, he says. Grandparents saw their main role in life as caring for their grandchildren. Now the elderly can expect to live longer but families are more scattered, and the children, by the time they start having children of their own, are more financially secure. So their children sit at computer or television screens. And the line of transmission of knowledge, from the old to the very young, breaks down. The elderly feel they have no one to talk to. From the park benches in Budapest and Bratislava, Prague and Warsaw, they watch, bemused, as their fellow pensioners from America and Britain, France and Austria sail past, dressed to the nines, flailing cameras and credit cards. An average pension in Hungary is £200 a month and many live on less.

With little to do with their time and little money for material goods, depression is a growing problem. Depression, not cancer, is the scourge of our age, says Ferenc Benkovich, founder of Saint Anna's old people's home in Gyor in western Hungary.

'I'm a priest, from a village, and the greatest gift

of my life is that from childhood I enjoyed the company of the elderly.'

29

Precious Life

John Simpson

Having a baby caused one correspondent to look at stories of violence and suffering through new eyes. (28 July 2007)

The explosion was just close by. The windows of my hotel billowed inwards like sails in a storm, and the walls shuddered. A pause, then the alarms and sirens started up all round. My camera team and I got there quickly. The stench of high explosive still hung over everything. The screaming had mostly stopped, and the rescue workers were dealing with the still living and collecting up bits of bodies. The police were starting to take out their frustration and anger on the photographers.

This was in Kabul just the other day, but I've seen these things dozens and dozens of times during my career. I've never been a great one for the kind of reporting that tells you how the journalist feels when something terrible happens. It seems to me that we need reporters to be crisp and accurate and unexcitable, like ambulance crews; and you certainly don't want an ambulance man leaning over you and telling you how he feels about your injuries. You just want him to say they'll get you sorted out in no time flat.

But in Kabul the other day and in Baghdad a couple of weeks earlier, I couldn't help noticing a change within myself. I tried to find out dispassionately what had happened, of course, but when I looked at the bodies on their stretchers and the injured moaning in pain I felt a new kind of anger.

I knew immediately what it was all about. Last year, after four miscarriages over a period of some years and virtually giving up all hope of having a baby, my wife and I had a son: a healthy, active, jolly little boy we've named Rafe (short for Ranulph). With six billion people on earth, having a child is scarcely a rarity. But in our case it was so unexpected, so gratifying, that Rafe seems to us like a miracle.

I already had two daughters by my first marriage and have always, fortunately, been close to them: even more so, now that we all, weirdly, have children of the same sort of age. But I confess that when my daughters were young I wasn't so aware of their uniqueness: everyone of my age seemed to have children then. I understand things better now.

And to see the miracle of other people's lives snuffed out wantonly on the streets of Baghdad or Kabul, or London for that matter, for some scarcely understood political or religious motive, seems to me nothing short of blasphemy. I don't just loathe the stench of high explosive, I've come to loathe the attitudes of people who use high explosive for their own purposes: insurgents, terrorists, the intelligence services of a dozen countries, governments which target towns and cities and always have a ready apology when they

104

kill the wrong people.

High explosive means hospitals with blood on the walls and corridors, and ordinary people like you and me lying on the floor or on a gurney, ears ringing with the noise of the explosion, nostrils filled with the stench of it still. The screams of others who are more seriously hurt than us. The fear and despair of the small number of doctors who have to deal with so many life-or-death cases and know that they're condemning many of them to a slow, painful death. 'The armed struggle,' said an African resistance song from the 1980s, 'is an act of love.' Try explaining that to the people lying in the hospital corridors.

The idea that some civilians are decent and righteous, while others deserve everything they get, or else shouldn't have been in the way, seems to me to be intolerable. I hope I never did think that attacks on civilians, any civilians, were justified; but now I know for certain they aren't.

Having been through the first and second Gulf wars, and watched the wars in the former Yugoslavia and the NATO bombing of Belgrade in 1999, I don't really care any longer what the cause is; it's the civilians on the receiving end who matter. I'm sorry if this sounds pious or sentimental; I don't mean it to be. But I have finally understood something, through the blessing of having another child late on. It's that life itself is immensely valuable. Not just the lives of people who think and look and maybe worship like you and me, people who are attractive or well educated or rich, people who are the right type of Christian or the right type of Muslim. All lives.

I realise this is terribly sententious: the moral

equivalent of a motto from a Christmas cracker. Still, just because something is obvious doesn't automatically mean it's totally lacking in value. I certainly won't stop going to the kind of places where these things happen. But, at the grand old age of sixty-two, my reaction to them has changed.

The fact is, my time reporting on violence and bombings in places like Baghdad and Kabul has shown me one essential thing: that the lives of the poor, the stupid, the old, the ugly, are no less precious to them and to the people around them than the life of my little son Rafe is precious to me.

30

Lessons in Love

Chris Hogg

There was an unpleasant shock for some of Japan's newly retired salarymen. A new law was introduced which allowed wives to keep half of their husbands' pensions if they divorced. But their men weren't giving up; they got together to try to find out how to become better husbands. (31 March 2007)

It's a cold Saturday evening and I'm standing in the rain in Tokyo's entertainment district. Glamorous girls in thigh-high boots strut past with barely a backwards glance at the men who can't take their eyes off them. This isn't what I've come to see, though. Instead I climb the steep stairs to the top floor of a small *izakaya*, or Japanese pub. Here a group of ten men have gathered to drink, to smoke, to eat and, most importantly, to learn how to save their marriages. This is the Tokyo chapter of what might best be described as the 'National Chauvinistic Husbands' Association'. Its founder, Shuichi Amano, made the long journey up from the southern island of Kyushu for tonight's meeting. He's a large self-confident man who sits, as befits his status, at the centre of the long table. This is a man comfortable with being the centre of attention.

They begin with a declaration of their three basic rules for love. They chant in unison: 'Say "thank you" without hesitation. Say "sorry" without fear. Say "I love you" without being ashamed.' People sitting at nearby tables go quiet, but then the women give them a round of applause. The chants begin again. The three basic rules for not winning. 'We do not win. We cannot win. We don't want to win.'

In the battle of the sexes these men are waving a white flag. But are they wimps? The man in charge, Mr Amano, doesn't think so. He started the group eight years ago after finding out that three or four of his friends had been told by their wives that they wanted a divorce. When he mentioned this to his wife, she told him he might be next. He was shocked. 'I started doing the household chores right away,' he told me. This was a new experience for both of them. At first his wife was suspicious. 'What have you done wrong?' she said. But then gradually their relationship improved. He started to share his techniques with other people. Word spread and today he says he has more than 1,200 members across Japan.

Mr Amano says he's created a network where for the first time men can share their problems and advise each other how to solve them. Women can always find a couple of friends to talk to when things are going wrong, he says. But men, Japanese men especially, find it harder to share their emotional concerns.

Listening to him talk was Yohei Takayama. He's twenty-eight. He's been married just six months, but he told me he'd joined the group because he was worried already that his wife might try to divorce him.

Why were Japanese men such bad husbands, I asked him. 'It's the way of the Samurai,' he replied without a smirk or a grin. Traditionally, he said, men went out to work, the women stayed at home and kept house. Even today, for many, that's still true.

That is a pretty fair description of a lot of Japanese marriages, particularly among the older generations. But now Yohei, like the others gathered around the table, is employing some of Mr Amano's techniques in a bid to save his marriage. He tries to win 'smileage'—one point for every time he makes his wife smile, by doing a good deed, or even cracking a joke with her. Mr Amano believes if you can build up a 'smileage' total of around forty a month you'll have enough credit for coming home drunk once a fortnight, for example.

Towards the end of the evening, certificates were presented. The association has ten levels of attainment and, much like in sumo wrestling, very few reach the highest levels. The criteria for the different ranks were written out on cards displayed at the end of the table. To be recognised as the lowest rank you have to love your wife after three years of marriage and help with the household chores. Mr Amano himself has only reached the fifth level, which you attain when you can hold hands with your wife in public. The highest or tenth level is reserved for those members who can say 'I love you' without embarrassment. It is an accolade many strive for but so far only a tiny proportion of the members has achieved.

It would be easy to poke fun at their earnest efforts to learn behaviour that many others find natural. But the men who'd gathered here to learn from their guru seemed as thirsty for his wisdom as they were for the beers. By nine o'clock, though, it was time to pack up and go home. When you're out drinking, and learning how to treat your wife well, it doesn't do to keep her up waiting.

31

Too Big for Paris

Caroline Wyatt

Obesity is a growing problem in many Western nations. Figures show that a quarter of all adults in Britain are obese, while a third of all children are overweight. But how come it's not a problem for the French, who are known to love fine food and wine yet remain in far better shape than the British? And they live longer too. What's their secret?
(24 June 2006)

109

My first memory of Paris is of arriving for a visit at the age of eleven. The weekend came courtesy of my French aunt Camille, a Parisienne from the tip of her perfect blonde bob to the kitten heels of her Charles Jourdan shoes. She was petite, not much taller than me at the time, and rather slimmer. She smelt of Chanel No 5, wore French designer clothes and, to my child's eyes, was the ultimate in sophistication. And she was taking me shopping to Galeries Lafayette, the Paris equivalent of Selfridges.

I was thrilled. Until the moment the Parisian shop assistant eyed my English boarding-school figure with that unique hauteur that only Parisian shop assistants can muster, and began an animated conversation. My aunt's grip on her Hermès-style handbag became quite steely and the discussion ended with the words: 'Well, the English are bigger for their age.' Years of sausages and chips and bread-and-butter-pudding at boarding school had taken their toll. Aged eleven, I was too big for Paris.

All these years on, little has changed. *French Women Don't Get Fat* was the title of a recent bestseller, written by a svelte and, dare I say, smug Frenchwoman keen to share her secrets of slenderness with the rest of the world. I read it in a post-Christmas haze of gluttony, lying on the sofa with a box of chocolates, though I did wonder a little why my best friend had given me the book. From memory, those French women's secrets seemed to involve eating less, and running up and down sixteen flights of stairs whenever a kilo threatened to pile on. She didn't mention Parisiennes' real secret, living on black coffee and

110

cigarettes, although it is a diet that appears to work for most, along with steely self-discipline. A fat Parisienne is clearly a crime against nature.

So, the other day, I found myself sitting in the waiting room of a French nutritionist, whose services of course come courtesy of the French health service. After three years of living in Paris, I have had enough. Enough of trying to squeeze a British-size bottom on to spindly French café chairs clearly built by a population of Lilliputians to repel the Anglo-Saxon invaders over the coming summer months.

The nutritionist, Dr Françoise L'Hermite, was surprisingly sympathetic. She looked horrified as I admitted that I often didn't get time to sit down for lunch. And that I grabbed snacks on the run. And certainly didn't take an hour for my main meal. Too much to do, too little time.

'No wonder!' she exclaimed. 'You must sit and enjoy your food, look at it and take in what you're eating. And you have to spend a minimum of twenty minutes on each meal.' As she patiently explained, there are good reasons why America and Britain are both suffering increasingly from obesity. For her, junk food is not the main culprit; it's the way we view sitting down for proper meals as a waste of valuable time, preferring instead to graze on the run.

Her advice was: everything in moderation; and two main meals a day, the biggest at lunchtime, and no snacks in between. Most French may not be quite so disciplined about what they eat, but many do still believe that sitting down twice a day for family meals creates better eating habits in children and healthier adults. Françoise

L'Hermite's advice was to have a long lunch, eaten slowly, savouring both the food and the company. Advice I now intend to put into practice on a daily basis.

'For France, a meal is a very particular moment in which you can share pleasure,' she said. 'From an Anglo-Saxon point of view, food is just fuel to give energy to your muscles. But if you take no pleasure in it, you're breaking all the rules of eating, and if you eat at your desk or too fast, your brain doesn't know when you're full.'

But what about all those French that I see at lunchtime, pigging out on steak and chips, with lashings of wine, followed by cheese or perhaps a little crème caramel? Well, there is another explanation and it's not really such a paradox, either. Researchers in the United States once spent months looking into why the French remained so much slimmer than Americans. After intensive study, they came to a remarkable conclusion: it was because the French ate less. Main courses, puddings, even drinks all come in smaller sizes. No super-size portions in Paris yet.

At lunch in a local restaurant this week, I looked around, in those few moments where I wasn't trying to commune properly with my food. All around me, French office workers were focusing on what was on their plates amid animated conversations, mostly about the food itself.

Yet as we left, the pavements were full of people grabbing a sandwich to eat at their desk. The queues at fast-food restaurants snaked out of the doors. And guess which country is home to McDonalds' most profitable franchise? Not America, not Britain, but France, which some forecast will reach US obesity levels by the year 2020.

As France slowly adopts our eating habits, the nation is getting fatter and starting to worry about it. Earlier this year, French schools banned vending machines. Children here, too, are bigger than ever.

Just as the French are trying to resist the perils of economic globalisation, they're also starting to realise that their old reverence for food—in the right place, at the right time, and in moderation—is something else worth holding on to. Fast food catcn on the run is the real Anglo-Saxon invasion that they should resist at all costs if the next generation of children is not to suffer agonies of embarrassment at the hands of haughty Parisian shop assistants.

32

Back to Chernobyl

Bridget Kendall

The catastrophic explosion at the nuclear power plant in Chernobyl in Ukraine triggered what turned out to be the world's worst nuclear disaster: the amount of radiation released dwarfed even that from the Hiroshima bomb. The blast sent a cloud of radiation over many parts of Western Europe and twenty years on arguments were continuing to rage not only about the consequences to health from the accident, but also about the safety of the damaged

113

reactor, which is now encased in a concrete shell.
(22 April 2006)

I well remember the spring of 1986, the year the Chernobyl disaster happened. I was in Moscow shortly afterwards and the city was awash with rumours. These were still Soviet times and Mikhail Gorbachev had only been in power just over a year, General Secretary of a Communist Party determined to keep its grip on power. No one was yet expecting the bold reforms that would turn the country upside down.

So in quiet conversations around kitchen tables, there was scepticism and anger about official pronouncements. Mr Gorbachev had gone on television to admit the situation was serious, though he said the worst had been avoided. Few at the time realised he was referring to the danger of a thermonuclear explosion.

In Moscow, the suspicion was of a cover-up to hide the extent of contamination: were Muscovites now travelling on buses used to transport irradiated Chernobyl emergency workers to hospital? Were the strawberries and mushrooms in the market from areas where radioactive rain had fallen?

Those in Kiev at the time tell the same story. In 1986, Ukraine was only a Soviet republic with limited local powers, not yet a separate country. Any serious emergency, especially one involving the centralised and highly secretive nuclear industry, was reported straight to Moscow. Even at Radio Kiev, part of the state propaganda apparatus, journalists had little information. Behind an officially proclaimed calm there was

114

unofficial panic. You couldn't find petrol anywhere. At the main train station there was chaos, as everyone tried to procure tickets for mothers and children to get them well away from the area.

Kiev became a ghost town of inebriated males, drunk on the red wine that rumour had it could strengthen your immune system. They fed each other's alarm with nightmarish speculation. The joke was you were more likely to die of exaggerated information in Kiev than of radiation.

Closer to Chernobyl and to the moment of the accident itself, the reminiscences are even more sobering. One woman who worked at the nuclear plant told me she'd been due to start an early shift on 26 April, but at 2 a.m. she got a call from her boss at the reactor telling her not to come in. 'I can't tell you over the phone what's happened,' he said. 'Just keep the children back from school and close the windows.' Pripyat, the workers' town, is only a few miles away from the plant. From one side, high up, the reactor would have been visible on the horizon, the damaged core smouldering red, and the black cloud billowing skywards.

All day she sat at home, while other folk, in festive mood, strolled in the April sunshine. Children played in the dusty streets and splashed in the frothy water that was sprayed periodically. Neighbours invited her on to the roof for a better view of the drama at the reactor. In vain she urged them to stay indoors.

'I'd heard the fear in my boss's voice,' she said. 'And I was an engineer. I knew the potential consequences of a nuclear accident.' Later, she and many other workers went back to the plant.

115

'We wanted to help,' she said. 'We were grieving for the loss of our beautiful plant we'd been so proud of. But above all we felt responsible.'

Not everyone in Pripyat was proud of the plant. In the summer of 1986, I tracked down the editor of the local Pripyat paper, a feisty independent-minded journalist called Lyubov Kovalevskaya. At the start of 1986, Gorbachev launched a new policy proclaiming no one was above criticism. She took him at his word and published a devastating critique of Chernobyl's nuclear power station, describing corners being cut and procedures ignored, with potentially serious consequences.

Her warning was of course prophetic: the accident took place a couple of months later. But she received no commendation from the party authorities. They saw her then as a troublemaker. And when I met her in August 1986, like everyone else in Pripyat, she'd been evacuated to Kiev where she was camping in temporary accommodation and worrying about the health consequences.

It was she who told me about the pets that had been left behind, the dogs who bayed through the apartment windows as they watched their owners line up to get on buses, taking at face value official advice that they'd be back in a day or two. Some animals seemed to know better.

Tatiana is now twenty-four, so she was four when her family left Chernobyl. She remembers her granny decided not to take the family cat. But as they boarded the bus, the cat threw itself at the folding doors, the last glimpse they ever had of it.

It seemed appropriate, for a trip into the Chernobyl zone twenty years on, to ask Tatiana if she'd like to come with us to revisit Pripyat, the

116

place of her birth. All she had, she said, was a vague memory of a gleaming white town, surrounded by woodland. Now, like the damaged reactor, the town is at the heart of an extensive contamination zone that has been fenced off, to keep most humans out. Only a few old souls have returned to their former villages. The wildlife is abundant. Past the first checkpoint, past the irradiated villages buried in cement that still cause the Geiger counter to click furiously, we came across a herd of Przewalski's horses, brought in to crop the grasses in the dry summer marshlands to reduce fire hazards.

Reactor number four is still an eyesore, a dark grey hulk encased in armour-plated coating of concrete and metal. But more weird still are the enormous cranes that twenty years ago were busy constructing two more reactors. Now they are frozen in mid-lift against the skyline, stuck in history. Like other metallic hardware that litters the site, they're too contaminated to be shifted.

We arrive in Pripyat and Tatiana shivers in anticipation. The town is still white, still surrounded by woodland, but it too is frozen in a bygone age. A massive coat of arms—a red and gold hammer and sickle—hangs from the roof of one sixteen-storey building, a reminder that twenty years ago this was the now-defunct Soviet Union.

Broken glass crunching underfoot, up sixteen flights of concrete steps, we reach the top floor. This is Tatiana's building. The wind whistles through the glassless windows. Faded pale blue wallpaper flaps. In one room there is a rusty children's chair. We open the door on to the balcony. In the distance, the grey slumbering

117

reactor is like a dragon, biding its time.

Down below, trees that have sprouted through the paving stones mark two untended decades. And beyond them is the unmistakable silhouette of a big wheel: the centrepiece of an unused funfair. By 1 May 1986, when it should have opened, the inhabitants had left for good. Unsettling images that prompt uneasy thoughts. But not for Tatiana. For her this is not bittersweet; it's a precious restoration of a childhood memory she feared lost.

'This is it,' she says, 'I remember the view. And it's still just as perfect!'

33

Return Visit

Brian Barron

Our correspondent was in Saigon, now Ho Chi Minh City, as the North Vietnamese forces burst into the city in April 1975 ending the eleven-year-long war. Thirty years later he was back, seeing what had changed. (28 December 2002)

Three times now I've been with American forces as they've gone to war in a major way. Twice, thanks to brilliant leadership and hi-tech weapons, they've triumphed: in the Gulf War eleven years ago and then more recently in the Afghanistan conflict. But the very first deployment I witnessed, the doomed attempt to prop up South Vietnam, spiralled into a shambles of betrayal and panic that scarred those running today's military and political establishment.

We sensed the end was near when the plaster began falling off the ceiling of the broadcasting studio at Saigon Radio. A renegade squadron of South Vietnam planes, which had defected to the Communist north, was bombing the presidential palace a mile away. As the capital shook to the explosions, the microphone suspended from the ceiling swung above our heads like a crazy pendulum. It was at this precise moment the BBC governors in London decided our team should evacuate. Their order to board the nearest helicopter crackled through the earphones in the dust-filled studio. No doubt they were well-intentioned, but of course we ignored them. What foreign correspondent would walk away from his biggest story to date? Anyway, the American Embassy, the airlift exit point for the fleeing Westerners and Saigon elite, was under siege from thousands of southerners wanting out as well.

We had a vast, ancient American limousine with the sort of chromium tail fins once favoured on Sunset Boulevard. Saigon was dissolving around us in a great splurge of looting as people staggered along the pavements pulling refrigerators from abandoned offices.

Aware a phalanx of North Vietnamese tanks was barrelling towards the city, we headed for the Saigon bridge to see them arrive. I was in the back of the car reading a book on guerrilla warfare by General Vo Nguyen Giap, the Northern Communist who'd defeated the French colonial army at Dien Bien Phu twenty years earlier. But now, from a roadside trench, jumped a heavily

119

armed South Vietnamese colonel and a dozen of his men. He was literally frothing at the mouth, and with guns pointed, accused us of being Communist spies. As he cursed and screamed I hid the book, a death warrant if found, among the broken upholstery and seat springs. Then the mad colonel forced us to block the Saigon bridge exit with our car. We shakily walked back to the city. The colonel was killed later trying to escape down the Saigon river.

An hour later, in a news agency office some 200 metres from the presidential palace, I heard gunfire and the rumble of tanks. The first North Vietnamese tanks were smashing through the palace's three-metre-high gates. There were bullets galore but they were being jubilantly fired into the air by the invaders. One tank commander brandished the Communist flag from the balcony. On the lawn, the Southern presidential guard knelt in submission. I found myself beside the last Southern president, General Duong 'Big' Minh, as he surrendered to a pistol-waving Northerner.

Across the capital, Southerners lined the streets as their highly disciplined conquerors passed. We headed back to the Saigon bridge. It was one vast traffic jam of Northern tanks and howitzers; the warriors from the jungle looked bewildered, for they lacked Saigon street maps. The remains of our car lay by the kerb, flattened by the first Communist tank across the bridge. On an empty road we found an abandoned South Vietnamese armoured convoy. With the enemy at the door, the Southern army had jumped out of its boots. They littered the hot tarmac, along with discarded uniforms and rifles.

Years later, the last American general to leave Saigon told me how he'd burned two million dollars with thermal grenades because it was too bulky to put in a helicopter. The very last American military presence was a small contingent of Marine guards fighting back tears of shame, lying hidden on their own embassy roof, even as the Northern tanks swept by us in the street below. Finally, just when the Marines feared they'd been forgotten, a helicopter appeared from the evacuation fleet in the South China Sea.

It was fantastic the war was over. For Americans, a catastrophe—and they'd failed to honour evacuation promises to thousands of Southerners who'd worked for the military. These individuals spent years in Communist re-education camps. For Hanoi, an incredible victory. But in the decades after, the Northerners failed to be magnanimous enough. In a sense, they won the war but fumbled the peace—or at least the chance of turning Vietnam into a modern powerhouse of ideas and industry . . .

Thirty years on and you have to pinch yourself at the transformation. The jungle marshes are fast disappearing, pumped out by a steel forest of cranes and engineering equipment hired by South Korean, Taiwanese and Hong Kong development companies. Where the Vietcong fired their 122mm rockets into this city—no longer called Saigon—is a rapidly expanding executive housing estate done out in the sort of pastel colours favoured in Florida coastal resorts. The concrete blocks are fronted by neat lawns and ornamental lakes with neoclassical statues. Traffic thunders past on its way to the Mekong delta and a mile away a new bridge takes shape across the Saigon river with Vietnamese engineers risking life and limb, precariously balanced on steel girders as ships slip by far below them. Fluttering from one bridge pylon is Vietnam's red flag with a yellow star. But then you notice that on one new street of shops there's a real estate sign. Next door is a pizza parlour. Saigon South, as this vast development is called, is for middle-class Vietnamese; for instance, Communist party officials with a decent income, or managers in the growing private sector, along with foreign businessmen back in Vietnam after the last recession.

I've seen earlier attempts at economic reform here come to grief, usually because of resistance from the revolutionary generation, the men who scooped up Saigon with the barrels of their guns. But this time the scale of the changes is so vast it will be difficult to block them. Maybe the best gauge of economic health in a country held back for far too long is the number of motorcycles in Ho Chi Minh City and Hanoi. It could be seven million, a sort of anarchic cavalry with each machine often carrying a complete family of four sandwiched between handlebars and rear wheel. It's a sign that money is trickling through even in the habitually frugal society of the north, and a pointer, perhaps, as to how the Communist Party is striving to stay ahead of public expectations. Today the Politburo has endorsed the path to economic reform blazed by its giant neighbour, Communist China. But the Vietnamese comrades retain absolute political control; hence the Soviet-style mausoleum in Hanoi for Ho Chi Minh, the veteran revolutionary who led them first against the French and then the Americans. He died in 1969 without seeing the final victory over the pro-American southern half of the country.

A party member solemnly assured me there were no political prisoners today. In fact, diplomats from European Union embassies in Hanoi try to keep tabs on twenty-one dissidents whom they call 'persons of concern'. There could be more. They're either in jail or under house arrest for opposing the government. I asked to see one prominent critic of the Communist regime who has been in and out of prison and was told no one knows his address. That was pure evasion.

Still, Vietnam is showing a more tolerant approach to religion, including evangelical churches, and during our visit it invited back a prominent Buddhist monk who had been in exile for forty years. He made the most of it by parading through Hanoi's oldest quarter at the head of a column of his followers, all from abroad.

The Politburo now takes a pragmatic attitude towards America, once its nemesis but now Vietnam's biggest trading partner. In the Mekong delta town of Ben Tre, where Graham Greene probably conceived part of his Indo-China masterpiece, *The Quiet American*, I ran into a group of American non-governmental advisers looking at the rice export industry. Near the same town thirty-five years ago I recall a spine-chilling night in an American encampment listening, over many cold beers, to CIA and military personnel discussing gruesome counter-terror measures. Now the delta is at peace exporting rice to the world and the Americans are back in small numbers. That's a wonder in itself after the horrors of war.

34

A Maoist Wedding

Charles Haviland

After years of fighting, Nepal's Maoist rebels were preparing to join the government. It wasn't clear what impact they would have on Nepali society. The Maoists had firm views on how life should be lived and even on how people should get married.
(2 December 2006)

It's evening in the hills. The sweet smell of herbs fills the air and the shadows lengthen. In this small village, built on a hill, military men and women, mostly young, troop into a school. Some wear camouflage fatigues, others garish T-shirts. Some carry rifles; others are empty-handed.

Surprisingly, this is a wedding party. Certainly not one as you or I know it. In fact, once they get to the school, the first thing on the menu for these sixty or so Maoist soldiers is their usual military drill. Village children stare from the rooftop as the troops get a lecture on marriage from their commander and hold a minute's silence for those they call their martyrs, all arms clenched in what the Maoists call their 'Red Salute'.

The wedding venue is to be the school veranda. It's decked with pictures of the iconic figures of Communism. But there's also a rough wooden table with garlands of mauve flowers and four candles.

Two grooms and two brides are sitting among the assembled company. They look deadly serious, and seem reluctant to get up as they're called to the podium amid rhythmic clapping and solemn drumming. The two grooms are to make speeches. The first, Comrade Samjok, now with a shy smile on his face, a red and black T-shirt visible under his uniform, urges workers of the world to unite and wishes long life to the People's Army. Then he comes to the point. 'Comrade Anima and I have fallen in love and request a wedding,' he says. It's then the turn of the other groom, Comrade Sayjan, but his speech is read by a senior Maoist while he and his fiancée stand giving the Red Salute. Comrade Sayjan firmly holds his gun throughout: it's clearly a fixture for him.

Then at last the couples allow themselves the luxury of a big grin. Each in turn lights a candle; bride and groom exchange garlands and apply red blessing powder to their foreheads. These are rituals from Hindu tradition but there is of course no priest, no incantation or reference to religion. Instead, there are firm handshakes between bride and groom.

The drumming gets faster and young men in the crowd start dancing. Suddenly, as if unable to restrain themselves any longer, the two grooms leap up to join in. Comrade Sayjan's gun swings alarmingly on its neck strap as they do high kicks around the schoolyard.

This is a rare moment of spontaneous fun in Maoist life. Like most Maoist activities, this double wedding is, in fact, spartan and economical. In these marriages they make a virtue, for instance, of outlawing the giving of dowry, a practice which in this part of the world has heaped misery on countless brides because their husbands' greedy families make ever more demands, often getting violent. In these Communist weddings, the wider families aren't involved. And they are love marriages, not arranged ones. The spouses have, however, met within the party, which strictly controls the whole ceremony. I talk to one of the couples, minutes after they've tied the knot. They are sanguine.

'I wasn't impressed by her beauty at first,' says Comrade Samjok. 'But we used to look at each other during battle, and then to support and help each other.' In a matter-of-fact way, he says an emotional relationship developed, then the two of them fell in love and proposed to each other.

His new bride, Comrade Anima, makes a wider reflection. 'We know we can't be together all our lives,' she says. 'It depends on the revolution, and where the party needs to send us. We'll cross whatever barriers there are between us. And even if we're not together physically, we'll be joined by our thoughts.' A woman Maoist official says much the same. 'A wedding is not a matter of personal romance,' she explained. 'Rather, the marriage is to combine the strengths of two people for the good of the party.'

By sponsoring weddings in their ranks, the Maoists want to prevent their troops from eloping together or leaving the party for an external lover. They also use the marriages to help enforce their own ban on sex outside marriage. If there are some Communists who believe in abolition of the family, they'll be disappointed by these Maoists, who want to keep the family but with, they say, full equality between men and women.

The zeal to promote marriage seems to have grown since April when the Maoist ceasefire began. There have been reports of mass marriages involving fifteen or twenty couples at a time. Naturally, a considerable number of children have been born into the Maoist movement and many have been raised sharing the parental lap with a gun or, in the past, living among bullets and shells. That's something which should end with the imminent move to lock up Maoist weapons under a peace deal.

In the mist, the morning after the double wedding, I saw the two newlywed couples stony-faced once more, back at their morning drill. It was clear there would be no honeymoon for them.

35

The Penis Restaurant

Andrew Harding

Chinese cooking is much loved the world over, yet the Chinese have a reputation for eating things which others might avoid. Plates of steaming dog, for example, have little appeal for the average British diner. And there's a restaurant in Beijing which serves even more unusual delicacies.
(23 September 2006)

The dish in front of me is grey and shiny. 'Russian dog,' says my waitress, Nancy. 'Big dog,' I reply.

'Yes,' she says, 'big dog's penis.' We are in a cosy restaurant in a dark street in Beijing. My appetite seems to have gone for a stroll outside.

Nancy has brought out a whole selection of delicacies; they're draped awkwardly across a huge platter, with a crocodile carved out of a carrot as the centrepiece. Nestling beside the dog's penis are its clammy testicles, and beside that a giant salami-shaped object.

'Donkey,' says Nancy. 'Good for the skin.' She guides me round the penis platter. 'Snake. Very potent—they have two penises each.' I didn't know that. Sheep, horse, ox, seal—excellent for the circulation. She points to three dark, shrivelled lumps which look like liquorice allsorts, a special treat apparently: reindeer, from Manchuria.

The Guolizhuang restaurant claims to be China's only speciality penis emporium, and no, it's not a joke. The atmosphere is more exotic spa than boozy night out. Nancy describes herself as a nutritionist. 'We don't call them waiters here. And we don't serve much alcohol,' she says. 'Only common people come here to get drunk and laugh.' But she does offer me a deer-blood and vodka cocktail which I decide to skip.

The restaurant's gristly menu was dreamt up by a man called Mr Guo. He's eighty-one now and retired. After fleeing China's civil war back in 1949, he moved to Taiwan and then to Atlanta, Georgia, where he began to look deeper into traditional Chinese medicine and experiment on the appendages of man's best friend. Apparently, they're low in cholesterol and good not just for boosting the male sex drive but for treating all sorts of ailments.

128

Laughter trickles through the walls of our dining room. 'Government officials,' says Nancy. 'Two of them upstairs; they're having the penis hotpot.'

Most of the restaurant's guests are either wealthy businessmen or government bureaucrats who, as Nancy puts it, have been brought here by people who want their help. What better way to secure a contract than over a steaming penis fondue? Discretion is assured: all the tables are in private rooms. The glitziest one has gold dishes. 'Some like their food served raw,' says Nancy. 'Like sushi. But we can cook it any way you like.'

Not long ago, a particularly rich real-estate mogul came in with four friends. All men. 'Women don't come here so often, and they shouldn't eat testicles,' says Nancy solemnly. The men spent the equivalent of £3,000 on a particularly rare dish, something that needed to be ordered months in advance. 'Tiger penis,' says Nancy.

The illegal trade in tiger parts is a big problem in China. Campaigners say the species is being driven towards extinction because of its popularity as a source of traditional medicine.

I mention this, delicately, to Nancy. But she insists that all her tiger supplies come from animals that have died of old age. 'Anyway, we only have one or two orders a year,' she says.

So what does it taste like? 'Oh, the same as all the others,' she says blithely. And does it have any particular potency? Nope. People just like to order tiger to show off how much money they have. Welcome to the People's Republic of China. Tigers beware. 'Oh yes,' she adds, 'the same group also ate an aborted reindeer foetus. That is very good for your skin.' My appetite is heading for the airport.

Still, I think it would be rude not to try something. I'm normally OK about this sort of thing. I've had fried cockroaches and sheep's eyes. So . . . there's a small bowl of sliced and pickled ox penis on the table. I pick up a piece with my chopsticks and start to chew. It's cold and bland and rubbery. Nancy gives me a matronly smile. 'This one,' she says, 'should be eaten every day.'

36

Please Speak English

James Coomarasamy

President Bush was forced to admit defeat when a plan for comprehensive immigration reform, to which he'd given his personal backing, collapsed in the United States Senate. But it wasn't just the politicians who had strong views about immigration. (30 June 2007)

Joey Vento sounded pleased to hear from me. Well, fairly pleased. 'Sure I remember you,' his voice came down the phone. 'You're the guy who put me through the wringer last year.' That's not quite how I remembered our previous encounter. I'd certainly quizzed him about his views on immigration, but he'd given as good as he'd got and been more than happy to talk about the need to defend the English language in today's America. With immigration back in the news, I asked him, could we have another chat? 'Sure,' he said, and with that I was on my way to Geno's, the Philadelphia cheese steak stall he founded forty-one years ago.

It's hard to miss on the apex of Ninth and Passyunk in the heart of Little Italy. It's just a takeaway stall really, but there's so much neon on the inside and outside that Joey affectionately calls it 'the Las Vegas of Philadelphia'. Which is appropriate, for a man who'd just hit the publicity jackpot when I last met him. Then, as now, immigration was the hot political topic of the day, and Joey had turned up the heat. He'd been reported to the authorities for having a sticker on the sliding door of his stall which featured a picture of an eagle and the phrase: 'This is America. Please speak English when ordering.' For some, he'd struck a chord, struck a blow for ordinary Americans. For others, this was brazen discrimination.

English is a language that Joey's Sicilian grandfather never mastered when he came to the United States in the 1920s. 'But he tried,' Joey told me, 'and he knew that was what it meant to come here.' Joey's not exactly proud of his family. He freely admits that his brother and father were gangsters, but he's proud of the notoriety he's achieved: as a defender of the English language. Somewhat disconcertingly he was brandishing a knife when I arrived, but it turned out he was in the middle of slicing the rolls for the day's food. 'I'm sixty-eight,' he reminded me, looking fighting fit in a black T-shirt, with a silver chain around his neck, 'and I've been up since three in the morning. Don't tell me Americans won't do the tough jobs.'

Geno's is one of Philadelphia's most famous landmarks. 'People visit us, then they see the Liberty Bell,' Joey jokes, placing his stall just above one of the symbols of American independence. Its signature, in fact its only dish, is a bun filled with thinly sliced rib-eyed steaks topped with chopped, fried onions and a choice of three cheeses: American, provolone and an amorphous, glutinous yellow substance called Cheese Whiz.

I wouldn't recommend the latter. As we were chatting, one of Joey's well-fed regulars popped in and asked for a double helping of Whiz. For breakfast. When he left, Joey confided that the Whiz could be speeding him to a heart attack. 'But in moderation there's no better stuff,' he added quickly, 'although I'd recommend the provolone.'

Twelve months on, the cheese choice remains the same and the controversial sticker is still there. Joey maintains that his stall has become something of a shrine, not just for cheese steak connoisseurs, but for English-first pilgrims, who get a free pen and sticker when they order. He seems unconcerned that the local authorities are taking him to court for placing what they argue is an offensive sign in his window.

'Bring it on,' he says, his eyes glistening almost as brightly as his diamond ear stud. 'What have I got to fear?' And with that, he glances up at the walls for reassurance. Staring back at him is a host of famous faces, from Bill Clinton to Justin Timberlake to Rudy Giuliani, some snapped in the act of rustling up cheese steaks at the stall themselves, all wearing huge, Cheese Whiz-eating grins on their faces. But none of those grins is as wide as Joey's, a self-made man who clearly loves the limelight.

Leaving a batch of rolls to languish unsliced, he scuttles away to a back room, looking for proof of the righteousness of his cause. He returns with a pile of folders, overflowing with letters and messages of support from all over the country. 'We're with you, Joey'; 'What you're doing is great, Joey'; even 'We'll vote for you, Joey'. To these writers, he's a true patriot, defending his countrymen from the threat to their identity posed by the growing influence of Spanish. And while that's not the only reason why the immigration bill failed, the letters to Joey give a sense of the grass-roots anger that senators from both parties have been hearing.

Unlike Joey, the immigration bill really has been through the wringer and failed to come out the other side. When I phoned him just after the Senate vote, Joey was triumphant. 'Looks like those politicians listened to Joey,' he said. Looks like they did.

37

A View from Burgundy

Caroline Wyatt

As France waited to see who would succeed Jacques Chirac as president, most French people had accepted that reforms were overdue. But still they believed it was important to retain those qualities which made France so special. (28 April 2007)

Earlier this spring, I found myself in the small sleepy Burgundy town of Donzy at 1pm and very much looking forward to a solid French lunch. The pale sunshine beat down on the main square, giving the honey-coloured stone a golden tinge. On the narrow cobbled main street was a host of cafés, their blinds shading the tables outside. For once, we had time to stop for a meal, and I could hardly wait. Until, that is, we went in to the first café to ask about lunch.

'Lunch? Oh no, Madame, we shut for lunch,' was the reply from Claudie, the owner, who raised her finely-pencilled eyebrows in arcs of amazement that anyone might think a café would serve lunch at lunchtime. The next place looked shut as well and the one after that. We grew hungry and slightly fractious, and returned to Claudie for advice.

'*Bah oui*—you just need to go a little way up the road to the next village. There's a restaurant there, and they stay open for lunch,' she said. 'But you'd better hurry, the kitchen shuts at two!'

The village she meant seemed dead, its one road silent and eerily empty. All that was missing at this French high noon was the tumbleweed. But, opposite the Romanesque church, whose bell tolled an ominous half past one, a lone restaurant was indeed open and absolutely packed. This was where everyone had gathered from miles around. Farmers in grass-stained overalls clinked hearty glasses of red wine, discussing the calving season as they tucked into bleeding steaks, while a stonemason earnestly discussed politics with a carpenter, gesticulating dangerously with his fork.

The restaurant's rather rotund golden Labrador bounded up eagerly as we arrived, wagging his tail.

Hot on his heels came the equally round chef, to welcome us almost as warmly and advise on what to eat. I felt as though we'd walked into a family party, as others turned to greet us with a *bonjour* and a smile.

On offer was a three-course meal for just twelve euros or eight pounds each, clearly created for a clientele with plenty of time for lunch. Anxiously, we asked the waitress how long the meal would take. She gave a not-unfriendly Gallic shrug, 'As long as it takes.' But that wasn't very long at all. With remarkable efficiency, we tucked into pâté on crusty warm bread, home-made chicken stew, and a fresh berry and cream pudding and were out of the door a mere hour later. Everyone else was still there as we left, looking faintly puzzled at our unseemly rush. Then we were back on the road to Donzy, to join Claudie and her customers for coffee.

At Claudie's, an unemployed builder was heatedly debating with a local teacher whether France needed to end its 35-hour working week. If it hadn't been for their clothes, I couldn't have said who was who. Both had been to the same village school, both could quote their philosophers and the history of the Fifth Republic with equal ease. The main divisions here were not between rich and poor but Left and Right, and just how radically each thought France must change.

'I think we have to reform things,' the builder, Jean-Francois, said. 'But not too much. Otherwise, we'd lose all of this,' and he gestured eloquently to the sunny street outside. 'This is our way of life, and I don't want it to disappear.'

This one small town still had a butchers, three

135

bakers, two doctors' surgeries, several hairdressers and two beauty salons. Yet unemployment was the same as in most similar French towns: hovering around ten per cent, far higher for the young. And all here wondered if there was some magic middle way that France could find to keep its way of life, and the things that matter here: family, friends, good food, and enough time to enjoy them all; to keep them and yet put France back to work without turning into Britain or America, a prospect quoted at me in horror by many on my recent travels.

Before I moved here, I'd assumed that the French were rather like the British, although with nicer wine and food, more mobile faces and a better class of shrug. But I've come to realise just how Mediterranean France really is, far more like Catholic Spain or laid-back Italy than its work-obsessed northern neighbours, where time is money, and time is to be raced against rather than savoured slowly.

In Paris, as I sat down for coffee with friends the other night, the waiter at my local café greeted me by name, and called me his 'petite'—I think with a certain Parisian irony. Even in the big city though, there's still the human side, the pleasurable dawdling along the way to enjoy a meal or a conversation. That night, all of us joined in the anguished national debate over France's future, after the elections.

And what came up again and again was the same sense of fear and hope that I'd heard in Donzy. The hope that France can keep what is good; a birthrate that's among the highest in Europe, hospitals and public transport that work

136

and a sense of civic pride. The fear is that banishing what's bad, the lack of jobs and a certain state-sanctioned idleness, could endanger what everyone likes most, the sense that people in France still matter more than money, and that a good lunch is worth making time for. Because the feeling remains that for all that's wrong with France, an awful lot is still just right.

38

Education and Stress

Carrie Gracie

The approach of the exam season in China was producing a rash of suicides and nervous breakdowns among the nation's over-stressed children. The government launched a campaign urging parents to be less demanding. (15 April 1997)

This year, spring came overnight to Beijing. One day the trees were brown and bare, the next they were shimmering green. Now the skies are blue, the air balmy and Beijingers are shuffling off their winter layers and blinking into the sunlight. My husband is a Beijinger, and he celebrated the arrival of spring by putting away his thermal underwear and suggesting we go out climbing in the mountains to the north of the city. We took our eight-year-old niece, Wang An. Hill-climbing is her favourite pastime and we had a great day. But we got back late and she didn't have time to do her piano practice, so she had a terrible row with her parents.

I was shocked. Why be so grim and joyless, I thought. But then I reflected on the family circumstances. An's father has just been laid off by his state-owned factory and her mother has been unemployed for several years, so they're very short of money. An's piano lessons are the one great luxury of their lives.

An's life is a round of school, piano and homework. School is all about iron discipline. She learned that on her very first day, when she was kept in for half an hour as punishment for twiddling her hair round her finger. The teachers still complain about her wandering concentration.

An had a birthday recently. Her parents gave her two Sindy dolls with long golden hair and blue eyes. But as an only child she has no one to share them with. And there was no birthday party with friends of her own age. Instead she was subjected to a collection of ageing aunts and uncles. Luckily, An likes her aunts and uncles, she enjoys playing the piano and doesn't take her homework too seriously. Nor does she seem to notice the lack of fun in her life. Perhaps that's because some of her contemporaries clearly suffer much more.

Every year at exam time, there are grim statistics of nervous breakdowns, suicides and children running away from home. Studies also show a high incidence of curvature of the spine in China, a result, specialists say, of children carrying too many school books around and bending over desks for too many hours in the day.

Then there are the beatings. Chinese parents still hold to traditional Confucian ideas of obedience and corporal punishment. A recent survey suggested that more than half of the country's primary-school children have been beaten by their parents. And every year, a few are even beaten to death.

Urban Chinese children have little spare time and little freedom. Parents are worried about safety in cities crowded with traffic, construction projects and migrant workers. They take their children to school and they often don't let them go out to play in the evenings or in the holidays.

But if they're locked in tiny high-rise apartments, it's hardly surprising that Chinese children are getting slower, fatter and weaker over time. Or that they should put their homework aside when no one's looking and think up unorthodox ways of amusing themselves. One thirteen-year-old, for example, spent the Chinese New Year holiday phoning international porn lines. Her parents were horrified. But it was they who'd locked her in, so what did they expect?

The government does worry about all of this. It's just issued a report telling parents they must give their children a more balanced education. It's time, warn the newspaper editorials, to stop behaving like the farmer in the Chinese proverb who pulls on his seedlings to make them grow faster and kills the whole lot instead. But it's hard to imagine government lectures making any difference. The stakes are simply too high. China is becoming an intensely competitive society and people are allowed only one child on whom to focus all their hopes and dreams.

What's more, today's parents are from the generation which came of age during the chaos of the Cultural Revolution. They themselves grew up starved of education and every physical comfort, and they are now determined their children will not suffer the same fate.

So, right from the beginning, urban children in China get the best their parents can afford, and often the best their parents can't afford as well. One young couple I know earn about £80 a month between them. Before they had a baby, it was a reasonable income. But now they spend the entire sum on imported milk powder and they're drifting deeper and deeper into debt to support themselves. The baby does indeed look fat and healthy, but his father and mother are thin and stressed.

Parents like this who work long hours of overtime, eat only leftovers and dress in cast-offs just so that their offspring can compete in the twenty-first century are simply not prepared to countenance a child who refuses to perform. But if parents expect their children to be grateful for the sacrifices made on their behalf, they are mistaken. Opinion polls suggest that most children in China think their parents lack a sense of humour. And what's worse, the same polls suggest that a clear majority don't like their parents at all.

39

The Louche Allure of Macau

David Edmonds

Macau, the peninsula in the far south of China with special autonomous status, was growing fat on the profits from casinos. Income was growing at a staggering 40 per cent a year.
(24 May 2007)

It feels like you're stepping into the pages of a Graham Greene novel. A seedy, shadowy, corrupt world with a dash of Catholicism and a generous sprinkle of greed. Less than an hour's jetfoil ride from energetic Hong Kong, Macau is altogether more laidback, more languid, more fun. The main source of fun for most people is, of course, the casino. Macau is minute—everywhere is within walking distance. But amazingly this slither of land has just overtaken Las Vegas to become the world's most lucrative gambling centre.

The big boys from Las Vegas are betting that it's only going to get bigger. Since the Portuguese left in 1999, the gambling business has been shaken up. Previously it was the monopolistic preserve of the colourful, now-octogenarian billionaire, Stanley Ho, known here as Uncle Stanley, who, as well as amassing an ever-expanding casino portfolio, acquired seventeen children by four wives. Vegas brand names, Sands and Wynn, have now moved in. In the next couple of months, the mammoth

Venetian hotel will open: a cathedral to über-kitsch, replete with canals and singing gondoliers.

The unprecedented growth in Macau is driven by three factors: the mainland Chinese are getting richer; they can now cross the border on individual visas, rather than in organised tours—twelve million flooded in last year; and their favourite pastime is gambling. This tiny toenail at the foot of China is fast becoming the mainland's playground.

The new casinos promise family entertainment —restaurants and live acts, not just dice and slot machines. You have to descend into the bowels of the oldest casino, the Lisboa, to see how things used to be, except you can't see much. The men, tightly packed around baccarat tables, are all puffing away, collectively creating wafting clouds of smoke.

The good news is that there's now full employment; indeed, they'll soon be a scarcity of croupiers. But not everyone is delighted by the chip revolution. In the heart of town, off a quiet square, is a Catholic charity run by a softly spoken, earnest, compassionate, middle-aged man, Paul Pun. He's based in a dingy, run-down building, the antithesis of neon glamour. Nearby are some elegant colonial houses with their pastel-shaded roofs.

Lose your shirt on the spin of a roulette wheel and the authorities might suggest you pay Mr Pun a visit. Mr Pun and his people offer counselling and enough money for the ferry ride home. 'We're getting busier every year,' he complains. He points to the next-door room. 'There's a woman in there, a factory owner from the mainland,' he says. 'She's just lost $100,000—that's nearly £50,000. We want

142

to speak to her, but every time she tries to talk she bursts into tears.'

Mixed up with the betting is the money laundering. The system works roughly like this. An apparatchik on the mainland demands a bribe from a businessman for, say, the granting of a licence. The official goes to Macau, where his bribe awaits him: a fat pile of chips. He squanders some on a game of baccarat, cashes in the rest and back on the mainland explains away his new-found wealth by boasting of his success at cards. One senior Hong Kong analyst told me that over a billion pounds a year is laundered this way.

I'm here to investigate a dubious family bank, Banco Delta Asia, BDA—part of yet another murky Macau tale. The United States has effectively shut BDA down, after claiming that North Korea was using the bank for illicit purposes. The North Korean regime is outraged. Whether or not it agrees to halt its nuclear programme may rest upon the fate of BDA.

Mr Joe Wong is spokesman for BDA—a risible misnomer really, since he doesn't speak. He won't answer our calls. He's always in a meeting. When we visit the bank in person, we're ejected by a burly Filipino security guard as soon as we mention his name. We wait outside and eventually spot him. 'Mr Wong, Mr Wong! Has BDA ever been used to launder North Korean money?' He looks aghast; his head jerks up and down like a frightened turkey. 'Can't talk, can't talk, I have a meeting.' And then he scuttles into the building; we never see him again.

The link between the hermetic Stalinist state of North Korea and louche Macau is surely the

143

strangest in international politics. But ever since 1974, when Portugal's fascist dictatorship fell and the new socialist government recognised North Korea, the North Korean elite have used this former Portuguese outpost as their gateway to the world. It's through Macau that they import their flat screen TVs and, we're told, President Kim Jong-il's caviar. Macau, it's alleged, has been used by North Korea to channel its counterfeit cigarettes and counterfeit US dollars. Until the Americans began to target this place, it was said to be peppered with North Korean spies.

Hong Kong has long prided itself on its rule of law. Macau, its near-neighbour, might be better known for its espionage, money laundering, its casinos and dodgy banks, but in an odd way that's all part of its allure.

40

Remember Mr and Mrs Nie

Rupert Wingfield-Hayes

As our correspondent prepared to leave Beijing for a new posting, he reflected on the eight years he had spent in the Chinese capital reporting on a period of extraordinary economic growth. (12 October 2006)

I recently wrote a piece for *From Our Own Correspondent* about a trip I had taken to India. In it I made some rather uncomplimentary comparisons between India and China, the general gist of which was that India was falling way behind and China forging ahead. A few days after the story went out, I was having dinner with the Chinese foreign ministry spokesman. Now the usual routine is for us to exchange pleasantries, then for my friends from the ministry to spend the rest of dinner complaining, politely, about the anti-China stories I've recently done. This time I was in for a surprise.

'We saw the story you did about China and India,' one of them said with apparent glee. 'An excellent story,' he said. 'We almost thought it had been written by a Chinese journalist.' I didn't know whether to laugh or cry. After eight years in China my foreign ministry friends clearly felt I had finally got it, I finally understood China. Sadly, for most of the rest of my time here, to their minds, I clearly had not. 'Why are you so down on China?' is a refrain I have got used to hearing. And not just from the foreign ministry.

I remember my brother visiting Beijing. It was his first trip to China in more than ten years. Not surprisingly he was astonished at the huge transformation of the city. Gone were the streams of bicycles and blue-clad workers he remembered from 1990. Now Beijing's wide new boulevards were clogged with cars, its skyline filled with gleaming office towers. At the supermarket he goggled at Chinese families stuffing the weekly shopping into their new hatchback cars. Out where I live on the edge of Beijing, he marvelled at China's new rich cruising home in their Volvos and BMWs to their mini mansions. 'Why do I never see any of this in your reports?' he complained. 'Why do you only focus on the negative things that happen in China?' Clearly, in my brother's opinion, I keep getting it wrong.

And he's not alone. I've heard the same complaints from businessmen, from friends, even from editors visiting from London. 'We need to reflect the huge changes taking place here,' one told me recently, 'not just what's happening to Chinese peasants in the countryside.' And they are right: China is changing, at astonishing speed. It's rapidly becoming an economic superpower. But there is a danger in looking at China's shiny new cities and airports and making the mistake of thinking that China has suddenly become a normal country. That new wealth is bringing a freer, fairer China. That democracy is just around the corner. That soon China will be just like us. Those sympathetic to that view might be interested to hear the story of Mr and Mrs Nie.

They are a couple I met last month at their little brick house in a village three hours south of Beijing. They perched on a couple of old stools in their tiny courtyard. Both are in their mid-fifties. But Mr Nie looks much, much older. He can barely hobble, with the aid of a stick, pain etched on his face with every step. Ten years ago, Mr Nie drank pesticide to try to kill himself. He was driven by madness and depression brought on by the death of his only son, Nie Shubin. Nie Shubin was barely twenty when he was killed by an executioner's bullet to the back of his head. He was just nineteen when he was pulled in at random by police looking for the murderer of a young woman.

'My son was no murderer,' Mrs Nie told me, fire and anger burning in her eyes. 'He was a good, quiet boy. He had a stutter. He never mixed with girls.' But after a week in police detention, Nie Shubin confessed to the murder.

'They beat him,' Mrs Nie tells me, tears now glistening in her eyes, 'they beat him until he confessed. They didn't care about the truth; they say you're guilty, so you're guilty.' Mrs Nie got to see her son only once before he went to his death. 'I found out which day he would be in court and fought my way in,' she told me. 'The police didn't want to let me in, but I pushed and screamed until they let me through. Then I saw him. In shackles, he was being led away. "Shubin!" I called. He turned and saw me. "Ma!" he shouted, tears flooding down his cheeks.' Mrs Nie rushed towards her son, but the police held her back. There would be no last goodbye.

Ten years after Shubin was executed, another man came forward and admitted he had murdered the young woman. Mrs Nie has appealed to the police to review her son's case. They don't want to know. The reason I tell you this story is that Mr and Mrs Nie are far from being alone. Across China there are tens, even hundreds, of thousands of people with similar stories to tell, stories of brutality and injustice at the hands of those in power. They are stories of a society that is profoundly troubled.

Twenty-five years ago, the Chinese Communist Party decided to scrap Marxist economics and pursue a capitalist free-market economy. But at the same time it refused, and continues to refuse, any form of political liberalisation. The result is what we see today: astonishing growth, combined with astonishing greed, where wealth means power and without power you are nothing.

Take the example of another story I recently did about harvesting organs from executed Chinese prisoners. This isn't a new story: China has been taking organs from executed prisoners and putting them into other people for the last twenty years at least. But what is happening today speaks volumes about the direction China is heading in.

An hour and a half's drive south-east of Beijing, in the city of Tianjin, stands the Tianjin First Central Hospital. It's a huge, heavy, grey building, typical of the public infrastructure built in China during the 1980s and '90s. But behind it, soaring to an even greater height, are two gleaming new white towers, with shining glass and acres of marble in the foyer. The 300 rooms contained in these towers are more like those of a five-star hotel than a hospital. Some even have sitting rooms and kitchens en suite. This huge new facility is devoted to one thing and one thing only: transplanting organs from executed prisoners into the bodies of wealthy foreign clients.

Foreigners in need of a transplant are flocking to China in ever-greater numbers. And who can blame them? Compared to America and Europe, transplant operations in China are cheap, the success rate is high and new organs can be had in a matter of weeks, rather than months or years. But most of those coming here probably don't enquire too closely about where the organs come from. If they did, what they would find might make them feel a little queasy.

China carries out the death penalty on an industrial scale. As many as 8,000 or even 10,000 people are executed here every year. Most, like twenty-year-old Shubin, will have been tried and

148

convicted in a court system that doesn't even pass the most basic of international standards, where torture is routine and where all too often convictions are based on confessions.

Death-row prisons maintain close contacts with a network of transplant hospitals around the country. Immediately after death, the prisoner's livers, kidneys and eyes are removed. The body is then cremated. All the family ever gets is a box of ashes and a bill for the bullet. The organs, meanwhile, are whisked away at high speed to one of the special hospitals to be transplanted into a waiting Chinese or, increasingly, a foreign patient. The hospitals charge foreign patients £40,000 to £50,000 for the operation. In addition the families are often asked to pay an extra £10,000 to the doctor who performs the operation. Where all the money goes is unclear. Most goes to the hospital. Some goes back to the prison, but none to the family of the dead prisoner. Where else but China would it be possible to find such a grim nexus of industrial-scale death, hi-tech medicine and untrammelled capitalism?

As I look out of the window of the BBC office in Beijing, I can see all around me the hustle and bustle of preparations for the 2008 Olympic Games. The vast Olympic stadium, shaped like a giant steel bird's nest, is nearing completion. An even vaster new airport, in glass and steel, is taking shape on the edge of the city. New elevated highways sprout overnight, while beneath the ground an army of mole-workers tunnel a multitude of new subway lines. The city is being remodelled to welcome the world to China and to welcome China to the world. The 2008 Olympic

Games will be China's coming-out party, where it will finally be accepted as a full and equal member of the international community.

Many who come will, no doubt, be bowled over by the vibrancy and modernity of China. They may even tell you it wasn't what they expected, not what they had seen on TV. To them, I would say: remember Mr and Mrs Nie and the tens of millions of ordinary Chinese who to this day are denied the basic freedoms of speech, of a fair trial and to equal treatment before the law.

My friends at the foreign ministry will, no doubt, think that after a brief moment of clarity, I have reverted to my bad old ways and that after eight years I still don't really understand China.

41

An Explosion in Lhasa

James Miles

Chinese security forces moved in to stop rioting in the Tibetan capital, Lhasa. Only one Western reporter was there to witness it. (29 March 2008)

Rarely, perhaps never in the careers of most foreign correspondents, will anything like this happen. A breaking story that grips the world's attention, in a place whose name in the Western imagination is synonymous with other-worldliness, and to be on one's own watching this crisis, this horror, unfold with no other journalists to be seen, from start to finish. It's an experience that belongs to a century ago, not today's world of high speed travel at a moment's notice, of media giants with global armies of staff.

It happens to me in Tibet not because of any foresight on my part, but by accident. It happens because China, for all its talk of opening up the country to the foreign media in the build-up to the Olympics, still keeps Tibet off limits. Foreign journalists need special permits to go there and they're not easy to get. After working as a foreign correspondent in China for many years, this is my first. Oddly, they agreed to let me in on 12 March. This is two days after the anniversary of the Tibetan uprising of 1959 that caused the Dalai Lama to flee into exile—it's always a sensitive time in the Tibetan calendar.

As I set off for Tibet the situation in Lhasa is already tense. Hundreds of monks from a big monastery on the outskirts of the city have staged a protest on the anniversary, the biggest in Tibet in many years. I expect my permit to be revoked, but there is no word. I board a train on the world's highest railway line. The service was launched two years ago and Tibetans are said to be unhappy that it's bringing in yet more ethnic Han Chinese migrants from other parts of China. As I look out over a breathtaking landscape of mountains and snow, yaks and antelopes, horses and herders, Lhasa is getting tenser. More monks have protested on the edge of the city.

In Lhasa, officials invite me to a welcome dinner at a luxury hotel.

'You've arrived at a special time,' says my host, referring to the recent unrest. 'You're the only

151

foreign journalist in Lhasa.' But, he tells me, the situation in the city is now stable. The next day, Lhasa explodes.

Locals say it started with a small fracas between monks and security personnel outside a downtown temple. I see people running in the alley near my hotel in the old quarter. Shops are suddenly shuttered. I go out onto the main road and I see Tibetans throwing stones at a shop. Then they're throwing them at taxis. Someone near me is smashing a piece of concrete. People are picking up the pieces and throwing them at passing cyclists, ethnic Han Chinese. It's a race riot. As a Caucasian I seem to be safe and as they start to pelt a Han Chinese boy on his bike I step forward and shout at them to stop. They do, thank God. But where, I keep asking myself—and others—are the police? Lhasa is normally crawling with them.

Rioters break into shops. They smash goods, haul out everything they can and set fire to the detritus and sometimes the shops themselves. Tibetan-run businesses are spared—they're marked out with traditional white scarves, but most shops are run by Hans.

Amid whoops of joy rioters toss gas canisters into the blazes. A monk worries I might be trampled by stampeding crowds trying to avoid the explosions. He grabs my arm and leads me inside a shrine. As we sit there a scared teenage boy runs up and prostrates himself before the monk. He's a Han Chinese and he's begging for protection. The monk hides him in a back room.

You could call it restraint or you could call it an appalling dereliction of duty, but the authorities let Lhasa burn. They wait for around twenty-four

152

hours until the rioters exhaust themselves before moving in decisively. When they do start patrolling the alleyways with guns, firing the occasional shot, they seem to meet little resistance. Soon the city is flooded with troops. It's very plausible that Tibetans are killed, but this doesn't seem like another slaughter like Tiananmen, which I also witnessed.

My mobile phone rings almost constantly for three or four days. The world's media want to know what's happening. China's state-run media want to talk too. They hope my accounts of the rioting will help their efforts to undermine international sympathy for Tibetans. It's certainly not easy to sympathise with racial violence that terrorises thousands of innocent people. I spent tense minutes in a darkened room with Han Chinese above their looted shop praying the rioters outside wouldn't hear us speaking in Mandarin. But China isn't asking itself, at least not openly, why people are angry. In Lhasa I saw Tibetan children throwing streams of white lavatory paper across overhead wires to celebrate the destruction. Why? And why are protests, many of them peaceful, erupting across a huge swathe of China populated by Tibetans?

There's a simple truth that the Chinese government doesn't want to face. Its policies in Tibet have failed.

42

Sixty Years On

Mark Tully

Six decades after the violence of its birth, independent India has not only survived, it's begun to prosper as the world's largest democracy. One of our former correspondents there has observed many changes in the more than forty years he's been closely involved with the country. (11 August 2007)

When I came to India in 1965 I was surprised to find that diplomats, at the end of their postings, would sell all the possessions they had imported, including partly used lipsticks and secondhand underwear. I soon found out why. The shops only stocked Indian goods and they were distinctly second class. I still remember the pain of shaving with an Indian razor blade and being taught how to remove the glycerin from Indian beer. The trick was to turn the bottle upside down in a glass and an oily liquid would ooze out, clouding the water. Now I shave in great comfort with Indian blades and pour beer straight into my mug.

When I went back to Calcutta, my early childhood home, to indulge in a bit of nostalgia, I found what had once been the commercial capital of India dying on its feet. One British town-planner had forecast it would be the first city ever to collapse. Trees were growing out of the offices of some of the once-great names in British commerce. At least Gillanders House, where my father had worked, was still reasonably well-preserved, but his firm was a pale shadow of what it had been in his days. Now Kolkata is enjoying something of a boom and a whole new city is springing up on the way to the airport.

I once complained to an Indian ticket inspector that I'd paid a surcharge to travel on a super-fast train, which wasn't very fast. He corrected me, saying; 'It is a super-fast train; it's only going slowly.' For years the Indian economy used to chug along at what was known as the Hindu rate of growth: 3 per cent with perhaps a little plus. Now it clips along at 8 per cent plus, which is by any standards fast, if not super-fast. All this has been brought about by the unscrambling of what was known as the licence-permit Raj. That was a siege economy, which kept out all foreign competition to India's nascent industry. But in the name of allocating scarce resources, one of which was power, bureaucrats—known as 'the abominable Indian no-men'—were also empowered to prevent competition within India. No one could start manufacturing without a licence given by the bureaucrats, and existing manufacturers would bribe them to refuse licences for potential competitors.

India started to dismantle the wall it built round its economy when, in 1991, it faced bankruptcy and the IMF demanded the reform of the licence-permit Raj as the price for bailing the country out. The demolition has released India's remarkable entrepreneurial talent. America has coined a new word, 'bangalored', to describe the fate of the large number of its IT employees who lose their jobs to

155

India's IT capital, Bangalore. The big international names in the motor industry now have plants here and they are all being given a good run for their money by cars designed as well as made in India. Indian companies are now taking over foreign companies such as the Anglo-Dutch steel manufacturer Corus.

But international business complains that the demolition job has not been completed. Foreign bankers, insurers, retailers and manufacturers compare unfavourably the restrictions India still imposes with the freedom they enjoy in China. India argues its specific political and economic problems mean that it must retain freedom to direct its economy and to control the market. Retail is a good example. The government rightly fears the political impact of destroying the livelihood of the millions of small shopkeepers who dominate the trade if Tesco and Wal-Mart, who are knocking on the door, are allowed in and given free rein. India is also a land of small farmers, and they cannot be left to fend for themselves against farmers in other parts of the world with their giant acreage farmed by one man and a tractor.

The biggest problem for India is that the rapid economic growth has only led to stunning changes in the lifestyle of the rich and the middle classes. There is still widespread poverty in the cities as well as the countryside. Many economists argue that the present top-down economic growth will never trickle down to the poor and so the economy needs to be directed more towards them. The trouble is that the direction has to be done by the government and that means the same abominable no-men who created the nightmare of the licence-permit Raj. No matter how many arguments there are for the Indian train going at its own speed, there can be no argument for allowing the abominable no-men to be on the footplate driving the engine.

43

The Wisdom of the Poor

Peter Day

As the Indian economy flourished, many people, particularly in the cities, were becoming prosperous. But India was also a place where seven hundred million still lived in the countryside, a world away from the nation's new shiny image.
(20 January 2007)

I've just been on a pilgrimage, on foot, across a bit of rural India. Not to get to a shrine, a saint or a temple. The point of the walk was the villages we encountered on the way and the traditional skills and knowledge locked up in them. I was with a remarkable professor called Anil Gupta, who teaches at the Indian Institute of Management in Ahmedebad; it is, by the way, the hardest management school to get into in the whole world. He's the moving spirit behind something called the Honeybee Network, a now-vast repository of often-clever rural inventions and village wisdom about plants and animals in danger of being forgotten in the new brand-name-driven India.

Honeybee celebrates this lore and tries to get financial backing for the best ideas. And for the past eight years, Professor Gupta has taken to the dusty roads of rural India on what is called in the ancient Indian language of Sanskrit a *Shodhyatra*, a walk to find knowledge. Twice a year in searing summer heat or chilly winter, Professor Gupta and sixty or seventy of the inspired, the curious and veteran rural innovators traipse out to remote places. The walks last about a week as the pilgrims journey from village to village along rutted ox-cart tracks and noisy main roads, honked at by endless motor horns, the fanfare of India. Being part of the *Shodhyatra* is an extraordinary experience, a confusion of travelling circus, revivalist meeting and Gandhi brought back to life. At walking pace in a country that lives outdoors, things happen. People who know inventors dash up to the pilgrims. The walkers themselves dive off the path into a field to clip off a twig of an unfamiliar shrub. In the middle of the crowd moves Professor Gupta, tall, bearded, dressed in white, an engaging smile and a compelling interest in everything.

We stop to admire the individual patterns the women create on the walls of the shelters they build to protect the precious store of handmade cow-dung patties used for fuel. A few miles further and there's another huddle as the prof launches into an off-the-cuff enquiry into the positive uses of the word 'crack', inspired by the parched earth before us. A farmer diverts the walkers to examine his new discovery: a rogue mustard plant that produces all its seed at once, not frond by frond. In

158

every village we are greeted and garlanded and then there's a meeting under the spreading neem tree in the schoolyard: two hours, three hours, in which rural knowledge is praised, inventors speak, local heroes are acclaimed. Then centenarians are rewarded with pashmina scarves to celebrate the wisdom locked up in old age, children are exhorted to listen to their grandparents (and inspired to write down inventions they'd like to see), and village drunks pledge to give up drink; one man smashed his full bottle of Mr India spirits in front of the whole gathering.

Walking with Professor Gupta is rather like being back in the New Testament: first-century disciples on the move with a great guru. Drums greet the *Shodhyatra* as it enters the village. We eat together from great vats of delicious food whipped up by a family of cooks travelling behind us in a truck. We all sleep on chilly schoolroom floors or barns; sanitation is primitive or non-existent, but no more primitive than the villagers experience every day of their lives.

Most of these knowledge walks are far from cities; this one was at times only twenty miles from the capital, Delhi. Even so, it was bandit country. In one village there had been dozens of vendetta murders, a place the local police stayed away from.

To get to the start, I drove out of Delhi on the first Indian highway built by the British. Along it, there's now a remarkable explosion of new real estate: multi-storey apartment blocks with alluring names, great shopping malls and new hospitals for medical tourists from abroad. The new India. The gap between the towering developments of this new industrial zone and the villages only a walk

159

away is of centuries, not miles.

Like Gandhi before him, Professor Gupta thinks that the Indian soul resides in the wisdom of the poor and he's seeking to make it flame up with new purpose. Much of the new India regards this with sympathetic scorn, the past dragging on the country's global future. The professor is frightened that in the rush to modernise, the wisdom of the poor will be wiped out and lost. And not just in India. In an extraordinary move, this spring Professor Gupta will be coming to Britain to do the same thing here. He'll walk from Liverpool to Manchester, a Lancashire *Shodhyatra*.

44

The Yellow Death

John Sweeney

Thousands of Russians, living in the far west of the country, had been poisoned by bootleg alcohol contaminated with a chemical which destroys the liver. It's thought the bootleggers added a cheap alcoholic disinfectant, intended for medical use, to their brew. It caused the drinkers' skin to turn yellow before they fell dangerously ill. (10 March 2007)

Pskov is the end of the line. I got off the Moscow overnight express and the earth started to buckle in front of me. On the Pskov express I'd played chess with a couple of Russians, the vodka bottles had come out, and soon every move of a pawn was

160

celebrated with a toast. If you're interested, I was about to win when the Russian bloke nicked my queen. Anyway, I'd had enough to drink to kill a small horse.

There's something about the light, or the lack of it, that eats the soul in Russia, that makes you drink. The dark days in winter, the grimness of ordinary life. They say one in six Russians is an alcoholic. That's why President Putin—the former KGB man is something of a puritan, at least in public—has brought in a series of laws, tripling the price of vodka and threatening dire penalties if people drink black-market moonshine, which they call *samogon*. And that is, of course, what everybody who can't afford shop-bought vodka does.

They called it 'the yellow death'. It started in the summer when dozens of people turned up in casualty units, a vile shade of yellow. The dozens turned to hundreds, then a thousand. The less severe cases recovered, but even they will die long before their time.

The more serious cases? Natasha is not yet thirty, she's got a seven-year-old boy called Maxim and she has less than a year to live. Her whole body has gone yellow, an instantly recognisable feature of toxic hepatitis. Something has destroyed her liver and now all the natural toxins in the body are stacking up. Her own body is poisoning her and there is nothing medicine, or at least nothing state medicine in Russia, can do about it. Natasha and everyone else in the hospital corridors had bought *samogon*, moonshine, as usual, but something had been added to it.

In Pskov, the authorities have tracked more than

161

1,000 poisonings with 120 dead. Across Russia as a whole there were no official figures, but some estimate 10,000 poison cases and 1,000 dead. So who is responsible for this mass poisoning? I had gone to Pskov to try to get to the bottom of 'the yellow death'. We made friends with a gentlemanly Russian, Alexei, who was also an alcoholic, gave him a secret camera bag and sent him off to buy the *samogon*. The plan was that we'd then get it tested and analysed to see what the problem was. He bought the stuff for 20 roubles (40 pence): a clear liquid in an old Coke bottle. I had a quick sniff. The bouquet: rocket fuel with a touch of boot polish. And a quick gulp. In the film *Flash Gordon* the heroine is given a slug of bright green alcohol so that she can bear to sleep with Emperor Ming the Merciless. It tasted something like that.

We filmed the local cops going round busting all the little people, the street traders in *samogon*. The local chief of police in Pskov, General Sergey Matveyev, a plump bureaucrat with a fatter gold watch, wasn't keen to tell me what was the most likely source of the poison. Not many in authority give much of a damn about the nameless wretches of the earth: winos, moral degenerates. The sense that many of the yellow people were ordinary Russians who had been poisoned through no great fault of their own seemed to be missing.

A doctor at the local hospital told me that the most likely cause was something which had been added to the moonshine: polyhexamethylene guanide hydrochloride. And that stuff had got on the market as a medical disinfectant, Extrasept: 95 per cent pure alcohol, tax exempt, making it cheaper than moonshine. Dodgy traders had mixed the cheaper Extrasept with the homemade *samogon* and made a killing.

It was only once I had learned about PHMG that I got seriously worried about the *samogon* I had drunk. It might have been contaminated too. Had I poisoned myself? Was I going to turn yellow too? We set off from Pskov to St Petersburg, to the Institute of Toxicology. They'd been feeding Extrasept to rats. The results were inconclusive. I brought along a little bottle of the stuff I'd drunk. They tested it and they found no PHMG, so I was clean.

The Extrasept factory was a vast sprawling mess in Alexandrov, a town associated with Ivan the Terrible. The technical director said there was nothing wrong with his product—and he even drank some to prove it. I asked him: 'You're not afraid of turning yellow, are you?' Later, when we got back to London, we had Extrasept tested on human liver cells and it killed every single one.

45

A Country with Two Faces

Steve Rosenberg

During fifteen years in Russia, this correspondent travelled across several time zones reporting from St Petersburg to Vladivostok, from the shores of the Black Sea to the icy tundra of Siberia. It was a time of breathtaking change in a country which often proved frustrating and dangerous—but one which he

163

grew to love. (12 October 2006)

People often ask me why I've stayed in Moscow for so many years. Well, one of the reasons is that, for me at least, living in Russia has been a bit like reading a bestselling novel. You know the feeling: the story's so gripping, the characters are all so colourful, there are so many twists and turns that you just can't put it down. You want to keep reading on and on, to find out what's going to happen next. And just when you think you've got the whole plot figured out and you're sure you know how it's all going to end—bang, there's yet another surprise and you just have to read some more.

Well, I've been 'reading' Russia every day now for the last fifteen years—I'll be quite honest with you, I still have no idea how this Tolstoyan epic is going to end. But I've decided it's time to take a break, put it down for a while and move on. One thing's for sure: the story so far has been remarkable. In a decade and a half, I've seen the Soviet Union collapse and witnessed Russia taking a cosmic leap from Communism to capitalism; I've seen Russian tanks shelling the country's parliament and the Russian army destroying the Chechen capital Grozny twice; I've seen the rouble crash, then bounce back; I've seen people enthused and then bemused by democracy; I've seen Gorbachev give way to Yeltsin, Yeltsin hand power on a plate to Putin, and Vladimir Putin restore if not the USSR, then at least Soviet-style state control and the country's self-respect. And in between all of this, I've married a Muscovite, had two wonderful children and fallen in love with

Russia.

My Russian story began on 29 August 1991, just a week after the bungled Communist coup which had failed to depose the Soviet president Mikhail Gorbachev. I flew into Sheremetyevo airport and took a taxi to the Moscow Machine Tool Construction Institute: a grey block in the north of the city where I'd come to teach English. I didn't know much about machine tools, let alone construction; but the Institute was grateful to have a native English speaker on the books, the bed bugs in the Institute hostel were grateful to have someone to chew on at night and I was grateful for the chance to come and work in Moscow and experience life in the USSR. I remember my first class: one of the students stood up and declared: 'Welcome to our Wonderland!' I asked him what he meant. 'Well, in our country,' he said, 'things happen that make Alice's looking glass look boring. Here you must always expect the unexpected!' I soon realised he was right. Just a few weeks later, the Soviet Union fell apart. The country I'd studied, travelled to, and whose name was printed on my visa, no longer existed.

And when this giant empire, this Slavic superpower, began disintegrating, the lives of many ordinary Russians began falling apart too, right in front of my eyes. The move to a free-market economy sparked hyperinflation. People's savings were eaten up overnight. There were goods in the shops, but prices were sky high and out of the reach of most Russians. Suddenly there were beggars on the streets, babushkas sifting through rubbish bins and long queues outside soup kitchens. As government subsidies dried up, many

165

state enterprises went bust.

Others survived, only just, by not paying wages. Russia was on its knees, relying on international loans and humanitarian aid. But when I think back to my students at the Machine Tool Construction Institute, I remember that the collapse of Communism had offered them hope. With the Iron Curtain consigned to history and the borders now wide open, third-year student Igor was planning to leave Russia and get a job in the United States. And then there was Oleg, still studying machine tools but now more interested in business and dreaming of becoming a tycoon. He'd convinced the dean of the Institute to let him open a supermarket in the Institute's foyer. And at the same time that Oleg was planning his food empire, other young Russian entrepreneurs were taking their first steps to fortune: one, by the name of Roman Abramovich, began his career selling rubber ducks. He ended up doing rather well for himself, owning an oil company, buying an English football club and becoming one of the richest men in the world. Oleg wasn't so successful. But then not everyone can become an oligarch.

I remember the early 1990s as a time when Soviet rules were replaced by Russian chaos. In 1994, I spent several months learning to drive a car at a Moscow driving school. Three times a week I'd diligently attend theory classes, where a smiling instructor with a big stick and a blackboard explained the minute details of the Russian highway code: how to overtake a tractor or how to behave when a tram conks out in front of you. Then at the end of the course he made this worrying confession to the class: 'One piece of advice—if you pass your test, just ignore all those rules I've been teaching you, everyone else on the road seems to.' And he was right. I got my licence, I bought a car (a secondhand Lada), but as I bumbled along, with Mercedes and BMWs cutting me up every few seconds, I soon realised that on the roads of independent Russia there was now only one rule: if your car's bigger and flashier than the rest, then everyone gives way to you.

Despite disorder on the roads and in the economy, it was an exhilarating time, a time when Russia was trying out new things, embracing the West, and when anything was possible. On one of my days off from teaching, I went on a tour of Russian State Television. In one studio, they were preparing for that night's Song for Europe competition, the qualifying round for the Eurovision Song Contest, in which Russia had only recently begun taking part. I happened to mention to someone that this was very interesting for me, that I was from Britain and was a big fan of Eurovision. Five minutes later I was offered a job co-presenting the whole show, just hours before it went on air. I was young, naive—I said yes. So that night, in an old jacket and a creased tie, I made my TV debut live on Russian television in front of thirty million viewers, babbling on about 'Boom Bang-a-Bang' and Abba in broken Russian!

Not surprisingly I was never invited back, but amazingly, after such an inauspicious start, the media became my career. First with American Television in Moscow and then with the BBC. As Moscow correspondent I've criss-crossed this, the biggest country in the world. Even after fifteen years I can't say I fully understand Russia, but I've learned to accept it for what it is, a remarkable country of enormous contradictions. A country where the winters are bitingly cold, the summers stifling hot, where stunning natural beauty co-exists with pollution and crumbling tenements; a country which once proclaimed social equality, but where the gap between the rich and poor is now as wide as the Volga river; and a place where you can experience such warmth and hospitality, yet witness such evil as the Beslan school killings. Nothing, I think, sums up Russia better than its national symbol, the double-headed eagle; this is a country with two faces pulling in opposite directions, and still struggling to decide where it belongs or even what kind of a country it actually is.

But it's the Russian people I'll remember most of all, for their stoicism and their eternal optimism. Just think, over the last hundred years or so Russians have been battered by everything under the sun: revolution, civil war, Stalin's terror, Nazi invasion, Soviet shortages and then the collapse of their country. But they've survived and so has their character. I'll never forget Mikhail Tamarin: he spent nearly a decade in the Gulag, one of millions of Stalin's victims, but he survived and, tough as boots, he's still going strong at the age of ninety-three. He values every minute of his life and makes sure he never wastes a moment; he regularly takes the bus to the theatre or to the concert hall. Or take Svetlana, manager of a furniture factory in deepest Siberia. Her enterprise was struggling to survive in the new Russia. Svetlana had been offered lucrative jobs elsewhere but, realising the town depended on the factory, she stayed put and was working round the clock to save the company. And then there were the monks I discovered in a little village near Kazan. Their local fire station had been forced to shut down because it didn't have any money, but the monks saved the day. They decided to train as fire-fighters, raising money to buy their own fire engine and uniforms. In the end they formed their own 'Friar Brigade' and all because they were determined to protect their parishioners.

So many characters, so many tales. But what's going to happen next in the grand story of Russia? Well, if much of the last fifteen years has been about chaos, confusion and the loss of empire, my guess is that the next few pages will be devoted to the rise of Russia. The plot already seems to be moving that way. The economy's booming, thanks to high oil and gas prices; the country's flexing its muscles on the world stage, determined to restore its superpower status. True, there are questions about the state of democracy under Vladimir Putin, but most Russians don't seem to be asking them, apparently satisfied with current stability. But how long that stability will last is another question. After all, this is the land of twists and turns, the 'Wonderland', where you must always expect the unexpected.

46

A New Life for Little Star

William Horsley

In all the countries of Eastern Europe which won their independence from the Soviet Union at the end of the Cold War, you could still see many of the old military bases and other reminders of the armed Soviet presence. But one particular object called Little Star which the Russians left behind in the small Baltic state of Latvia is now proving to have a special charm as well as great scientific value.
(20 May 2000)

Today, Little Star stands in a clearing in the pine forest that stretches for miles along the Baltic Sea coast near Ventspils, the huge port which still handles much of Russia's oil exports. Actually, Little Star is lucky to have survived the break-up of the Soviet Union. On the lonely forest road that leads to it there are signs of desolation on every side: telegraph poles leaning over at crazy angles; a large rusty-brown pipeline beside the road, of which many sections are completely missing; and a whole ghost town of gutted apartment buildings which used to house 2,000 people—Soviet technicians, intelligence officers, soldiers and their families. Among the empty buildings the ground is covered with jagged broken glass and splintered wood from the torn-out windows. A glimpse inside confirms that everything has gone, even the electric wiring and the lavatory seats.

I had already seen a picture of it, but my first sight of Little Star still took my breath away. It's the most powerful radio telescope in Northern Europe. For years it was at the heart of a top-secret Soviet listening post, eavesdropping on NATO's communications. Now it's part of an international effort to map the universe and search for extraterrestrial life. It stands fifty metres high, soaring far above the pine trees, with the body of a giant windmill and its magnificent, yellow ochre-coloured dish gleaming in the sun. Within a couple of minutes, as we watched, the great thirty-two-metre dish swivelled gracefully around to face us almost directly.

And then, even more impressively, it seemed that Little Star began to sing. It was a transcendent sound, like something from a film about close encounters—a piercing, metallic note, accompanied by other harmonics which echoed through the forest, and I told myself: 'Now I know why the ancients spoke about the music of the spheres.'

Our reception committee at the ground-floor entrance was a group of Latvian astronomers who have now spent six years rescuing Little Star from the scrap heap and putting it back in working order. The youngest and probably the brainiest was Karlis Berzins, an intense but friendly man of twenty-six. He showed me how the Russians, before they left, had opened the engines that power the big dish and poured in acid to disable them. He and his colleagues pulled up a trapdoor in the floor and showed me how the Russians had cut through scores of thick cables used for powering and controlling the delicate scientific instruments. The only way to bring Little Star back to life had been by laying new cables through the rusty hulk.

We climbed up through the telescope, as if through a huge submarine, with its vertical ladders and portholes looking out. Right in the middle I saw the monstrously huge cog-wheels which physically rotate the dish. Here, Russian soldiers had literally left spanners in the works, iron rods and tools wedged in among the cogs. If they hadn't been taken out before the wheels were powered up again, they could have caused irreparable damage.

Then came a moment to savour. I had never before stood on the dish of a mighty radio telescope, but Karlis said it was all right. Of course you can't see the ground, because the high sides of the dish block the view. It is like standing in the middle of one of those steep-sided halls where rollerbladers zoom up and down the curved walls, only here we were at bird-height, high above the trees, under the hot midday sun.

The aluminium compound of the surface is strong enough to walk on, but a few steps away from the centre the dish was so steep it was hard to stand upright. I heard how during the Cold War Little Star had helped the Soviet authorities with critical military tasks; for example, it helped to measure the bumps in the earth's surface, in order to target nuclear missiles accurately on New York and other cities in the West. The Soviet authorities had wanted to blow up Little Star, to make sure its advanced technology would not be used against them after Latvian independence. In the nick of time an agreement was reached that it would be left intact but never again used for military purposes.

'What exactly is it doing?' I asked. Karlis became visibly excited as he told me: 'It's searching for quasars, black holes and many intergalactic objects.'

From the dish we climbed up about forty more steps on a rickety ladder to reach the top platform, a kind of eagle's nest raised above the dish itself. From there we could see not only the Baltic coast, several miles away, but we had a bird's-eye view of how the whole infrastructure around Little Star—supply routes, pipes and a large underground tunnel—had been destroyed. Now the twenty or so scientists who are repairing and operating Little Star have no amenities, not even running water or winter heating. Latvia is still poor and has other priorities. They desperately need money to reconnect the supplies and upgrade the outdated electronics.

Coming down again towards the ground I asked another of our guides: what is it that makes that celestial noise when the dish is at a certain angle? He smiled patiently and explained: 'It is the selsyns. They are the transformers which tell you when you've locked on to the target object in space, and give off electronic signals at fixed frequencies. You see, they vibrate.'

That evening as we drove away and looked back at Little Star deep in the forest, framed against the setting sun, its dish was again pointing up. It was too far off to hear the music of the spheres. 'But still,' I thought, 'Little Star is back in business, surely those selsyns must be vibrating now!'

173

47

The Trafficker

Jill McGivering

Thousands of women in the Baltic states and in Lithuania in particular were being tricked by phoney job offers before being sold and then forced to work in brothels abroad, many of them in Britain.
(9 July 2005)

She was clearly frightened, sitting hunched on the bottom bunk of a bed which almost filled the tiny room. As she spoke, she fingered the large crucifix round her neck. Her hair was coloured with a defiant streak of red.

Last summer, she'd been approached by a childhood friend, she told me. He said he knew someone who was recruiting women to work as prostitutes in Holland. Prostitution is illegal in Lithuania, but in Holland he said she'd make big money. Trusting him, she agreed. Within weeks, she arrived in Holland—only to find herself a prisoner in a brothel, sold by her friend to a Lithuanian gang. For months, she endured beatings, sexual abuse and a constant stream of clients. She saw little of the money she'd been promised. When she escaped back to Lithuania, her childhood friend tipped off the gang members. They beat her so badly, she almost died. Today she's in hiding, terrified that her attackers will return.

174

Her story is common here. Lithuania joined the EU last year. Since then, the trafficking of young women into Western European brothels has increased dramatically.

British investigators, struggling to keep up with what for them is a relatively new development, say the criminals are making millions. Trafficking young women is as profitable as drugs and arms sales—without the same risks. And increasingly the young women are being recruited by people they know and trust. I heard of women sold by childhood friends, neighbours and even cousins. And although many of the women know there'll be sex work involved, there are others who simply expect to work as waitresses or au pairs.

Local case workers told me about two teenage girls in a small village whose neighbour personally reassured their parents the girls would be safe overseas and then sold them. When they finally escaped from a foreign brothel and returned to the village to accuse her, no one believed them. Many of these cases are simply one person's word against another's. And in Lithuania anyone involved in sex work, even a victim of trafficking, is unlikely to be taken seriously.

In a sprawling prison in rural Lithuania, I met one of the few traffickers to be convicted. Haroldas slouched in his chair, his prison number round his neck, watched by an armed guard. Yes, he shrugged, he'd trafficked women. He'd lost count how many; maybe twelve to twenty. He described how he travelled round villages, asking about young women who might need jobs and befriending them. First I just offered work locally, he said. Then I'd invite them to a party and get to

175

know them. Finally I'd offer them a job abroad. Of course they ended up in brothels, he said, but they must have known what they were getting into. I asked him if he thought the amount of trafficking was increasing. Definitely, he said. In fact it's growing so fast, he's worried. 'I've got a daughter,' he added. 'I'm frightened she might get caught up in it too.' He'd made roughly £20,000 selling girls—a fortune in Lithuania. He was sentenced to two and a half years in prison.

Lithuania is trying to improve contacts with British investigators, but doesn't yet have an anti-trafficking unit. The police seem confused about the distinction between trafficking and prostitution. In the capital, Vilnius, I joined two police specialists who tipped back lazily in their chairs and, with a smirk, showed me pictures of semi-naked women offering themselves on the Internet. They had to balance their anti-prostitution work, they said, with other duties: stopping illegal disposal of oil and prosecuting people who owned more than one cat or dog.

Finally, they telephoned one of the online prostitutes, agreed a price and set off to trap her. Their sting took place in a set of cramped rooms in a filthy housing block. When I arrived, two young women were slumped dejectedly on a low sofa, filling in arrest papers. The wallpaper was damp and peeling. Pictures of naked women, cut from porn magazines, were stuck to the walls.

Back at the police station, two other women—these were Ukrainian women in their twenties—had just been arrested for prostitution. They said they had arrived in Lithuania the previous week, expecting to work in a massage parlour only to find they'd been sold to a brothel owner. Afterwards, the police officer shook his head. He didn't believe a word of it, he said.

In the meantime, young women are being sold into UK brothels in steadily growing numbers. Catching the traffickers is one way of tackling it. But reducing demand is another. In Lithuania, I was asked: 'What's Britain doing to change attitudes towards prostitution?' Or, as one case worker asked me: 'Why is trafficking so profitable—and why do British men want to buy sex with very young, very terrified women?'

48

Lonely Mountains

Nick Thorpe

When Romania joined the EU, its farmers had to ensure that their produce conformed to the strict food safety standards laid down by the European Union. (27 February 2007)

The small road winds steeply up through a valley beside a stream, past beech trees, oaks and further up, thick stands of pines. It should be almost impassable in this season because of the snow. But this year there are only a few stray strands of distant white, like wool caught on the rocks, as we reach Tilisca, then Gales, then Poiana Sibiului—the largest of the shepherding villages. And finally Gina, our destination.

Everything has the sweet, musty smell of sheep here: the main street, the mayor's office, but most overpowering of all, the cheese cellars. Elena and Sawa, sisters whose families own 250 sheep or so apiece, scoop great square ingots of rich cream-coloured cheese out of the pine barrels for me to sample. It tastes rather like Greek feta.

The cheese rests here, in salted water, waiting for the trip to market in Bucharest, six hours' drive to the south. Those in the village who don't have sheep drive the cheese and do the selling, in twenty or so big open markets in the capital where sheep's cheese from Sibiu—*brindza*, they call it here—is especially prized. In fact it's a key ingredient grated into Romania's national dish, polenta.

From the window of the mayor's office every green hilltop, as far as the eye can see, is neatly fenced off into sheepfolds. But there's hardly a sheep to be seen. The men take them down to the plains each October, as they have done for centuries, to escape the mountain snows and ice. Georghe walks for two months, to Baia Mare in the north. Others herd them down to the Danube delta, where their charges bleat beneath the honking geese from Siberia, who winter there also. In Prince Michael of Wallachia's time, in the fourteenth century, the shepherds of this strip of the Carpathians had the right to pasture their sheep as far away as the Crimean peninsula. Sometimes they were gone for years.

Under the Austro-Hungarian monarchy, they carried carved wooden passports showing the number of sheep in their care. For centuries they've battled with the wolves and bears which still cling, like them, to these mountains. But now they face the biggest danger yet: the long-toothed bureaucrats of Bucharest and Brussels.

'I'm not against traditional producers,' says Marian Avram, the head of the Food Safety Inspectorate in the Romanian capital. 'But I am against extremist traditionalism.' For a moment he makes it sound like the latest front in the war on terror. 'The peasants only have themselves to blame,' he continues, 'squandering their income on luxury cars instead of investing it in milking technology.'

Over mouthfuls of salty cheese in her cellar, I ask Elcna about luxury automobiles. 'I married at seventeen,' she says. 'We've got a horse, but we've never had a car.' Her family makes roughly 2,500 kilos of cheese a year, ten kilos per sheep, in the milking months from May to October, which they sell to the merchants for up to £2 a kilo. It's their principle source of income. And they have to pay for fodder in winter and the rent of the meadows in summer. The men bring the sheep back to the mountains at Easter, and all the family helps in the sheepfolds, milking morning and evening, and making the cheese. The most remote folds can be six hours' walk from the nearest road. But now the new regulations encourage the building of cheese factories with stainless steel vats, instead of wooden barrels, within easy reach of the inspectors.

'In the summer heat, how are we going to get the milk to the main road?' ask the shepherds. 'And where will the money come from to build factories?' 'And anyway,' an old man outside the mayor's office tells me, 'the cheese wouldn't taste the same.'

179

The new regulations leave one loophole: to register as 'traditional' producers. But can all the documents be filled out in time? Will inspectors have to check each and every sheep? Thirty-nine thousand belong to the shepherds of Gina alone, and nearer 50,000 in the biggest village.

The system seems tilted, as ever, to factory production, supplying spotless, sanitised supermarkets with identical items. 'But do you actually like the taste of *brindza*?' I asked the chief inspector. 'Yes,' he replied, 'if I'm sure it's not going to poison me.'

In her front room in Gina, Maria Sterp sings of life in the mountains in her youth: the handsome, flute-playing shepherds, the maids-a-milking and the children rounding up the animals. Young people want to watch television and play on computers nowadays, not look after sheep, she laments. The new law will speed up the end of a way of life already in decline. Year by year, the mountains are getting lonelier, she sings. Soon the only people left will be tourists.

49

The Honey Hunters

Alastair Lawson

Honey-hunting in the south-western jungles of Bangladesh is by no means the gentle rural pastime it may sound. It's a task fraught with danger, and not just because the bees are among the largest and most

With a broad flashing grin, Latif Dhali was the grateful recipient of a pair of white women's tennis shoes on the last day of our trip to the jungle of Bangladesh. They were given to him by a tourist who had spent a week accompanying him collecting honey from cones amid the stifling heat of the Bangladeshi mangrove forests. Like other honey hunters, he had, up until then, ploughed his way barefoot through the thick vegetation in search of the wild bees that provided him with a living. But now he had a pair of shoes, the first that he had owned in his life.

Latif Dhali, like most honey hunters, or Mowalis, is from the Sundarbans. He is an inhabitant of one of the numerous villages that surround the waterlogged mangrove forest, which is criss-crossed by rivers and waterways. For two months of the year during the honey-collecting season, he lives on a seven-metre-long boat which resembles a giant canoe, deep in the heart of the forest. We followed him and other Mowalis on a honey-collecting odyssey by boat into the far south-west, close to the border with India.

Latif Dhali is small, thin, with the skin of a man who has spent most of his time in the great outdoors. The only clothing he has is on his body, which is why a pair of ladies' tennis shoes is such a welcome addition to his wardrobe.

He is extraordinarily fit, often running through the jungle in search of the honey cones, shouting with delight every time one is found. When that happens there's a flurry of activity. Torches are prepared from the abundance of thick vegetation:

181

the smoke irritates the bees and makes them fly away. But only for a short time. Many realise they're under attack and will repeatedly sting any invader who isn't holding a torch. The honey hunters ignore the stings to collect the cone and wax in a large basket, taking care to leave part of it so that the bees can return and rebuild. On a good day the hunters can find seven to eight cones. But it's hard work. Frequently they're knee-deep in mud and have to cross numerous rivers, creeks and streams while simultaneously remaining aware of the ever-present tiger menace. Evidence of tigers is everywhere: we came across footprints which my guide said were less than an hour old. Latif Dhali and the other honey hunters were too busy working to let that worry them.

When not braving the jungle, Latif Dhali is a master storyteller. He is one of the few people in his village to have had access to a television during his life, and spent one memorable evening under the stars on the deck of our boat recounting every twist, drama and nuance of an American soap opera that he had recently seen on Bangladesh Television. His storytelling made compulsive listening.

It's unlikely that Latif Dhali and his fellow honey hunters have heard of the Greek myth of Jason and the Argonauts. But I think he would agree that they have a lot in common. Jason searched for the elusive golden fleece hanging from a tree, travelling a long way by boat to a remote area. The honey hunters, like the Argonauts, also have to travel long distances by boat in search of a trophy that hangs from tree branches. They too are looking for a golden prize—some of the most highly valued honey in Asia—and are up against equally formidable enemies, including giant-sized bees and the famous Royal Bengal Tiger. And, like the Argonauts, the honey hunters often have to pay with their lives in search of the final prize. But it's a reward worth winning: honey hunters can earn as much in two months as farm-workers do in a year.

Latif Dhali faces the dangers of the Sundarbans with remarkable equanimity. He and hundreds of other unarmed honey hunters would be paid danger and hardship money if they lived in the West. The bees of the Sundarbans don't take too kindly to having their homes invaded, and five stings is enough to give most people a severe fever. Every year, between ten and fifteen Mowalis die after being attacked by tigers during the honey-hunting season. It's not known why there are so many man-eating tigers in the Sundarbans; one theory is that the high salinity in the water there makes the animals more aggressive.

'We know there is always a risk that we won't come home,' Latif told me, 'but this is a job which we and our ancestors have been doing for hundreds of years and we are well aware of the dangers.' He said that in the West he had heard that there was a high mortality rate among pilots who spray fertiliser on crops using single-engine aircraft. 'I suppose our job is like theirs,' he suggested, 'dangerous but very exciting.'

For a time, Latif Dhali was able to do his job with the added luxury of a pair of women's tennis shoes to protect his feet from the notorious Sundarbans thorns. But tragically he didn't have long to relish the experience. Within twelve hours

183

of receiving them, he was attacked and killed by a tiger. But for a short while they were his pride and joy, one of the few indulgences he had ever experienced.

50

Absorbed by Saffron

Daniel Lak

An ancient harvest was continuing up in the troubled valley of Indian Kashmir, undisturbed by time and years of militant separatist violence. More than 100,000 Kashmiris join in the region's autumn saffron harvest, picking, stripping and sorting the crocus flower and the stigma within that make up the world's most expensive spice. The saffron of Kashmir has been known as the most fragrant and expensive in the world for more than 2,000 years.

(21 November 1998)

Imagine a vast plain of grey-brown earth, shaded here and there with willow and almond trees, surrounded by snow-capped mountains gently warmed by the late autumn sun. Then cover that plain with swaying purple flowers, each exuding the most lush and beguiling scent. Now people the fields with tens of thousands of villagers wearing homespun clothes, picking flowers at a furious pace and heaping them into wicker baskets. Their chatter and laughter rings through the clear air,

184

old men smoke hubble-bubbles under the trees and all you can do is marvel at a sight like no other, anywhere in the world.

These are the saffron fields outside the small town of Pampore in Kashmir, just about half an hour's drive from the summer capital, Srinagar. For most of the year they're barren, as the bulbs of the *Crocus sativa* germinate beneath the dry earth. But come late autumn the fields turn purple. It's been this way for more than 2,000 years, according to some. Certainly the way the people pick and produce the saffron hasn't changed much. They may arrive at the fields in a bus or a car, but from there on, everything else about saffron is authentically ancient.

The crocus flower is a lovely shade of pastel purple, but its real value is found within the petals. Every flower has at its heart three red stigmas— the female part—two stamens, which perform the male role, and a long white stem connecting all of this to the main flower. The job of the saffron pickers isn't finished until they've plucked several hundred thousand flowers out of the ground. That's how many they must pick if they're to see any reward at all for their efforts. And a day or two's picking is just the beginning.

The sacks of flowers are taken home, or to labourers who toil through the night, stripping away the insides of the flowers. Nothing is wasted. The petals are eaten as a vegetable. Animals are given the stems, and of course, the market—the world—covets the rest: stigmas alone for the purest saffron; stamens the next most-sought-after grade; and finally a mixture of all the bits for the cheapest saffron, the kind the growers and pickers keep for themselves.

All life revolves around saffron during the harvest. The flowers become currency for those few short days. Beggars roam the fields with small plastic bags, offering a blessing to pickers who give them a handful of flowers. One raggedy man, Farooq he called himself, told me he walked more than ten miles every day, from picking family to family, and he earned about £2 selling his sack of crocuses at the end of the day. Fruit sellers also move through the fields, selling bananas and apples in exchange for petals. The mood is jolly; you never see any quibbling over the size of the clumps of flowers offered in payment.

No matter how busy the picking gets, there's always time for prayer. Kashmir is known as the Valley of Saints, the heart of Sufi Islam in the subcontinent. In ancient days, it was on the silk route to China and was the favoured playground of the Moghuls. Its religious influences are rich and the line between the Hindu and Muslim faiths is almost indistinguishable. Prayers during the saffron season are offered at a golden-domed shrine in Pampore, the joint tomb of Khwaja Masood Wali and Hazrat Sheikh Shariffudin. These two wandering Sufi holy men apparently arrived in Kashmir about 800 years ago, carrying flower bulbs from Asia Minor. After a local chieftain cured one of them who was ill, he was given a bulb in payment. And thus, according to legend, did the saffron crocus come to Kashmir.

But Kashmir's more secular historians beg to differ. Mohammed Yusuf Teng, a poet and expert on the ancient culture of his land, told me the indigenous people of Kashmir grew saffron more

186

than 2,000 years ago, a fact that's mentioned in the epics written during the era of Tantric Hindu kings. Kashmiri traders also took saffron to ancient Athens, Rome and classical Persia, long before the Islamic age dawned, according to Professor Teng. This delightful and hospitable man also makes the best *kava*, Kashmiri saffron tea, in the entire valley. There can be few experiences more sublime than sitting with a steaming cup of the professor's aromatic brew, listening to him recite poetry in Urdu, the language of the Moghuls. He also claims that saffron is an aphrodisiac, something I haven't had a chance to verify yet.

I can vouch for his poetry though. His favourite couplet goes: 'My love went down the Pampore Road and there he was absorbed by the flowers of saffron.' I'm getting to know the feeling.

51

Renaissance in the Cinque Terre

Christian Fraser

The Cinque Terre, on the coast between Genoa and La Spezia, is one of Italy's most striking stretches of coastline. For years the five villages strung out along a series of largely barren cliffs were poor and had a high level of unemployment. But their fortunes were transformed when the area was accorded National Park status. (6 January 2007)

The slopes of the Cinque Terre rise in such

dizzying fashion that in Riomaggiore you can take a lift up to the second level of town. Some of the vineyards around the region are on hillsides so steep and so close to the sea that the grapes have to be harvested by boat. Since Roman times, the farmers here have been conjuring small miracles from these slopes. Their sweet dessert wine was so popular that amphoras bearing their insignia were found during excavations in Pompeii, hundreds of miles to the south.

Yet this has always been one of the poorest regions in Italy. There is still only a single road that connects the five villages of the Cinque Terre, and access is mostly by boat or by train. But the last few years have seen the local economy booming. In fact, so successful is it becoming that in recent years the residents of Riomaggiore and the other hamlets strung out along the Ligurian coast have been enjoying a lifestyle their predecessors could only have dreamed of. Courtesy of the National Park they now receive free natural medicine, massage treatments and health screenings. There is a free shopping service for elderly residents and subsidised childcare for working parents. Cars are banned, replaced by electric buses.

It's become a farming utopia, a place where tourists and others from outside are in the front line of conservation. The driving force behind these changes is Franco Bonanini, the former mayor and now head of the National Park. Generations of his family have farmed this land, but like most people in Riomaggiore, Franco grew up in poverty. 'When I was little,' he told me, 'the worst two weeks of the year were when the wine speculators arrived. It was always a painful

188

process,' he said. 'The merchants would taste my father's wine and spit it out in disgust. They would tell him the wine was no good. And then they'd carry it off at half price. It was the saddest night of the year.'

So when the Cinque Terre achieved its National Park status and the first property speculators arrived, Franco and his team swore that this time, the Cinque Terre would not be cheated.

The Park began to buy up the cottages in the villages as they became available. Prospective buyers have to cultivate at least 3,000 square metres of vines, fruit trees or vegetables before they're allowed to settle.

British ex-pat Paula Pecuria has been living in the Cinque Terre for thirty-one years with husband Mauro. They live in the house in which he was born. They farm their land, coaxing vines, lemons, olives and basil out of a plot that defies gravity. It towers over the sea on such a steep gradient, I wonder how anything grows. 'Over the years I have done it all,' she says. 'Stamped the grapes, plucked the basil and carried these heavy baskets down the slopes. People who come here,' she says, 'may come with a dream of the good life, but they quickly realise how much hard work is involved. The rules for new buyers are essential,' she says. 'Without the land you have no home! This is not natural farmland. It has been chiselled from the cliffs. And if it was left, it would quickly disappear.'

The farms of the Cinque Terre are propped up by hundreds of miles of drystone walls. The locals tell me the work that has gone into maintaining this steep terracing is comparable to the building of the Great Wall of China. Those farms

189

abandoned in the 1980s have either collapsed down the hillside or disappeared under the wild alpine vegetation. But now some of them are being reclaimed and repaired by outsiders. I met students from Australia and Germany who, in return for free lodging and food, are rebuilding hillsides.

With their help, the co-operative farmers are growing basil, garlic and pine nuts for a local factory, which makes pesto sauce for pasta. And they have all sorts of wild herbs to work with, including saffron, still by weight the most expensive spice in the world. And in time, with a bit of encouragement, this could provide a further lucrative sideline for the ambitious Cinque Terre.

The money from this organic produce, and from the visitors who pay to walk the coastal paths, means there's now virtually no unemployment and for the residents of these five small communities, no end of opportunity.

As I sailed away from the harbour of Riomaggiore, looking back at those impossible steep terraces behind me, I marvelled at what Franco and his team have achieved in such a short space of time. Yet this is a land that also stands testament to the iron will of his predecessors, the farmers back through the generations. And I am guessing that if they were here today, they would be well satisfied that so many people have come from so far to help protect the place which they once worked so hard to cultivate.

52

A Hygiene Inspector Calls

Imogen Foulkes

*Moving house is one of life's more stressful
experiences, but in Switzerland, the tension was
compounded by strict requirements on the condition
in which you must leave your old home.*
(5 March 2005)

I have to confess, I've always been a bit intimidated
by the Swiss devotion to cleanliness. It all began
not long after I arrived in Switzerland, when, as a
new mother, I was invited for coffee by a woman
who had had her baby in the same hospital as me. I
found myself sitting in a kitchen which seemed
more suited to open-heart surgery than a cosy chat
about feeding routines and nappy rash. The
surfaces gleamed, the floor was spotless, even the
babies were squeaky clean—apart from mine, who
was only squeaky.

But, a few years on, I've become more used to
Swiss hygiene standards, so when it came to
moving house, I knew I was expected to leave my
old home immaculate. Sure enough, I got a letter
saying the hygiene inspector would be there at ten
o'clock on a Monday morning. He arrived,
punctual to the nanosecond, a dapper little man in
a maroon jacket and beautifully pressed trousers.
His name was Herr Schweizer, or Mr Swiss in
English, and he'd even brought a spare pair of

shoes to wear inside the house. I should have recognised the warning signs when I noticed that Herr Schweizer, who was no taller than me, somehow managed to look down at me over the top of his glasses. But I had spent the best part of three days cleaning and I was confident I'd pass the inspection with flying colours.

'Let's start in the kitchen,' said Mr Swiss, and I trotted eagerly after him. I was particularly proud of the kitchen: old postcards and invitations were gone from the walls, so too was the odd blob of spaghetti sauce, vintage 2002. The oven shone, the cupboards were bare. But Herr Schweizer was not impressed, he was too busy unscrewing my taps. 'Look,' he said, pointing to the inside of a pipe I'd scarcely known existed, 'all these calcium deposits, you'll have to get rid of them.'

We moved on to the ceramic hob. Mr Swiss bent over it. I could see his reflection in its pristine surface; he could see something else. He produced a razor blade from his pocket and scraped gently: a tiny black speck floated upwards. 'Still dirty,' he said. An hour and a half later we were still in the kitchen, but mercifully almost finished, just one drawer to go. Too late, I realised I couldn't actually remember having cleaned that one. Herr Schweizer pulled it open, to reveal three old fish knives, a cork, two bottle openers and what looked suspiciously like a lock of child's hair. This time he said nothing, just sighed and added the drawer to his list.

On it went: behind a radiator he discovered half a spider's web; in the bathroom, dismantling the toilet cistern revealed yet more calcium deposits; and downstairs in the cellar, the ventilation shaft was smudged.

The list grew ever longer, and I realised I had at least another day's cleaning ahead of me. A chance, during the scrubbing and polishing, to reflect on why it is the Swiss attach so much importance to cleanliness. A friend of mine says it's the crowded nature of this country. Switzerland is small and mainly mountainous; space is limited; most of the seven million inhabitants live in apartments. Keeping things clean and tidy is necessary just to live comfortably. Another friend, more unkindly, suggests that the Swiss are not exactly noted for their achievements in art and literature—perhaps, he says, because they pour their creative energy into cleaning.

My own interpretation has to do with the role of women in Swiss society: those with children often do not work. That means hundreds of thousands of women in small apartments with no gardens have time on their hands. A recent survey revealed that the average Swiss woman can spend at least two hours every day on housework. The very idea exhausts me, but it probably saves them the ordeal I went through at Herr Schweizer's hands.

When the inspection ended, I was given a six-page list of improvements I needed to make, and as I ushered him towards the door, he had one last comment. Passing the fuse box, he pulled it open. 'Look,' he said triumphantly, 'dust!'

A week later, the house is clean, my muscles ache and my hands are sore from cleaning fluids. But I'm happy, because I know that should a pair of heart surgeons move into my old house, they need never go to the hospital—they can perform operations in my kitchen and store their instruments in my fuse box.

53

The Boy Who Sleeps in a Tyre

Humphrey Hawksley

The United States was promoting democracy in societies previously ruled by dictators. But in one such country, Morocco, not everyone was benefiting. (24 December 2005)

'How many of you go to school?' I asked the group of children gathered round. Behind us was an open drain, then shanty huts, which crept back along the grey rocky landscape. There was a mild aroma of rotting rubbish. Across the road, two men from the Interior Ministry, sitting on wooden chairs, eyed us but said nothing. We were just outside the Moroccan capital Rabat, in a slum called Akrash. The children put their hands up—all except one, a boy in a filthy yellow shirt, arms marked with little scratches, his face filled with a child's awe and innocence, but his eyes firm as if he knew that if he lost his confidence he might not survive.

'Why don't you go to school?' I asked. His parents, although alive, had abandoned him and for some reason that meant he wasn't at school. 'So what do you do? Where do you live?' 'Up there,' he said, pointing to the top of a hill misted with smoke. His name is Souffian Baghari. He's eleven. We drove up and turned the final corner of the

194

road to his home, a rubbish tip. Seagulls and crows swooped down. The birds landed on the backs of goats and sheep and pecked at their wool which was soiled and dangling with rubbish. Birds and animals alike foraged for food. People, too—many children, rags hanging, heads down, hacking with pitchforks or their bare hands.

I'd come to Morocco not just to look again at more developing-world poverty but to test America's policy of pushing for democracy in societies which for years have been ruled through dictatorship. Can it really be done without first building mature political parties, an uncorrupt civil service, a fair court system—institutions which take not months but generations to create?

'But where do you actually sleep?' I asked Souffian. He walked over to a huge old tractor tyre, lying among weeds. 'Here,' he said. 'Like this.' He climbed in it, curling round inside where the inner tube would have been, put his head on two clasped hands, closed his eyes and pretended to sleep. 'I do whatever I can to eat. I work on the dump all day and at night I come here to rest,' he said. 'What I really want is for someone to adopt me so I can have a normal life.'

Back down the hill, Souffian and I visited the local school. Walking into the playground, his head turned left and right, his expression relaxing as if he thought he could now suddenly become a child again. 'Can he enrol in the school?' I asked a teacher. 'Of course, of course,' she said. 'He can come any time.' But he couldn't right then because the headmaster wasn't there. Nor were Souffian's parents.

So we went to ask the two Interior Ministry

195

officials we'd seen earlier. 'Let me tell you something,' said one of them, peering at us through dark glasses. 'A delinquent child like this represents a big danger to society. We have a list of people like him which we forward to our head office. His parents aren't here, so what can we do?' 'Hold on,' I said. 'You're saying that because he has no parents, you can't help him.' 'The problem is with the child,' said the other, pushing a dirty white baseball cap back on his head. 'It's pointless to talk about it.'

That evening, I tracked down the education minister, Habib El Malki, a suave French-speaking politician with perfect manners, dressed in an immaculate cream suit. I asked him why an eleven-year-old boy wasn't at school. 'Yes,' he said, 'there is social marginalisation, it's true. But the policy we've put in place is to set up strongly representative local committees which we help to find solutions to put back all the children who've fallen through the education net.' We talked for some time, but never once did he ask where he, or his staff for that matter, could actually find Souffian, until we told him.

For the next few days I talked to dozens of people in Morocco about democracy. It had little or no resonance. 'Elections,' scoffed one young mother. 'During the voting the politicians come, the street light works and water flows from the taps. As soon as voting stops, nothing works again.' 'You don't need elections to have a responsive government,' said a farmer. 'They're just an excuse.'

Back in London, I reread the UN Convention on the Rights of the Child to which Morocco is a

196

signatory. Article 20 states that a child deprived of a family environment shall be entitled to special protection and assistance provided by the State. Article 28 recognises the right of the child to education. At a primary level it should be compulsory and free. A couple of weeks later, I asked a colleague to check on Souffian. He was still sleeping in his tyre. Still no one had come to help him.

54

A Minor Modern Miracle

Richard Hamilton

The Baja family were so poor they lived in a lavatory for seven years. But their lives changed after their story was featured on the BBC. (7 July 2007)

The Bajas looked like a normal family when I saw them in their new apartment in the maze-like old medina of Sale, a city not far from the Moroccan capital, Rabat. They offered me couscous, tea and cakes as they sat happily with their children on an embroidered red sofa in front of the television. In fact they are a normal family, but for seven years they did something extremely abnormal: they lived in a public toilet.

Their problems started many years ago when their daughter was kidnapped by child traffickers and they spent all their money getting her released. They could no longer afford to rent their home and as Aze Adine Ould Baja worked as an attendant in the public lavatories they thought they could stay there, just as a temporary measure. The local authority promised them somewhere else to live, but the promises never materialised and their pleas fell on deaf bureaucratic ears.

This is a story of mice and men. In the toilet the family lived among the mice, which would nibble and tear at their clothes. And men who had drunk too much would stagger in and shout abuse at Aze Adine's wife, Khadija, and her daughter. Khadija even gave birth to her third child in the lavatory block. Her middle child was teased at school. They called him simply 'the boy from the toilet'.

Morocco is not a poor country by African standards. But there's a gap between the haves and have-nots. Well, it's not really a gap—more like a chasm. In the main cities you can see the lush surroundings of the royal palaces and palm trees shading the immaculate villas of government ministers and diplomats. But then there are the poor quarters in places like Sale, a dormitory town that supplies Rabat with its workers. Take a train out of the city and you will see rows of corrugated iron rooftops held down from the wind with rocks and stones. These are Morocco's shanty towns. They have bred alienation, discontent and suicide bombers who blew themselves up in Casablanca four years ago and in April this year. They found no earthly paradise in the slums, so they sought it in the afterlife.

Meanwhile, the local authority didn't do much in terms of finding the Bajas a new home, but they were extremely good at paperwork. They printed up a neat-looking identity card for the family which gave their official address as: 'Toilets, Sale.'

When the Bajas told their story to a local newspaper, the authorities were embarrassed by the media attention and finally took action, concrete action: they evicted the family and blocked the lavatory's entrance up with cement and concrete. When I first met Aze Adine I found him crying by the wall. 'I am dying of hunger and my children are dirty and suffering,' he told me then. 'I think I shall find a boat and sail away. Maybe we will find a place where it's easier to get something to eat or maybe we will just die in the middle of the sea.' At this point a police officer came up to me. He took my press card and escorted me to the police station before letting me go. I then went to the government to find out why the authorities had blocked up the lavatories, but the man there wouldn't answer; he just blew smoke into my face.

And then a minor modern miracle happened. When they read about the family on the BBC website, hundreds of Internet users from as far afield as the United States and Kuwait sent e-mails expressing concern. Dozens offered money. 'I have been unemployed for some time now,' wrote one reader, 'but I have a roof over my head and would like the same thing for the Baja family.' More than £1,000 has so far reached the Bajas, wired through a money transfer service. The family say their prayers have been answered and it's the work of God; others might say it's the power of the Internet. 'I don't think we would have survived without this charity,' Aze Adine told me. 'I want to thank all those who gave us money. May God give them a place in heaven.'

Aze Adine plans to get a job selling sandwiches on the beach at Sale. He dreams of buying his own house, using money he's received as a deposit. 'Living in the toilet was a nightmare that we have just woken up from,' he said. 'It was like a dark cloud or a fog passing in front of our eyes. When you have no job, no house and cannot provide for your family, you are not a real human being,' he said, 'but now I am a human being once more.' It was early evening when I said goodbye to the Bajas. The sun was setting, bathing the old medina in a peaceful orange glow. I left them sitting quietly on their sofa with their couscous, tea and cakes, pondering the kindness of strangers.

55

A Nation Brought to its Knees

Martin Plaut

The Basotho people in the mountainous kingdom of Lesotho were facing a triple crisis: a sharply reduced demand for their labour; a rising tide of HIV and AIDS; and a declining agricultural sector as erosion and drought devastated crop yields.
(17 December 2005)

The plains of South Africa's Orange Free State are flat and featureless, stretching as far as the eye can see. But gradually, as you approach Lesotho, the landscape changes. Rocky outcrops, then hills appear. It prepares one for the mountains that have been the sanctuary of the Basotho people since the birth of their nation in the early nineteenth century. It was King Moshoeshoe who united the disparate remnants of tribes crushed by the Zulu into a fighting force to defend their mountain strongholds. After the Zulu came the Boers, who took much of the best farming land.

But Moshoeshoe was one of the shrewdest southern African leaders, and when final defeat stared his people in the face, he appealed to Queen Victoria for assistance. In an act that neither Boers nor Basotho truly understood, the queen magnanimously extended her sovereignty to the beleaguered people. As Moshoeshoe put it, she spread her blanket over them. Whatever it meant, it did the trick. The Boers retreated, leaving Lesotho an independent island in the heart of South Africa. And the Basotho repaid their debt, loyally sending 20,000 men to fight Britain's enemies during the Second World War.

And so this anomaly continued: a free nation, a refuge for those fleeing apartheid, earning its keep by sending its men to the gold and diamond mines of South Africa. All of which makes the current plight of these people so poignant.

I met Christine Kehoele at her home, which was perched on the side of a steep hillside on the outskirts of the capital, Maseru. The modest two-roomed house looks out over the clothing factory where she once worked. But, like many Basotho who came to town looking for work, she is now unemployed. 'We were told to go home,' says Christine. 'Sometimes we were not paid because the factory had no money. It eventually closed.'

The Chinese owners simply locked the doors

and took the next plane home. No redundancy pay, no final salaries, even the sewing machines were left where they stood. Ten thousand jobs lost in the last year. Some blame it on changes resulting from international textile agreements, others on currency fluctuations. The local newspapers call it the Chinese tsunami, which swept away a once-thriving industry.

For women like Christine, the future looks bleak. And returning to the rural areas is hardly an option. Driving south of Maseru, the villages gradually become smaller and increasingly poor. This land has been so intensively cultivated by one generation after another that it has little left to offer. The topsoil has been washed downstream, providing South Africa with a precious gift that Lesotho cannot afford to give. With their agriculture now in terminal decline, some villagers simply sit and wait.

Lesotho was always poor, but never like this. I learned to walk in this country, and we returned for holidays throughout the 1950s. Basotho herd boys took me out with the cattle. The bulls fled before their long thin sticks and shrill whistles. They hunted pigeons, bringing them down with whirling sticks. I would swap the birds, roasted in anthills, for the sandwiches my mother packed for me. I sat by the streams and tried to imitate the boys as they skilfully moulded clay into oxen. Theirs were wonderfully lifelike, mine never more than lumps of mud.

But above all I remember pushing my sister's pram through the tall fields of maize to visit the local villages. Women would come out of the thatched huts to admire her and we never left empty-handed. We would arrive home with the pram full of presents: an egg from one, corn from another, flowers from a garden. The villages were full of laughter, the women endlessly generous as they waved us off, their children on their hips.

Of course these are the rose-tinted memories of youth. But cold statistics dished out by the United Nations confirm the general picture. Lesotho is in a steady decline and HIV and AIDS are taking a deadly toll. Life expectancy has dropped from sixty to just thirty-five.

At a time like this you might have expected that Britain, the former colonial power, would have stepped up its presence in Lesotho. Yet in January, London decided to close its High Commission, transferring its functions to Pretoria. Many Basotho see this as a symbolic rejection, an old friend turning his back in an hour of need. 'How can they do this?' one old man asked me.

People here now sit and stare at barren fields and unploughed lands, waiting for handouts from the international community. A once proud and independent nation has been brought to its knees.

56

An African Crisis

Will Ross

Weeks of mass protests in the West African state of Guinea saw more than a hundred demonstrators shot dead by police and troops. The protestors were saying the country's ageing president, Lansana Conté, had let corruption overrun the country while people struggled to meet basic needs. They wanted him to resign. (15 February 2007)

I realised early on that this was going to be an eventful trip. The car broke down on the way to my hotel from the airport and, along with half a dozen children, I was soon pushing a battered Mercedes Benz through the filthy streets as the driver tried to jump-start it. 'Don't stop! One more try' was the repeated refrain. But I was far from optimistic when he popped the bonnet open. I am no mechanic, but the sight of an upturned, punctured can of tomato purée serving as a part of the engine would surely look out of place in any car. I eventually arrived, drenched in sweat, at the hotel reception and since that moment it's been far from dull and often chaotic. But Guineans are used to that.

Since independence from France almost fifty years ago the country has had only two presidents. The current one, Lansana Conté, a diabetic chain-smoker in his seventies, seized power twenty-three years ago, but even as his health fails he shows no sign of stepping down.

Guinea is mineral rich but as in so many African countries, as the raw materials leave the port, the population sees little benefit. Meanwhile, the economy has gone from bad to worse, in step with the president's health.

Ministers learn of their fate on the evening news, which usually abruptly interrupts endless hours of music videos. Last May, the state television newsreader announced the latest presidential decree—a cabinet reshuffle which included increased power for the prime minister. The very next morning the reshuffle was overturned and the prime minister was jobless. Guineans have often wondered who's in charge here.

But with massive unemployment and a civil servant's salary barely covering the cost of getting the bus to work and feeding the family, people are saying enough is enough.

I won't forget the name Hamdallaye in a hurry. This suburb in the capital Conakry was where demonstrations against President Conté began over the weekend. Driving with a BBC colleague, Al Hassan, we passed groups of angry young men keen to yell into the microphone a rude word or fifty against their president. We sat beside a wall as gunfire rang out from not far away. Plumes of thick black smoke filled the air where protestors had burnt tyres.

Al Hassan and I found ourselves in looters' alley. Panting men passed us with souvenirs from ransacked homes—air conditioners, glitzy light fittings—and one looter who hadn't set his sights too high pulled a light bulb out of his pocket. All over the country law and order was breaking down, and it was no coincidence that the homes of several government ministers were targeted.

Hamdallaye didn't look like the best place to spend the night, so before sunset we set off for the city centre. No way through. Accompanied by a gang of teenagers, a two-metre-tall giant in an orange T-shirt with eyes as red as traffic lights stood in our way. His name—Taliban. We turned round and found a place to sleep, or at least try to

205

between the rounds of gunfire.

Shortly before dawn we tried again; on the back seat, a frightened woman we had offered to drive to safety. The main road was strewn with boulders and we drove over hundreds of pairs of secondhand women's shoes, presumably looted from a truck the night before. Then, as we turned at an impassable pile of wood and rocks, three men ran towards the car. One, wielding a machete, smashed the back windscreen, but thanks to my colleague's heavy foot on the accelerator we made it away, although not far. The rocks had caused so much damage, the engine oil was pouring out so we had to abandon the car and walk to safety.

As I prepared to send the report of the violence to the studios in London, Al Hassan stopped me. 'Do you mind deleting those bits where you can hear the lady screaming in the back of the car?' he asked me. 'You see, my wife will worry who that woman was in my car.' A bit of careful editing and the shrieks were gone and Al Hassan looked a little more relaxed.

As I write this it's increasingly hard to guess what will happen next. The president has declared martial law and the army chief has imposed a curfew. People are only allowed out of their homes between the hours of noon and six in the evening.

In the hotel reception, a Moroccan waitress is bidding a tearful farewell as her country sends in a military plane to evacuate her and her colleagues. A Japanese businessman is doing lengths of the hotel swimming pool in between glasses of red wine, while an Indian pharmacist, who wonders whether his contract with the Ministry of Health will be worth the paper it's written on, has approached me with his latest evacuation plan.

'Ah, Mr Will, Mr Will. What about a speedboat?' he asks.

As for eight million Guineans, they too can only guess, but they can't leave.

57

The Snake's Gaze

Tim Whewell

There were many in the Democratic Republic of Congo who refused to believe that a new power-sharing government would mean an end to years of civil war; certainly the country still had numerous militia commanders, like the man our correspondent travelled a long way to meet. (15 November 2003)

It was hard to avoid glancing at the general's crotch, because stuck through the middle of his low-slung military belt was a shiny silver pistol. Wasn't it a bit uncomfortable down there? And could that be why he rocked back and forth on his chair during our interview, just like I don't let my children do at dinner? Why on earth couldn't Jerome Kakwavu wear his firearm on his hip like other self-respecting warlords? But much as I wanted to know, that was just one of many things I never asked the general.

In fact he wasn't really a general. But then no one was going to argue. Seven years of war in central Africa came to an end this summer with the installation of a new power-sharing government in the Democratic Republic of Congo. But even now, many Congolese do not believe the war is really over.

General Jerome was a former traffic cop who'd risen a few ranks in the military and then rewarded himself with four gold stars on each of his scarlet epaulettes. He acquired a private army and a lucrative kingdom in one of the remotest parts of Africa, where Congo meets Uganda and Sudan. He controlled a large open-cast gold mine, forests of valuable timber, and customs posts which, according to UN investigators, net him thousands of dollars a week.

You wouldn't know it from taking a guided tour of Aru, the grid of red dirt roads, banana trees and thatched huts that serves as the general's capital. It's as quiet as the grave; perhaps because, according to many accounts I'd heard, the corpses of his victims are dispersed around the town's chief attractions—under the football pitch, in the back garden of his official residence and so on—dispatched by that shiny weapon he keeps down his front. But that was another subject I didn't raise with the general.

We arrived six hours late in a tiny old Soviet aircraft that last saw service in Siberia, and found the general lethargically sucking on a Fanta in one of Aru's three dingy cafés. He was a lean, restless young man with frighteningly loose limbs, striped in bright colours like a snake in a child's picture book. At the top was his red beret—the shade of very fresh blood—then an imperious black moustache, the flashing white teeth, the red epaulettes, the green fatigues, that strategically placed silver weapon and so on down to the patent black boots.

He met my gaze. But you couldn't tell from his eyes what he thought he was looking at. There was no firm evidence he recognised a fellow human being. And so I didn't just pull my journalistic punches; I held them back for grim life. What was the illegal business network he ran with officers from neighbouring Uganda? Why had his men mutinied against him? And just how bloodily had he crushed the revolt? None of those questions I'd come so far to put were pressed very hard. And so it was off on the 4x4 tour of Aru after dark.

I didn't ask to see the football pitch or his back garden. Instead, we sent dozens of female cyclists careering into ditches as Jerome proclaimed: *'Vous voyez! Vingt-quatre vingt-quatre!* Twenty-four out of twenty-four! Even women feel safe at night!' Under the general, Aru has already achieved that non-stop round-the-clock status that Ken Livingstone still dreams of as mayor of London. The general toyed with another Fanta as we gulped down a few lagers at the Aru dancing club. Then— noblesse oblige—he delivered us to our *gîte*.

It wasn't the kind you may have rented in the Dordogne. There was no light in the loo or water in the basin. A well-built, impenetrable clod of a youth in green fatigues lumbered repeatedly around my room, rummaging under the bed for boots and other military paraphernalia. But before we retired for the night there was a most unexpected revelation.

A very pretty, slightly shy young woman appeared from the courtyard and smiled at us. 'I'm Eunice,' she said in perfect English, 'the general's wife.' So we sat and chatted for half an hour as the TV screen alternated forlornly between blank and buzzing fuzz. She'd been educated in Kenya. She wanted to be a paediatrician. Her dream was to visit London. I hadn't felt able to ask her any of the questions that now bothered me—why on earth had she married the general? And which wife was she? But somehow, her charm and sheer normality had emboldened me—that and the prospect of leaving early next morning.

And so, when the general came to pick us up after breakfast, I had to find out what he did with that pistol. 'Do you have capital punishment?' I ventured insanely. He pretended not to understand. 'We are a well-organised movement,' he growled. 'For us, impunity does not exist.' And yet, hypnotised by the snake's gaze, I couldn't move away. 'Death?' I whispered. Surely he wouldn't gun me down in front of Eunice. But the general wasn't answering. 'You're already late,' he said. And I realised with relief that he was right.

58

Meeting a President

Mark Doyle

Interviews with heads of state don't always go as anticipated. On this occasion it was the president who was keen to question our reporter.
(4 December 2004)

It was a correspondent's dream. Or, at least, I briefly thought it was. I was hanging about in the marble corridors of the presidential palace in Kinshasa, waiting for what I suspected would be a rather unexciting briefing about a meeting between the Democratic Republic of Congo president, Joseph Kabila, and some visiting United Nations diplomats. They were talking about the fragile peace deal in Congo and the UN peacekeeping force which is trying to glue it all together. But then I got a tap on my shoulder.

I turned round to find an immaculately dressed Congolese official asking me if I was Mark Doyle. 'Er, yes,' I replied, rather tentatively. 'Good,' he said, 'follow me', and he started bounding up a marble staircase. Turning round to check I was following him, the man in a perfect Parisian suit said: 'You asked to see President Kabila, right?' 'Er, yes,' I replied, lying through my teeth. I simply could not believe it. I guessed that there had been some mix-up somewhere and as a result I was going to get an interview with the president of Congo without even having asked for one.

We turned a corner at the top of the stairs and there he was, waiting for me, President Joseph Kabila. He was standing near the edge of a thick red carpet. When he saw me, he gestured me into a room and politely took a step backwards to allow me to go in first. He stumbled slightly on the edge of the carpet and for a terrible moment I thought he was going to fall over and crack his head open on the marble floor. That might have been a cue for every machine gun in the palace, and there are plenty of them, to be pointed at me. Luckily he did not fall, but nevertheless other things then started

211

going wrong with my plan.

'Thank you so much, Mr President,' I started hopefully, 'for agreeing to be interviewed.' 'Oh, I don't want to be interviewed, Mark,' he replied, looking at me with his piercing eyes and waving away my microphone. 'I just wanted a word with you about what you've been writing about Congo.' Oh dear. I was alone in a room with a powerful man who appeared not to be happy with me. I must have looked worried, but the president smiled. 'You see, Mark,' he continued, using my first name again as if we had been friends for years, 'you see, I was not very happy when I heard you say that the idea of holding fair elections in Congo in six months' time was—what was it you said—a bad joke?' I had indeed said that, in a BBC News website feature article. I was quoting well-placed sources, of course, but I had said it. And the president of Congo, unfortunately, appeared to be a BBC News website reader. Shifting his weight in his chair, the president of the Democratic Republic of Congo pointed his dark eyes at me again and said: 'Why did you say that, Mark?'

I swallowed hard and decided on the honest approach. 'Well, I've just been in eastern Congo for a week,' I began, 'and it's obvious to me that your national army is still split between opposing factions. There's no police force to speak of, foreign armies are still present in the region and there are no lists of potential voters, and frankly, in these circumstances, I don't see how you can hold fair elections in six months' time.' 'Mark', the president said, using my first name again, 'you've been around a bit, you've got to take some other things into account.' It was then that I realised that this first-name stuff was not some clever public relations tactic designed to flatter me, but a genuine feeling on the president's part that he did know me, because he had been listening to me on the radio for years. I have experienced this before. It is testimony to the power of radio in Africa— lots of people feel they personally know correspondents because they have heard them so often.

'Look,' President Kabila continued, 'if you had come here two years ago, there was no peace process at all and we were still fighting in the east. Things aren't perfect now, of course, but we are making progress. Please be fair.' 'But that still doesn't mean,' I said, 'that fair elections can be held in six months' time.' But, hang on, I thought, what's going on here? Why was I having this private debate with the president of Congo? I am a journalist and I was supposed to be recording an interview with him. 'Of course,' I said, 'of course we'll be fair, but couldn't I just record a little interview with you saying that? Only take a few minutes. Then I can use your voice saying you think there has been progress and . . .' 'No thanks, Mark,' the president replied, 'I'm tired.' 'Later, then,' I implored, 'any time, any place, just before I have to leave tomorrow morning?' He shrugged. 'Oh, all right then.'

I was amazed at the informality of all this. 'All right then,' the president of Congo said. 'Come to my place at seven tomorrow morning. I'll send someone to your hotel to collect you.' I never did get the interview. My plane left earlier than we thought it would, and my messages to the president, asking for a different timing for the appointment, got confused in the protocol channels, as messages to heads of state so often do. But if you are reading or listening to this report, Mr President—Joseph—maybe we could do the interview some other time?

59

The Beloved Colonialist

David Willey

The remains of the nineteenth-century Roman nobleman who gave his name to the capital city of the Republic of Congo were to be reburied in a white marble mausoleum specially built for him in Brazzaville. Africans aren't generally known for their affection for the European colonialists and adventurers who ruled and mapped their countries and often made their fortunes there. But Pietro di Brazza, the only European colonialist still honoured by having an African capital named after him, is different. (23 September 2006)

In the so-called 'scramble' by European powers for the mineral wealth, the rubber and ivory and the territories of Africa at the end of the nineteenth century, Italy didn't come out terribly well. The British, the French and the Belgians all grabbed what they could, but curiously it was an Italian, Pietro Savorgnan di Brazza, who has emerged as the only European explorer and colonialist to be honoured at the beginning of the twenty-first

214

century for what he gave to Africa rather than for what he grabbed.

Pietro di Brazza was born in the mid-nineteenth century into a well-to-do Italian family who lived in a rather grand palace in the centre of Rome. Three years after his birth Dr Livingstone, the Scottish missionary and explorer, reached the Zambezi river. Di Brazza's imagination was fired by this story when he was still a child and later by an atlas in his father's library containing a map of Africa with a big blank space in the dark heart of the continent. 'Would be interesting to visit,' di Brazza scrawled on the map in his own hand.

He ingeniously managed to join the French navy as the newly established kingdom of Italy hadn't yet acquired any ships, and he got himself sent on an official French mission to West Africa where he travelled by river several hundred miles into the unexplored interior. There he met the local king who received him warmly. More than a century later, the descendants of King Makoko and the descendants of Pietro di Brazza have also become friends.

Di Brazza's ideas on sustainable development were ignored in his day by greedy European businessmen and governments in quest of easy profit. In fact, di Brazza died on the journey home after a last visit to his beloved Congo just over a century ago.

In the meantime he had become something of a celebrity with his handsome strong features, his brooding dark eyes and aquiline nose. He was photographed in the studio of one of Paris's best-known photographers, posing barefoot and wearing a headscarf and tattered robes, looking for

215

all the world like an early version of Lawrence of Arabia. His image was later used on advertisements for well-known French brands of soup, chocolate and cheese.

During this last visit to Africa he drew up a report for the government for which he worked, that of France (for by that time he had become a French citizen), denouncing the crimes committed by the colonial merchant companies which exploited Africa's wealth for the benefit of their shareholders. The report has never been published and to this day remains locked away in the archives of the French Foreign Ministry. Its frankness about forced labour and cruel punishments handed out to African workers in the rubber plantations was apparently the reason why it was never made public.

A copy of the report was discovered many years after di Brazza's death locked inside a portable desk commissioned by the explorer for his African travels. The desk, which folded up and became a trunk during the sea voyage, was specially designed for him by Louis Vuitton, the well-known French luggage manufacturer. A photograph of it has been on display in Rome, next to di Brazza's original folding camp bed constructed by the same company, and which he used on many of his explorations. The rusting American portable typewriter on which di Brazza tapped out his reports from Africa is also on show.

One of di Brazza's descendants, a great-niece, showed me a film of her taking part last year in an African dance, touching toes with the current king as they both sway to the rhythm of the drums.

Pietro di Brazza's constant pursuit of ideals of

freedom and justice for Africans aroused criticism from his masters in Europe. When he died, the French government did grudgingly decide to give him a state burial beside some of France's most illustrious and greatest military, political and literary heroes in the Panthéon in Paris, but his widow declined and di Brazza was later buried in another former French colony, Algiers. And it's from here that his remains were to be flown to Brazzaville, their final and certainly most appropriate resting place.

60

King of the Cocos

Nick Squires

For 150 years, the Clunies-Ross family, originally from Scotland, ran the Cocos-Keeling Islands in the Indian Ocean as a private fiefdom. The one-time heir to this tiny coral kingdom was still living there— only now in rather reduced circumstances.
(7 June 2007)

From the air, they look like a chain of pearls wrapped around a giant opal: twenty-six tiny islands enclosing a turquoise and jade lagoon. Stepping out of the aircraft, I was enveloped by tropical heat. Palm trees rustled in the breeze, there was the distant sound of surf crashing on a reef, and the locals were either barefoot or in flip-flops.

217

Adrift in the middle of the Indian Ocean, the Cocos-Keeling Islands lie halfway between Australia and Sri Lanka. Home to just 500 people, they're an Australian territory, but on many maps of the continent, they don't even feature. Which is a shame, because the islands have an intriguing history. They were uninhabited until the 1820s, when a small settlement was established by a Scottish adventurer named John Clunies-Ross. He was originally from Shetland and must have delighted in exchanging his frigid homeland for these balmy, sun-kissed isles. He set about planting hundreds of coconut palms and brought in Malay workers to harvest the nuts. Successive generations of Clunies-Rosses built up a business empire based on copra, the dried flesh of coconuts traded for its oil. Their tenure over their exotic adopted home was confirmed in 1886, when Queen Victoria granted them possession of the islands in perpetuity.

They styled themselves the 'kings' of the Cocos. Remarkably, their rule lasted right up until 1978, when the last 'king', also called John Clunies-Ross, was forced to sell the islands to Australia for two and a half million pounds. He'd come under pressure from the Australian government and its trade unions, as well as the United Nations, none of whom was too enamoured of his feudal regime.

The Clunies-Ross family lived in a grand colonial mansion which stands to this day. To reach Oceania House I took a ferry from West Island across the lagoon to Home Island, the only other inhabited scrap of land in the territory. Arriving was like suddenly stepping into south-east Asia. The island is home to 350 ethnic Malays, the descendants of the original plantation workers. Women wear headscarves, street names are in Malay and there are several mosques. Which makes Oceania House all the more incongruous— it has the look and feel of a Scottish country estate. Wandering through the overgrown gardens, I came across a stone Celtic cross inscribed with the names of Clunies-Ross ancestors.

John Clunies-Ross used to stride around his tiny coral kingdom barefoot, a dagger tucked into his trouser belt. He paid his Malay workers in Cocos rupees, a currency he minted himself and which could only be redeemed at the company store. Workers who wanted to leave the islands were told they could never return. Despite such strictures, opinion among the Malays today is divided as to whether the Clunies-Rosses were exploitative colonialists or benevolent father figures. Wages were low, but water, electricity and schooling were free. Sixty-seven-year-old Cree bin Haig worked as a boatman back in the old days. 'Mr Clunies-Ross was a good man,' he told me, throwing scraps to the chickens in his backyard. 'Although we have better houses and food now, the Australian government doesn't let us shoot birds and hunt turtles like the family allowed us to.'

After being forced to sell his beloved islands, John Clunies-Ross eventually went bankrupt through a failed shipping line. Now approaching eighty, he lives in suburban obscurity in Perth, in Western Australia. But his son, Johnny Clunies-Ross, still calls the islands home. Back on West Island, it didn't take long for me to track him down. He and his four siblings grew up amid the grandeur of Oceania House, but he now lives in a bungalow overlooking the airstrip. Parked outside was a battered jeep riddled with rust. In place of his father's immaculate white shirts and pressed trousers, he was in a faded T-shirt and shorts.

Had his family's reign not come to an end, he'd now be the sixth 'king' of the Cocos. So, is he disappointed? 'I was upset at the time,' he admitted with a shrug. 'I was twenty-one and I'd been brought up to do the job. But even in the old man's time, it had become anachronistic. It had to change.'

Where his forebears made a fortune from coconuts, Johnny is now forging a more modest living from another island resource—giant clams. He breeds them in tanks and sells them to the aquarium trade in Europe and the US. It's an unusual line of work, but one which enables Johnny to remain on the islands his family has inhabited since 1827.

The man who would have been king seems content with his lot. On my last evening I met him again in the islands' only watering hole, the Cocos Club. He was still in shorts and a T-shirt, drinking a beer, chatting with friends. An ordinary bloke, with an extraordinary past, in one of the most beautiful and unspoilt places in the world.

61

Ocean's Thirteen Plus One

David Willis

Our man in Los Angeles was being advised not to give up the day job despite landing a small part in a new Hollywood film starring George Clooney, Brad Pitt and Matt Damon. (9 June 2007)

A few days after I registered with a casting agency, the phone rang. The woman at the other end introduced herself as Cathy. Cathy sounded excited. 'We're casting a movie called *Ocean's Thirteen*,' she said breezily. 'Are you by any chance available tomorrow?' I did my level best to appear calm. 'Just hold on a moment, Cathy, while I check my diary.' I put the receiver down and circled the room twice, punching the air with my fists and mouthing 'yes, yes, yes', and then picked it up and said as matter-of-factly as I could: 'I think I can manage that—what time do you want me?'

Ocean's Thirteen is Hollywood's holy grail, without question one of the most sought-after gigs in town. I'd taken a break from writing about movie stars for the BBC in order to become one myself—or at least that was the plan—and a wise man had told me that the best way to make it as an actor in Hollywood was to start as an extra, or 'background artiste' as they're known, and then shin your way up the ladder. Every extra in town wanted the chance to say they had worked alongside Brad and George and Matt and so a call from Cathy was a bit like rummaging through the pockets of an old suit and finding the winning lottery ticket.

Which would explain why everyone was perky and polite at five o'clock in the morning, waiting to board the bus that would sweep us through the gates of one of Hollywood's most famous movie studios, Warner Brothers and on to the set. We were taken to stage sixteen, the biggest soundstage on the lot and the scene of some of the most memorable moments in cinema history. This was where Bogart wooed Bergman in *Casablanca*, James Dean battled teenage angst in *Rebel without a Cause* and the caped crusader and his sidekick Robin restored order to a lawless Gotham City. The huge Warner Brothers sign that you see just before the opening credits clung to the side of the building—a reminder, if one were needed, that we were entering a citadel to the big screen, a shrine to the moviemaker's art.

Crossing the threshold was truly like venturing into another world. The set designers had built a four-storey Asian-themed casino so lavish it would have put many a Las Vegas gambling den to shame. Ornate pillars carved with oriental dragons stood like sentries around a rock pool stuffed with real koi carp; blood-red Chinese lanterns hung from black bamboo frames which lined the walkways between roulette tables; and surrounding the slot machines and blackjack tables were croupiers in canary-yellow waistcoats, cocktail waitresses with expansive cleavage, high rollers, pit bosses, card sharks and dealers. All of them were extras—sorry, background artistes—600 in total,

222

one of whom was me.

I was to play a photographer at the launch of this new casino. The owner was about to become the victim of an audacious heist, masterminded by Danny Ocean, played by George Clooney. I'd been given a real camera and was told to take shots of Clooney as he and others arrived for the grand opening. The sight of him drew audible gasps from many of the female cast and crew, some of whom started to giggle like overgrown schoolgirls.

The cameras rolled and we did our thing. Me, George—oh, and the rest of them. And then we did it again. And we did it again. Until the camera around my neck felt like a noose and I had lost the will to live. And throughout all the retakes Clooney remained personable and funny and of course irritatingly handsome. When it finally became time for lunch, he slipped out of his tuxedo and took to the makeshift basketball court next to stage sixteen. He was good at that too, pausing just long enough to blow a kiss to a bog-eyed tour group before plopping the ball perfectly into the net.

I came to grief during a break in filming by sitting somewhere I shouldn't. Barely had my bottom touched the canvas chair than an assistant director called Jody was on to me like a heat-seeking missile. 'What's your name?' he demanded. 'Um, David Willis,' I replied. 'Whose name is on the back of that chair?' I walked around to the back to take a look. 'It says Al Pacino.' 'Exactly!' snapped Jody, 'and when your name is Al Pacino you can sit there—now get lost!'

I mentioned that experience to George Clooney when we attended the premiere the other day, and he laughed in that wickedly handsome way of his. I asked him if he had any advice for aspiring actors. He flashed a grin and said simply: 'Stay out of my shot!'

Clooney and Willis: coming soon to a cinema near you. But don't blink or you'll miss me.

62

Under Fire

Jim Muir

Israel, in an assault on the Lebanese militia Hezbollah, was bombarding the border areas of southern Lebanon. The Israeli operation began after the capture by Hezbollah of two of its soldiers. (22 July 2006)

Going round the hospital wards here in Tyre is a depressing experience, as hospital visits usually are. Here's a thirty-seven-year-old woman from the border village of Aita Shaab in a deep coma from a head wound which she's not expected to survive. Here's Fatima, a pretty twenty-seven-year-old teacher from the village of Srifa. She lived through a night of bombing which demolished a whole quarter of her village. Between thirty and eighty people are believed still to be buried in the rubble: no rescue mission has been able to get there. Fatima and her mother joined neighbours fleeing in pick-up trucks the next morning; her vehicle fell into one of the huge craters punched by

Israeli bombs in roads throughout the area. Then the jets attacked again and she was wounded, but she's going to be OK.

And then there are the dead. In the rubble of a flattened two-storey house in a smart suburb of Tyre, normally just a five-minute drive from where I am now, I found the identity card of Zahia Kudsy. Like so many of the Lebanese caught up in this conflict, she was from here but living abroad. She'd brought her three children and mother back from Sierra Leone for the summer holidays. Now they and their Sri Lankan maid have been lying crushed beneath the fantastic tangle of rubble since last Monday. Also in there are the bodies of a Nigerian civilian employee of the United Nations forces here, UNIFIL, and his wife. The UN's tried hard to get heavy-lifting gear in to retrieve the bodies, but the roads have all been damaged by bombing and are under continual attack.

It's hard to come up with an answer to the question you read in the eyes of the wounded survivors that you also hear echoing up through the piles of debris where the dead still lie: 'Why us?' No doubt that same question is being asked by equally innocent Israeli civilians in hospitals across the border, wounded by Hezbollah's random unleashing of rockets and missiles: 'Why us?'

But there is a difference, one of many in this conflict. Israel's stupendous firepower comes from one of the most sophisticated hi-tech war machines in the world. Wherever we go here we have Israeli drones constantly buzzing through the sky overhead sending back images probably clear enough to count the hairs on your head. The targets that are being hit are taken out with laser precision. The building where Zahia Kudsy and the UN bodies lie buried was reduced to a tortured heap of rubble while the buildings around it were barely touched. So again that question: 'Why us?'

Near the main emergency hospital in Tyre we found at least part of the answer. Literally a stone's throw from the hospital, another building's been similarly flattened. Nine people remain buried there. But another stone's throw away from that in the banana grove alongside, we saw evidence strongly suggesting that Katyusha rockets had been fired from there. The UN forces have also reported that several of their positions were hit by Israeli shelling after rockets were fired from nearby. So Hezbollah hits and runs and the building closest by takes the brunt of Israel's wrath. So too has anything else that might be regarded as a target in a situation of all-out war between two countries: roads and bridges, petrol stations and fuel dumps, factories, anything remotely suspicious moving on the roads.

But all this awesome power and destruction have so far been impotent to stop Hezbollah fighters pointing their missiles at Israel and firing them off. And when Israeli ground troops have crossed the border, they've been engaged by Hezbollah in fierce battles which have cost them far more lives than those of the two captured soldiers in whose name this war was launched.

This is Israel's dilemma. How far does it go? Does it just keep bombing and destroying, hoping to get lucky? Hoping to put so much pressure on the region's weakest government that it can somehow do something that the region's superpower, Israel itself, can't do to control

Hezbollah. Does it invade again? It did that in 1982 right up to Beirut. But that was against the Palestinians. Yasser Arafat and his fighters were eventually put on boats and sent to Tunis, though he ended up as president of Palestine.

This is different. Hezbollah are not Palestinians. Encouraged by Israel's regional enemies, Syria and Iran, it emerged as a Lebanese Shi'ite reaction to the Israeli occupation. It's deeply rooted in Lebanon's largest community. It cannot be destroyed without destroying that community. It cannot be put on a boat and sent away. Any inch of Lebanon the Israelis now occupy will provide another sacred cause, a magnet for never-ending resistance.

The reason this conflict has already run as far as it has, this unbridled exercise of force with no serious international ceasefire effort to restrain it, is because other things have changed too. In the past, similar bouts have been curbed eventually by intervention from the only power that can do it: the United States. But this time there's been a startling degree of permissiveness. The Americans, with their own hi-tech war machine, are embroiled in a struggle in Iraq where their own power is impotent to impose control. For President Bush, Israel is simply waging another part of that same war on terror. A regional balance of power is being fought over here: Syria and Iran, America and Israel. And it's the people buried in the rubble and lying in their hospital beds in northern Israel who are paying the price.

63

Kidnapped

Alan Johnston

Alan was nearing the end of his BBC posting in Gaza when he was kidnapped in March 2007. He was eventually released after 114 days in captivity. (25 October 2007)

The kidnappers had forced me to lie face down on the floor. But after they left, and the small, bare room had fallen silent, I rolled over and pulled myself slowly into a sitting position. My wrists were handcuffed behind my back, and a black hood had been pulled down over my head. And as I sat there, in danger and afraid, I had a great sense of being at the very lowest point of my life.

It had begun out in the spring sunshine, on the streets of Gaza City. A saloon car had suddenly surged past mine, and then pulled up—forcing me to stop. A young man emerged from the passenger side and pointed a pistol at me. I had reported many times on the kidnapping of foreigners in Gaza. Now, as I always feared it might, my turn had come. The figure with the pistol and another gunman forced me into their car, and as we sped off I was made to lie on the back seat. A hood had been shoved over my face, but through it I could see the sun flickering between the tower blocks. I could tell that we were heading south and east, towards the city's rougher neighbourhoods.

Most kidnappings in Gaza were carried out by disgruntled militant groups seeking the attention of the authorities in some minor dispute. And always the Westerner was freed within a week or so, shaken but unharmed.

But the game had changed last summer. A much more sinister group had emerged and seized two members of a team from the American Fox News network. They were freed, but only after being forced to make videotaped denunciations of the West and a public conversion to Islam.

Of course this was serious. In the claustrophobic, intense, violent sliver of land that is Gaza, there was now a shadowy organisation that thought in terms of waging jihad on the West. I knew it was likely to strike again, targeting the few dozen members of Gaza's foreign community. And so, with the help of the BBC's security experts, I did everything I could to reduce the risk of capture. I moved to a better-protected apartment. I filmed less in the streets, switched cars and made sure that my movements in the city were always random and unpredictable.

And set against the danger, I felt that Gaza's story was important. It is at the centre of the Palestinian drama which in turn lies at the heart of the rising tensions between the East and the West that have become the defining story of our time.

So, in consultation with senior colleagues, I decided that the risks were worth taking and I stayed in Gaza. And I did manage to keep out of the grasp of the kidnappers almost to the end. When the man with the pistol emerged from the white saloon, I had just sixteen days left until I was due to leave for good.

As I lay on a thin mattress on the floor, late on the first night of my captivity, the door opened. Its frame was filled by a tall figure in a long white robe. He stood for a moment looking down at me, swathed in a red chequered headdress that completely masked his face. The jihadi leader had arrived. He stepped into the room and sat down heavily on a white plastic chair. 'Alan Johnston, we know everything,' he said in English.

He said that my kidnapping was about securing the release of Muslims jailed in Britain. Later, my captors, the Army of Islam, would describe me as a prisoner in what they see as the war between Muslims and non-Muslims. When I started to say that Britain wouldn't negotiate, the man in the chair cut me off. He said that the British would be forced to listen.

But mostly the voice emerging from the mask was calm and even kindly. He said that I wouldn't be killed, that I would be treated well, in keeping with Islamic codes of conduct towards prisoners. Crucially, he said that I would eventually be allowed to leave. I asked when, but he just said: 'When the time is right.'

Did he mean weeks, or months, or longer? It was impossible to say. But I was left with a disturbing sense that what was about to happen would be protracted and life-changing. When it was over, he said, I would write a book about my experience and even that I would finally get married.

But how far could I trust the masked man? Did his word really count for anything—couldn't he simply change his mind? And I wondered if he really was a leader of the group. Perhaps, in reality,

230

others would decide my fate.

I did fall asleep again, but I was woken by two men coming into the room. They handcuffed me and put the black hood back over my head and led me slowly out into the cold of the night. There was no word of explanation, and as my mind searched for one in that terrifying moment of uncertainty, I feared, as I walked into the darkness, that I might be going to my death, that I was being taken somewhere to be shot. But the tension eased as I began to realise that the men were only moving me to another building and what would, for a time, become my cell.

In that room, on the roof of an apartment block, all I had was a narrow, sagging bed and two plastic chairs. There was no television, or radio, or book, or pen, or paper. I'd been stripped of my watch; I could only tell the time by the passage of the sun and the five calls to prayer from nearby mosques. I had had to throw away my disposable contact lenses on the first day, and my eyes are weak. And so, in this blurred, empty room I began to try to come to terms with the disaster that had engulfed me.

I paced backwards and forwards across the cell. Five strides, then a turn, and five strides back. Mile, after mile, after mile. Imagine yourself in that room. Imagine pacing, or just sitting for three hours. For five hours. For ten hours. After you had done twelve hours, you'd still have four or five more before you could hope to fall asleep. And you would know that the next day would be the same, and the next, and the one after that, and so on, and on, and on.

As one empty day slid slowly into another, the

231

seriousness of my situation became more and more apparent. It's hard to strike at Britain from Gaza. There's no British business there, and the British Council library was burnt down last year by an angry mob. Almost all that Britain had left in Gaza was the BBC. And in the BBC there was only one British citizen: me. And the jihadis had me, like a bird in a cage. Britain never does deals with kidnappers so why, I couldn't help worrying, would I ever be freed? I thought of the Western hostages who had been held for years in Beirut in the eighties, and I wondered if their fate might now be mine.

The first crisis came in the form of a bout of illness. The food was quite reasonable, Palestinian-style rice or beans or vegetable dishes apparently cooked in a flat just below my room. But my European stomach couldn't cope either with what I was eating or the dirty water. Soon I could feel a swelling just below my ribs and there were many trips to the small, foul-smelling toilet attached to my room, where the floor was always awash with water. I was frightened that I would just get sicker and sicker and I decided I must try to get some control over my diet. In the first weeks I had occasionally been given potato chips and I knew that even the toughest Gazan bacteria couldn't survive the sizzling oil that they were fried in. So I asked just for a plate of chips each day and for my water to be boiled. And those simple elements, along with bread, tomatoes, some fruit and later eggs became the basis of my rather dull, but safer, two meals a day. There was, though, never quite enough food, and I eventually lost ten kilograms. And always I worried, especially when I had a serious allergic reaction later on, that I might fall dangerously ill. I was sure that, if it came to it, the Army of Islam would just let me fade away slowly rather than call off the kidnap because I was sick.

In those first, terrible days, the hardest that I have ever known, I worried very much about the impact my abduction would have on my elderly parents and my sister at home in Scotland. And of course, with that wonderful clarity of hindsight, I deeply, deeply regretted having stayed in Gaza so long and having taken the risks that I had.

One of my lowest moments came during a power cut. I lay in a dwindling pool of candlelight, listening to the shouting, rowing neighbours and occasional gunshots that are all part of the noisy clamour of Gaza's poorer neighbourhoods. I felt very, very far from home, trapped and aghast at how dire my situation was.

Things were, however, just about to get a little better. Desperate for some distraction to ease the psychological pressure, I had repeatedly asked for a radio and amazingly, on the night of that power cut, a guard brought one into my room. Suddenly I had a link with the outside world a voice in my cell, and something to listen to other than my own frightening thoughts. And through the radio I became aware of the extraordinary, worldwide campaign that the BBC was mobilising on my behalf. It was an enormous psychological boost. And, most movingly, I realised that the vast majority of Palestinians were condemning the kidnappers. Many people in Gaza seemed to appreciate that I had chosen to live among them for years in order to tell their story to the world.

But the radio also brought dreadful news. In

those calm, measured tones of the BBC, I heard reports of a claim that I had been executed. It was a shocking moment. I had been declared dead—and I thought how appalling it was that my family should have to endure that. But of course, I knew that I was far from dead, and after a few minutes I couldn't help recalling the famous Mark Twain line about how the reports of his death had been exaggerated.

I was worried, though, that perhaps the announcement of my execution was just a little premature. I knew that my kidnappers' demands were not being met, and I thought that perhaps they had decided to kill me. I felt that I needed to prepare myself for that possibility in the hours ahead. I was sure that if I was to be put to death, the act would be videotaped in the style of jihadi executions in Iraq. If that was to be the last image my family and the world was to have of me, if at all possible I didn't want it to be one of a weeping, pleading, broken man. So through that long night, I lay listening to every sound that might signal the coming of my assassins and tried to gather the strength that I would need if the worst were to happen. But at last the silence was broken by the dawn call to prayer. The night was over. Somehow I felt the danger had passed, and I fell asleep.

But that wasn't the last time that death seemed a possibility. A few weeks later my guard barged into my room with a set of manacles. My wrists and ankles were chained together. And the guard shut my window and put off the light, leaving me in the dark to swelter in Gaza's summer heat. He told me that it was being decided whether I should be put to death in the days ahead. If that was to happen, he said, my throat would be cut with a knife. I didn't quite believe the threat but again, I had to prepare myself for the worst. I'm sure that different people approach something like that in different ways. But I chose to rehearse in my mind exactly what might happen, hoping that somehow that would make the lead-up to any execution a little less shocking, a little less terrifying, and hoping that that might make it easier to preserve some kind of dignity in my final moments. But mercifully, the crisis passed. In fact, the chains came off after just twenty-four hours and as the days went by, the threat of execution seemed to recede again.

Through all this I gradually came to know my guards. One of them, a man in his mid-twenties called Khamees, with a dark, quite handsome face, would be with me almost every day, right through to the kidnap's frightening climax. Like many young men who I had met in Gaza, Khamees was the son of a family that had either fled or been driven from their home in what is now Israel. He had been raised in the poverty of one of Gaza's intensely crowded cities and been drawn to the militant groups that had fought the occupying Israeli army. Khamees had matured into a battle-hardened urban guerrilla. He walked with a limp and had a slightly misshapen torso, the legacy of a wound inflicted by the Israelis. But they weren't his only enemy. He had trouble too with both of Gaza's main factions: Hamas and Fatah. He was a wanted man and he almost never left the succession of flats that were my prisons. He lived confined to the shadows—almost literally in the second of our hideouts, where the shutters on the windows were kept closed and I didn't see the sun or the sky for nearly three months.

Khamees would exercise by pacing up and down the gloomy corridor, counting the laps on his prayer beads. He spent countless hours flipping through the Arabic satellite television channels, and often, far into the night, he would sit in a pale blue robe, reading aloud from the Koran. Occasionally he would let me go through to his room and watch television for an hour or two. And one day he allowed me to see my parents make a televised appeal for my release. After worrying about them so much it was a vast relief to see my father make a powerful and dignified address. And although my mother didn't speak, when I looked into her eyes I was somehow sure that she too had the strength to cope. I felt very bad at having brought the worst of the world's troubles crashing through my parents' peaceful lives, far away on the west coast of Scotland. My kidnappers, the most frightening kind of people, were putting them under appalling pressure and all of Britain was watching. But my parents weren't being broken. They were, in Dad's words, 'hanging in there,' and for me it was their finest hour.

To let me see my parents on television was an act of kindness on the part of my guard and there were certainly others. In the second of our four hideouts, where I was held longest, Khamees allowed the regime to become quite lax. My door was left unlocked so that I could go to a bathroom and even use a kitchen next to my room, where eventually I was boiling water and fixing very simple meals for myself twice a day. And there were moments when Khamees would be friendly, when we would talk a little about Gaza, and about politics or Islam. But mostly I will remember Khamees as a dark and moody figure. Often, for days at a time, he barely spoke to me, refusing to respond if I said hello. Handing me my food, he would just glare at me hard, saying nothing, and a number of times tiny things sent him into frightening rages that I came to dread. It was often easy to imagine that he saw me as a great burden and that he loathed me. And when he smashed me in the face in the final moments of the kidnap I felt that, with Khamees, perhaps all along violence had never been far below the surface.

As the weeks drifted by, and I paced through my wasteland of time, my thoughts often ranged back across my life. I filled many empty hours reflecting on periods in my childhood and phases of my career. I tried to work out the roots of certain aspects of my character and I thought hard again about why one or two important relationships in my past had worked but then eventually lost their way. But much of my mental energy went into the huge effort to confront my many anxieties: the struggle, as I saw it, to keep my mind in the right place. I felt very strongly that in the kidnapping I was facing the greatest challenge of my life and I knew that I would perhaps always measure myself by the way I met it, or failed to meet it. I told myself that in my captivity there was only one thing that I might be able to control, my state of mind. And I struggled to persuade myself that bouts of depression did nothing to change the hard realities of my situation, they only weakened me. I tried to strangle damaging, negative thoughts almost as they emerged, before they could take hold and drive me down. And positive thoughts had to be encouraged. Of course, at first glance, there wasn't much to take heart from in my situation.

But the fact was that I hadn't been killed and I wasn't being beaten around. I was being fed reasonably and I decided that my conditions could have been much, much worse. Whatever else it was, my Gazan incarceration wasn't what some Iraqi prisoners had been forced to endure at Abu Ghraib jail. It wasn't the Russian Gulag and it certainly wasn't the Nazi death camps. I felt that I wouldn't be able to pick up a book again about the Holocaust without feeling a sense of shame if I were somehow to break down mentally under the very, very, very much easier circumstances of my captivity. I thought too that, unfortunately, every day around the world, people are being told that they have cancer and that they only have a year or two to live. But the vast majority of them find the strength to face the end of their lives with dignity and courage. I, on the other hand, was just waiting for my life to begin again, and I told myself that it would be shameful if I couldn't conduct myself with some grace in the face of my much lesser challenge.

And in its search for inspiration, my mind took me down what may sound to you like some rather strange paths. But for me, as impressive as any story of endurance is that of the explorer Ernest Shackleton. After his ship was crushed by the Antarctic ice nearly a century ago, he took a tiny lifeboat and set out across the great wastes of the stormy Southern Ocean. He aimed for an almost unimaginably small island far beyond his horizon and eventually he reached it. And in my prison, I

238

felt that I needed some kind of mental lifeboat to help me cross the great ocean of time that lay before me, aiming for that almost unimaginable moment far beyond my horizon when I might go free. And so I took all the positive thoughts I could muster and lashed them together in my mind, like planks in a psychological raft that I hoped would buoy me up. And in some ways it did. It was one of several mental devices or tricks or props that helped me get through.

In this way, I fought what was the psychological battle of my life. God knows it was hard. And lonely. And there were many dark passages when I edged close to despair. But I was always in the fight, and there was no collapse.

Eventually Gaza's violent politics suddenly shifted against my kidnappers. The powerful Hamas and Fatah factions began a fight to the death. Hour after hour I lay listening to machine-gun and rocket fire in the streets around the apartment block where I was being held. Bad enough, I felt, to be kidnapped, but worse still to be lost in a place that had descended into all-out war. Eventually, though, Hamas managed to seize complete control. It immediately set about imposing what it would regard as order in Gaza and it made ending my high-profile kidnapping a priority.

For the first time my captors seemed shaken and uncertain, but they had a plan. Khamees came in with a plain black briefcase, of a kind that you might see any accountant carry on the London Underground. But he opened it to reveal a suicide bomber's vest, with panels of explosives that closed tight around my stomach as I pulled it on. In a letter the leader, the masked man from the first night, said that I needed to be afraid. He said that Hamas was planning an assault that would turn the hideout into what he called 'a death zone'. The message I had to give via a video camera, dressed in my deadly contraption, was that if there was an attack, I too would die.

But still Hamas was closing in and the Army of Islam prepared for a showdown. A machine-gun nest was set up just under the room where I was being held. And I could hear the group's fighters scramble to their battle stations below me during an exchange of fire as Hamas forces probed their defences. I knew that if Hamas stormed the apartment block they would come all guns blazing and I might well die in the assault. And even if Hamas didn't kill me accidentally, then there was a danger that the kidnappers, furious and frightened, and about to die themselves, might shoot me to prevent my being rescued alive.

Then suddenly one night I was taken downstairs. A hood was put over my head and I was led stumbling out into the darkness as members of the gang began to hit me and slam me against walls and the side of a car, before I was shoved into its back seat.

The kidnappers and the powerful clan that was protecting them seemed to have buckled under Hamas pressure. They had agreed to deliver me up in return for their survival. But I didn't know that as the car began to move slowly towards the Hamas lines and the most terrifying ride of my life began. My guards, with their Kalashnikov rifles on either side of me, were screaming angry; furious no doubt at the failure of the kidnap and scared perhaps that Hamas would kill them anyway, whatever the deal. Khamees struck at my face, and I could taste blood in my mouth. At one of the checkpoints, through the wool of my mask, I could see the muzzle of a rifle inches from my eye and I knew that the guard on my right was roaring that he would put a bullet in my brain if the Hamas men didn't back off. In the extraordinary tension and the confusion it seemed that a gun battle might erupt at any moment and the car would be filled with bullets.

Eventually though, we came to a halt and Khamees dragged me out into the road. I looked up to see an alleyway filled with armed men standing in the street light. Two of them stepped forward and led me away. I was afraid that this was some new gang to which I had now been passed on. But actually these were Hamas men and as we turned a corner, there, standing in a garden, was my old friend and colleague, Fayed Abu Shamalla of the BBC Arabic service. And only then did I know that my kidnap was over and that I was free.

Days later I was back in Scotland, taking that road that I know so well, heading at last for the hills of Argyll and my family. And there, in our house by the sea, in that beautiful, peaceful place, all that happened to me in Gaza began to slide into the past. But the experience of incarceration does have a way of lingering, of haunting the nights. I dream sometimes that I'm in captivity again and I cannot tell you how good it is to wake and gradually realise that, actually, I'm free, safe, back at home, on the shores of Loch Goil. But the nightmares come less frequently now. And although psychologists might say that these are still

241

quite early days, I very much believe that I'm going to be fine.

And the kidnap's legacy is not all bad. With its locks and chains, its solitary confinement and moments of terror, it was a kind of dark education. I lived through things which before I would have struggled to imagine and maybe, in the end, I'll be stronger for that. I've gained too a deeper sense of the value of freedom. Perhaps only if you've ever been some kind of prisoner can you truly understand its worth. Even now, more than three months after I was freed, it can still seem faintly magical to do the simplest things, like walk down a street in the sunshine, or sit in a café with a newspaper. And in my captivity in Gaza, I learnt again that oldest of lessons: that in life, all that really, really matters are the people you love.

64

Room at the Inn

Matthew Price

The continuing hostilities between Palestinians and Israelis meant that Bethlehem, previously a popular Christmas destination for pilgrims and other tourists, was preparing for a bleak festive season.
(22 December 2005)

I don't think I'd fully appreciated quite how little the Little Town of Bethlehem was before I first went there. Of course I'd sung about it as a child at school carol services and on countless occasions since. This weekend you too will possibly hear it and sing along. Sitting here in my Jerusalem home, just a fifteen-minute drive from the Little Town, I've tried to remember what images the song brought to mind as a child. They are certainly very different from the reality I now know of Bethlehem. I think the carol once conjured up a picture of a rather pretty town, a hopeful place, full of smiles and Christmas cheer. The everlasting light shining forth from its streets.

And for the handful of Christian pilgrims who still travel to Bethlehem, there is still that sense of joy in visiting the birthplace of Jesus. A few days ago I stood in Manger Square and watched as a group of Korean tourists formed a circle, joined hands and sang 'Silent Night' in beautiful strong voices. I can't claim to be a regular churchgoer, but I still find myself drawn by Bethlehem. The dark peace of the Church of the Nativity. The incense lingering in the air. The quiet echo of footsteps. In the grotto where Christians believe Mary gave birth to Christ, the squeak of a pulley system as a nun slowly raises a candle to the ceiling.

Last week, I stood in a cold Manger Square, dusk painting the dull buildings an even duller shade of grey. A few hundred local people had gathered to watch the mayor switch on the Christmas lights. We stared up at the poplar tree the people of Bethlehem hang their lights from, and listened to a couple of brief speeches. Not so much about Christmas. More about military incursions, settlement-building, the wall Israel has almost completed which now separates Bethlehem from Jerusalem. We listened to the mayor voice what has now become an annual hope that the New Year will bring peace. Then he switched on the lights. There was a ripple of applause. And the audience wandered home.

As you might have sensed, there is little Christmas cheer in Bethlehem. In the last month, Israel has opened up its new checkpoint at the northern entrance to the town. To get in you now pass through a grey concrete towering wall with a mammoth iron gate. Sitting at dusk in a traffic queue there the other day, I chatted to one of the jewellery sellers who hang around hoping to make a little cash.

'What do you think?' I asked Khaled, pointing at the wall.

'Like Berlin,' he shrugged back.

Israel's argument, of course, is that the wall protects it from the Palestinians. The obvious effect, indeed intention, is that it is getting harder for Palestinians to travel into and out of the town. Added to which, the wall is hardly a welcoming image for the few tourists who still make it here.

There is today plenty of room at the inn. Before the conflict started up at the turn of the millennium, more than 90,000 tourists visited the town every month. Last year the number was less than a tenth of that. As darkness set in, I wandered to the souvenir shops around the back of the nativity church on Milk Grotto Lane. Down either side, stone walls, and set into those walls, shop after shop—closed, locked tight behind green metal shutters. A light spilled out of one doorway; the owner was sweeping an already clean floor. Further up the lane the Milk Grotto Art Store was open. Inside, three men chatted, sipping tea. The owner told me he couldn't afford to pay his rent at the moment. Sometimes he only sees one tourist a day.

You can feel the despair in the Christian community of Bethlehem. People are worried, not just about Israel, but increasingly about law and order and jobs. As life gets harder, local Muslims are turning towards Islamic movements like Hamas for solutions. Many Christians who can afford to are moving abroad. Within the last five years about 10 per cent of the local Christian population has emigrated. Two Bethlehem Christian friends who once spoke about 'if I ever leave' now speak about 'when'.

No, it doesn't feel much like Christmas in Bethlehem this year. There's not a lot of money to buy a tree with—or even presents. The owner of the local radio station says he hasn't bothered to dust off the Christmas jingles this year. The spirit, as one resident told me, has gone.

So now when I listen to 'O Little Town of Bethlehem', the everlasting light shines slightly less brightly. When I hear of 'the hopes and fears of all the years', it is the fears that shout loudest to me. Outside the Church of the Nativity, I asked Father Amjad Subara if he had a Christmas message. 'Pray for us,' he said, 'and don't forget Bethlehem.'

65

A Furious Vitality

Paul Adams

Sixty years after the birth of Israel its people still seem plagued by the past, uncertain about the present and fretful about the future. The decades have seen half a dozen wars, countless governments, the gathering in of Jews from all over the globe, the revival of a language and the creation of a state from the ashes of the Holocaust. (10 May 2008)

Israelis have been called the 'proud doers'. And even now, after sixty years, the sense of Israel as a nation of achievers has barely dimmed. They may not be creating whole new communities at a rate of one every three days, as they were at the beginning, but there's still a furious vitality about them. From the grand, sweeping lines of its new international terminal at Ben-Gurion airport—a far cry from the shabby building I first encountered more than twenty years ago—to Tel Aviv's proliferating skyscrapers, and even the way Israel's imposing security wall weaves its way through the suburbs of eastern Jerusalem in a billowing ribbon of grey concrete: these things are all, in their own way, impressive. They testify to qualities of energy, determination and ingenuity that Israelis have shown, in abundance, throughout their history.

Ten years ago at Kfar Hanasi, a kibbutz north of the Sea of Galilee, we met Michael Cohen, who, at seventy-six, described himself as a retired pioneer. The kibbutz which he helped to found is an oasis of green amid dun-coloured hills. At the bottom of a narrow gorge, the Jordan river flows down to the nearby Sea of Galilee. The bleak uplands of the Golan Heights rise suddenly to the east.

A Scot by birth, and a code breaker at Bletchley Park during the Second World War, Michael had helped to found the kibbutz. He spoke of clearing rocks with his bare hands. 'Look,' he said, pointing to a picture of himself standing beside Israel's first prime minister, David Ben-Gurion, both men in shirtslccvcs, 'We even looked like pioneers. We were the poor elite of the country.'

There is no poor elite any more. Michael Cohen admitted that the collective ethos of the kibbutz had already served its main purpose—bringing people together for the single-minded business of forging a state. Today's elite are not the kibbutzniks or even the soldiers, whom Israelis continue to hold in high, but no longer exalted, esteem. Today's elite are a bit less interesting, less distinctive, less Israeli. They're the super-rich.

And that, for many older Israelis, is a little disappointing. It's not that they mind living in a place which sometimes feels like a little fragment of the West, perched on the shores of the castern Meditcrranean. It's just that they recognise that this is not quite what they grew up believing in, or, in the case of those who were born elsewhere, not what drew them here.

'Sometimes I forget why I came to this country.' My friend Robert sounded nostalgic as he recalled his first days as an immigrant from Holland. It was the 1970s. Israelis all dressed alike—in jeans and

247

check shirts; they drove the same cars—just a few models, and all white; and there was only one kind of shampoo in the shops. Luxury goods were expensive, the wine was undrinkable and there was only one non-kosher restaurant in Jerusalem. After Europe, Robert said he found Israel austere. But it's very asceticism appealed to him. It was an egalitarian place, he said, with a single Israeli identity.

Of course, the Israel of the '70s was already a more complex place than that. Internal tensions between oriental and Western, secular and religious Jews had been there from the start and were beginning to drag the country in different directions. But when it came to the big national project, Israelis seemed to know what they were about. And while they forged their state with such single-minded determination, the Palestinians were swept aside. Hundreds of thousands became refugees; many of the villages where they had lived for generations were wiped off the map. As Israel grew and prospered, Palestine withered. Robert put it succinctly: 'We made mincemeat of them.'

Eerie fragments remain. On the north-western edge of Jerusalem sits the deserted Palestinian village of Lifta, abandoned by its frightened inhabitants during the fighting that preceded Israel's declaration of independence in 1948. Lonely, ruined houses clinging to the rocky slopes, bypassed by new roads which no longer need to go there. Today, Lifta is frequented by picnickers and drug addicts, few of whom will know that one village family still owns the title to the land on which Israel's parliament, the Knesset, is built.

Or what about the nearby village of Deir Yassin,

248

scene of the most notorious massacre of Palestinians by members of the pre-state Jewish underground? Only a handful of buildings remain, now forming part of an Israeli psychiatric hospital, sandwiched between an industrial zone and an ultra-orthodox suburb. It's where victims of what's known as the Jerusalem Syndrome are treated. This is when people suffer mental illness as a result of visiting a city with enough history, religion and politics to drive almost anyone to distraction. Call me superstitious, but I always thought that taking someone in the midst of a psychotic episode to a place haunted by the ghosts of a massacre was asking for trouble. But like Lifta, Deir Yassin is part of a Palestinian past simply swallowed up by today's Israeli reality.

You might think Israel's evident success, set against an almost unbroken record of Arab defeat, would make the Jewish state supremely confident. But it doesn't, and it never has. Throughout its existence the country has, not surprisingly, been plagued by the darker episodes of Jewish history and, despite biblical associations with the land, remains uneasy about its geographical location in the heart of the Arab world. The Middle East is, as Binyamin Netanyahu is fond of reminding us, a 'rough neighbourhood'. Territorial conquest may have bought it some strategic depth, but it's come at the cost of moral and political confusion. Israelis have grappled psychologically with being victors, not victims, powerful not powerless. And when their undoubted military prowess is called into question, as it was during a summer of fighting in Lebanon two years ago, they're assailed by doubts, a few even wondering if the Jewish state has already passed its peak. Sixty years on, Israelis remain 'proud doers', but the pride sometimes feels a little fragile.

66

José Antonio Goes to War

Fergal Keane

Not all of the American soldiers fighting in Iraq were born and bred in the United States. José Antonio Gutierrez was an orphan living on the streets of Guatemala City. After arriving in the US, he was fostered by a Latino family which helped him through high school. Then a career in the military beckoned and he joined the US Marine Corps. His unit was sent to join the troops fighting in Iraq. (5 April 2003)

The boy was eight years old when he and his sister were orphaned. It happened during the civil war. The parents were poor people who lived in the vast slums around Guatemala City. I haven't been able to find out how they died. But their children, José Antonio Gutierrez and his sister Encina, were left to look after themselves. The children drifted on to the streets. In the world of the slums, a world with no safety nets, no social security, where the extended families of the countryside have been broken down and dispersed, there's often no alternative but the begging, stealing, prostitution, the desperation of the streets. José Antonio might have become one of the vanished thousands had it not been for the intervention of one of the world's more remarkable charities.

Casa Alianza runs homes and schools for street children in Honduras and Guatemala. José Antonio's sister, Encina, had been taken in by another family. But someone told the boy about Casa Alianza. When he found his way there, he was hungry and exhausted and dirty. But I've seen a photograph of him taken after he'd been there over a year. In this, he's a smiling, healthy and robust child. By now, he'd become a good soccer player. He was learning English. Later, Casa Alianza would help him to learn the basics of technical drawing, preparation for his dream of becoming an architect.

There was a dark period when, after an argument with a teacher, José Antonio left Casa Alianza. He ended up on the streets once more, sniffing glue, surviving. But he did come back. Those who knew him say there was something powerful driving him, something inside that wouldn't allow him to self-destruct as had happened to so many of his friends. There was too, they say, a sadness in José Antonio. Bruce Harris, the Englishman who runs the Casa Alianza programme, remembered the quietness that would overtake the boisterous young footballer.

At the age of twenty-two, José Antonio decided to make the journey of his life. He knew that in Guatemala he could never afford the university education needed to become an architect. So he said goodbye to his sister Encina and to his friends at Casa Alianza and he took the roads and the rails north to the United States, a journey of 2,500 miles. Across the steaming valleys and the mountains and the dry deserts he went, hitching lifts and jumping freight trains until he became one of the so-called 'wetbacks' and crossed the Rio Grande into the United States. Some 50,000 street children and teenagers make this journey every year. In the US borderlands, the ranchers hunt down the illegals and turn them over to the immigration service. The 'wetbacks' are not wanted.

José Antonio was picked up and detained by the Immigration and Naturalisation Service, the fabled and much-feared INS. But he was a persuasive boy, and he looked much younger than his years. He told them he was only seventeen. They believed him. As a minor, he was entitled to asylum, so he got to stay and he was fostered with a Latino family in Lomita, California. So began the story of his American life. He went to high school and he studied hard. What he wanted most of all was American citizenship. This, in order to be able to bring his beloved sister Encina to join him in America.

He decided eventually to sign up with the US Marine Corps, knowing that military service would help his citizenship application; and then, on New Year's Eve last, he called his sister in Guatemala City. He told her he was going to war. As Encina remembers it, this is what he said: 'Take good care of yourself. I'm going to war. Pray to God a lot for me. God willing, I'll return alive.' Last week, with the grand attack on Iraq in its opening hours, José Antonio was with his unit in the port of Umm Qasr when he was struck in the chest by a high velocity bullet. He died instantly.

This week, the street children of Casa Alianza gathered with old friends of José Antonio and his sister Encina at a quiet plot close to the coffee plantation of Antigua, Guatemala. Here are buried scores of murdered street children. They said prayers for José Antonio and they remembered his life among them. Encina says she's proud of her brother, but she is heartbroken. You could, if you wanted, jump to all kinds of conclusions about this story and what it tells you about the world and how it works. But that is the stuff for philosophers and social historians. On the shaded slopes of Antigua, Guatemala, it was the loss of a beloved brother and friend that was at the heart of things.

There is a brief postscript: a few days ago, the US government announced that it was granting posthumous American citizenship to José Antonio Gutierrez.

67

A Long Nightmare

Jim Muir

As Tony Blair prepared to stand down as prime minister, a debate about his legacy was under way. No issue had affected his image and standing more than the decision to join the Americans and send troops to Iraq. Jim Muir, who has been a correspondent in the Middle East for decades, believed Mr Blair's military intervention was a serious mistake. (10 May 2007)

I've never written to a politician in my life. But I very nearly made an exception for Tony Blair. It was towards the end of 2002, when it was already clear that the invasion of Iraq was inevitable and only a matter of timing.

I found myself deeply torn. I had no illusions about the nature of Saddam Hussein. I'd followed his brutal antics for years. I'd been to his Iraq and felt the all-pervasive fear instilled by his vigilant and ruthless police state. What a relief it was to get on the plane and feel that oppressive weight lifted off your shoulders, an experience that most Iraqis were denied. But when Saddam's excesses were at their worst, during the war with Iran in the 1980s, he was actually being discreetly supported by the Americans. Washington was turning a blind eye to human rights reports from its own State Department detailing how Iraqi children were being tortured in front of their parents to get them to confess or inform. In 1988, when the Iraqi air force dropped chemical bombs which killed thousands of Kurds at Halabja, I remember phoning the Pentagon and being told: 'We think it was the Iranians who did it.'

So on a personal level, I would be glad to see the end of Saddam Hussein and his harsh dictatorship. But the impending invasion was clearly not about to happen because he was a bad man. It might be the right thing, but it was being done for the wrong reasons—reasons that had more to do with the global ambitions of the ascendant neoconservatives in Washington and their desire to engineer a New Order in the Middle East.

The chosen pretexts for the war—Saddam's alleged weapons of mass destruction and links with international terror—turned out to be simply invalid. I've often thought, over these past four years, of that regular cartoon slot in the satirical magazine *Private Eye* entitled 'Things We Seldom See'. It features situations which would be blindingly logical, but just never happen. I wanted to propose one where President Bush addresses Saddam Hussein and says: 'Mr Hussein, you were right. There were no weapons of mass destruction, and no links with terrorism. We'd like to apologise and give you your country back.'

Apart from misgivings about Washington's real motives and objectives it was clear, long before it happened, that this was going to be a terrible mess. It had to be. Iraq is a patchwork country, an ethnic and confessional cocktail, of Arabs and Kurds, Turkomans and Chaldaeans, Sunnis and Shi'ites. Such countries are usually held together by a strong centralised dictatorship, which could be benign or tyrannical. As soon as you admit the concept of democracy and take the lid off, it's bound to be difficult and chaotic in the best of conditions, in a place with no democratic traditions or culture. To blow the regime and all its control mechanisms away virtually overnight, through the massive use of force by people from halfway around the world, would inevitably plunge the country and the region into a long period of chaos, whatever exact form it would take.

That's why I lay sleepless in my bed that night, mentally composing that letter to Tony Blair that I never wrote. I was going to tell him, on the basis of three decades living and working in the region, that he was on the brink of a massive historical blunder. I never sent it, because I knew of course that it wouldn't make a blind bit of difference, apart from perhaps salving my own conscience and allowing me to say: 'I told you so'—something that would bring no satisfaction at all.

And so, four years on, look at what a terrible mess Mr Blair can now say goodbye to and hand on to Gordon Brown. Where there used to be tight state control, there is massive terrorism on a daily basis. The Americans have been bombing Baghdad again, to quell Sunni militants and Shi'ite militias. They're building walls to separate districts, euphemistically calling them 'gated communities'. Millions of Iraqis have fled the country. In the south, British troops are trying to stifle Shi'ite militias which know they only have to wait, because the British will be gone before long.

A transition of leadership in London isn't going to make much difference on the ground in Iraq. Gordon Brown will be locked into a situation which he might or might not have chosen to get into in the first place, but will now be stuck with, and his options will be limited. At the end of the day, the British are minor players, politically important partners brought in on the coat-tails of the Americans. It's the outcome of their last-ditch struggle to control Baghdad and central Iraq that is crucial to the country's future. If it doesn't work, the coalition troops may start pulling out. And we may find that Iraq's long nightmare has only just begun.

68

A Stolen Dream

Hugh Sykes

America's most senior commander in the Middle East was warning Congress not to set a timetable for the withdrawal of troops from Iraq. General John Abizaid, testifying before US senators, said he was optimistic his soldiers could stabilise the country. But life for most Iraqis just seemed to be getting worse. (18 November 2006)

The law of unintended consequences applies by the caseload in Iraq. I met a man in his home; he was using wireless Internet. They didn't have that under Saddam. As he clicked his mouse to open a document, he inadvertently returned to a website that he'd just been visiting. Hard-core full frontal naked young men. They didn't have access to that under Saddam. It reminded me of a Baghdad cinema that I visited shortly after the fall of Saddam Hussein. Faded posters in the lobby of *Top Gun* with Tom Cruise. I was compiling a report about entertainment in the new Iraq. I slipped into the auditorium to collect some sound effects for the radio report. It wasn't *Top Gun*. The music was climaxing. So were the naked men and women on the screen. 'Did you show films like this when Saddam was in power?' I asked the cinema manager. 'No, never,' he replied.

The vortex of violence in Iraq was also,

presumably, not an intended consequence of the invasion. The intense crime wave which disfigured daily life in Baghdad and Basra and other Iraqi cities in the early days of the occupation has evolved into car bombs, roadside bombs, suicide bombs, sniper attacks, drive-by shootings, sectarian killing, mass abductions, minibus ambushes with the victims found dead in a field or floating in the Tigris river, torture followed by murder, severed heads left in cardboard boxes, and hundreds of bodies found dumped in the street, often partially eaten by dogs. Bombs have exploded in crowded markets, main shopping streets, mosques, churches, police and army recruitment centres, even buried under football pitches where children with no shoes play soccer in the dust.

The invasion was called Operation Iraqi Freedom. Ask ten-year-old Mohammed what he thinks of Iraqi freedom. Mohammed was playing in the garden behind his house one evening after sunset. His father found him on the ground, moaning, with blood coming from his neck. A stray bullet hit Mohammed and went through his spinal cord. At first, he was paralysed from the chest down, but able to move himself about in a wheelchair. Now, his arms are also paralysed. Mohammed's father, and many others I have met, say life was better under Saddam Hussein. Brutal and terrible, but nowhere near as bad as it is now. Iraq has become hell. The horrors are so searing, so frequent, that fear is a rampant virus, destabilising normal life so that even a trip to the shops or the walk to school are tainted with deep anxiety. Is there a suicide bomber on this minibus? Is that parked car a bomb? Is that bag in that bicycle basket somebody's vegetables or explosives? Under Saddam, they say, you knew where the 'red line' was. Now there is no red line.

'Stuff happens,' the outgoing American Defense Secretary Donald Rumsfeld once said about the anarchic disorder which developed in Iraq after the invasion. But they were all warned, by opponents and by friends alike, that 'stuff' would happen. A Pentagon adviser and former US ambassador, Peter Galbraith, foretold: 'chaos . . . breakdown of law and order'. General Eric Shinzeki, former army chief of staff, advised that security in Iraq could only be maintained after the invasion if America committed between 300,000 and 400,000 troops; he was slapped down by his superiors and accused of being 'wildly off the mark'. A prediction by an Arab friend of mine, made before the invasion had begun, sounded a clear warning bell to anyone who cared to listen. 'If the Americans do this,' he said, 'there will be such a wave of suicide bombings and attacks on Americans that you will not believe it.'

The Baghdad government now estimates that the number of Iraqis who have been killed since the invasion in 2003 is 150,000. This year, the death toll has been about 100 every day—3,000 a month. That's 36,000 known dead in a year. The Iraqi government estimate feels about right.

In April 2003, as looters rampaged through Baghdad and hundreds of thousands of Iraqis found themselves without work, a man in a crowd said to me: 'We were dreaming of freedom. They have stolen our dream. What use is freedom of speech if I cannot work or feed my family or walk safely in the street?' The stolen dream has now

259

become a terrifying, endless nightmare.

69

A Baker and a Barber in Baghdad

Andrew North

The US military was suffering a growing number of casualties in Iraq. But many more civilians were being killed in an increasingly vengeful sectarian conflict. (21 October 2006)

This is a snapshot of life for two people in one Baghdad neighbourhood. Before I introduce you to the baker and the barber, though, a little background: they both work in Karada, which sits on the east bank of the River Tigris. It's one of the wealthier parts of the city and right now it's seen as something of a haven. That means there are bombings and shootings only once or twice a week, rather than every day, as is the case in other city suburbs.

This is a majority Shia area, but many of its residents are Sunni and there are large numbers of Christians too. So far, though, it has avoided the fate of other traditionally mixed neighbourhoods which have become ever more homogeneous as death squads and militias drive out whichever group is in the minority. However, the question everyone in Karada now has at the back of their minds is: how long before it starts happening here too?

Hussein, the baker, is a Shia. Sami, the barber, is a Christian. These are not their real names. There is nothing fancy about Hussein's bakery: no cakes or pastries on sale here, just one kind of traditional flatbread. He works incessantly as he answers my questions, flipping diamond-shaped pieces of dough from a tray and on to a long wooden paddle. Once full, he plunges it into a cavernous oven beside him. I soon feel myself starting to sweat with the intense heat coming from within. Hussein keeps cool though with the aid of two large fans attached to the wall behind. It's not long before he whips the paddle out again. Almost in the same movement, he sweeps the freshly cooked bread down a chute and starts filling the paddle again.

A colleague at the other end of the chute scoops a bundle into a bag and hands it to a customer waiting at the window. It's a wonderfully efficient process; it's just minutes between the dough going into the oven and a customer walking away with steaming hot bread for the evening meal to break the Ramadan fast.

Hussein is a tough-looking character with a boxer's face and forearms shaped like bowling skittles. But he is nervous; he's not just keeping watch on his bread, his eyes flick constantly towards the street outside.

He's frightened because bakers have become the latest casualties in Iraq's seemingly unstoppable slide into communal bloodletting. The reason is simple: traditionally most bakeries in the city have been run by Shia families. So, for Sunni insurgents trying to stir the sectarian demon, or seeking revenge for Shia attacks on their own communities, bakers make an easy target.

The stern face of one of the most revered Shia imams staring down from the wall leaves no room for doubt as to the kind of Muslims who work here. 'We will stand up to these people,' says Hussein. 'We are doing a good thing, making bread for the people. The government has to protect us,' he says. Yet his tone suggests he has little hope it will. It's hardly surprising: Iraqi government and American security plans for Baghdad have come and gone, but the number of killings only increases. We don't stay long. They are concerned that the presence of our foreign faces will attract undue attention. 'Hurry, hurry,' says the man at the bread chute, as I finish talking to Hussein.

Sami has the same concerns when we visit his barber's shop a few streets away. He's also at risk now, although you wouldn't know it when you walk in: business is good; he snips away as he talks. The leather seats are full of waiting customers, including a screaming little boy with his father. But in recent months a growing number of barbers have been killed or intimidated—on religious grounds. They're accused of breaking Islamic codes by cutting hair in a certain way and shaving men's beards, an echo of similar edicts issued by the Taliban in Afghanistan.

The threats are coming from both Sunni and Shia extremists; the same people are behind much of the sectarian violence. 'I am very worried,' says Sami. 'I know what has happened to barbers in other districts.' For the moment, though, he is benefiting from these attacks on his profession because in some areas all the barbers' shops have closed and their customers are coming to areas like Karada. But, like Hussein the baker, he keeps an

262

eye on the street outside. 'It's very sad,' he says. 'Before the war, we would just cut hair the way people wanted. Now we're not allowed to.' And he went on: 'Before, we would never talk about whether someone was Sunni or Shia or Christian. You would never hear those words; we all lived peacefully. I don't know what is going to happen now.'

Then, with another furtive look at the street outside, he calls for the next customer, the father with his small boy, still screaming, to come and take his place on the red leather barber's chair.

70

Don't Take Us for Granted

Martin Bell

Thousands of British troops remained on duty over the Christmas period in Iraq. It was a busy time for the army padres charged with trying to provide some festive spiritual cheer. (23 December 2006)

There isn't much to be said for war. But one thing it does is to allow the military chaplains to hold their Christmas services at the right time, with the men and women of the armed forces all around them. At home, the services would be held days or even weeks before the event, in garrison churches, before the regiments dispersed for Christmas. By contrast, the twelve chaplains, eleven from the army and one from the air force, serving more than

7,000 troops in southern Iraq will be in the thick of things. They will hold midnight masses tomorrow, and carol services in every unit for those who wish to attend provided they are off duty.

For the rest, Christmas is like any other day. Those attacking them don't take the day off and the defenders will, if anything, be extra-vigilant. Rocket and mortar attacks on British bases occur every day; three rockets fell on the Shaibah logistics base while we were with a padre visiting a sentry on a watchtower. An artillery battery which went home on the last rotation lost four men killed out of 110; in modern soldiering, those are not light casualties.

Some of the young men, eighteen- and nineteen-year-olds, are on their first operational duty, and even in their first foreign country. Others have had one, two or even three previous tours of duty in Iraq. All of them are facing six months of concentrated reality amid conditions of hardship, danger and boredom which most of us, who live in peace and comfort, can hardly imagine.

Their homes are tents and their churches are Portakabins. In such conditions one of the few advantages of being an army padre rather than a village vicar is that you can rename your church if you want to. The Reverend Andrew Martlew, chaplain to 40 Field Regiment of the Royal Artillery, holds services in a metal hut behind ten-foot-high blast walls which, when he arrived, was the Church of St Paul in the Desert. It is now the Church of St Jude. St Jude is known, among his other functions, as the patron saint of lost causes.

The chaplains are frank about it: their task is harder because the soldiers feel more isolated, and have more questions to ask, because they are serving in a cause that is either unpopular or misunderstood at home. The padres also wonder: 'What are we doing here and why?'

Andrew Martlew adds: 'This is quite a difficult thing to say and an even more difficult thing to think, but almost by taking the queen's shilling we're putting elements of our consciences into cold storage, and in order to help the guys we might be not necessarily economical with the truth, but we might want to give them encouragement and help rather than pull them down.'

Another sign of Christmas is the seasonal migration of chiefs of staff and politicians. Like birds of passage they fly into Basra and then out again. As a disaffected soldier put it, they stay for the length of a fag break. Tony Blair, on his fourth and last pre-Christmas visit, actually spent three hours with them. The theatre of war, an aircraft hangar at Basra air station, was decorated with two Challenger tanks outside and two Warrior armoured personnel carriers, a Lynx helicopter, and 300 serving men and women of all three armed forces inside. These things are not left to chance. The prime minister's travelling party of thirteen, excluding bodyguards, included seven whose job was in one way or another to deal with the press. Twenty reporters were also on the plane. That's a ratio of more than one to three of sheepdogs to sheep. On what is still a controversial conflict, presentation matters.

The prime minister insisted there was no change of policy: 'British troops will stay until the job is done.' Yet the soldiers themselves know that the Shaibah logistics base will be handed back to the

Iraqis in the spring or early summer. The three British bases in Basra will close. Forces will be concentrated around the airport. The visible symbols of occupation, such as tanks in the streets, will diminish to little or nothing. The conditions will be in place to declare victory, or at least something less than defeat, and leave the field.

The troops just get on with it. They always have. They always will. If there's a message from them this winter, it is more than one of seasonal goodwill. It is: remember we're here. We're here to stay or better still to go. And please, don't take us for granted.

71

Baghdad is Gone

Lyse Doucet

The United Nations appealed to the world to take notice of a huge refugee crisis in the Middle East caused by the bloodshed in Iraq. It was the biggest movement of displaced people in the region for sixty years. Four million Iraqis fled their homes. Many of them ended up in neighbouring Syria, a country which was struggling to cope with the scale of the problem. (21 April 2007)

'Baghdad is gone.' That's what I hear now. 'This is Baghdad,' asserts Hussain. We're sitting on brightly coloured plastic chairs on the sidewalk of Sharea al-Iraqi, Iraqi Street, in the Syrian capital,

266

Damascus. The street used to be called something else, but no one remembers that now. And it doesn't look like it used to. The shop signs tell this story. There's Baghdad Bakery doing brisk trade. Sulaymaniyah Sweets. Fallujah Restaurant. Billboard after billboard announces transport to and from Iraqi cities. The signs are all Iraqi, so are the accents, so is the way women arrange their headscarves.

I ask Hussain why he left the real Baghdad. He raises one leg of his black and red tracksuit to reveal a round dark circle, a scar. Then he pulls up one sleeve and shows me another, the marks of bullets meant to kill him when he was working at the Ministry of the Interior, a place reputed to be dominated by Shi'ite hit squads. He's a Shi'ite himself. And here he sits with Basel, a Sunni Muslim. Why did Basel leave? He makes a slitting motion across his throat. I look at them and realise this line of men sipping glasses of hot sweet tea along the side of a shop isn't just a grim sign of joblessness but a sad reminder of what has been lost. 'You're all sitting together here,' I say, 'Shi'ites, Sunnis, Christians.' It coaxes the faintest of smiles and then a grimace. They shake their heads at this horrific sectarian violence threatening to tear their country apart.

'This is the new Iraq,' declares Basel, with a kick in his voice meant to convince himself and everyone else. He fled to Damascus last year but then went back to Baghdad a few months ago, hoping the new US-led security plan for his capital would work. But now he's back in Syria and doesn't want to return again to what he calls 'my death'. That seems to be the view, however reluctant, of

267

many of the more than a million Iraqis now in Syria. And some 800,000 more in neighbouring Jordan. But where will they go? Most Western countries, including the United States and Britain, have so far kept their doors shut to the vast majority of asylum seekers. Syria and Jordan euphemistically speak of 'visitors' or 'guests'. They don't want a new Iraq created on their land. Sixty years ago, Palestinian refugees flooded across their borders in the 1948 Arab-Israeli war and they still haven't left.

This movement of Iraqis, the biggest displacement of people since then, is a massive exodus that will change the face of this region. Just how still isn't clear. But the scale of this human wave is staggering. Iraqis now make up about 10 to 15 per cent of Jordan's tiny population of fewer than six million. Arab neighbours don't dare speak out publicly against a sacred notion of Arab unity, but Jordan is quietly tightening its borders and Jordanians and Syrians grumble discreetly about the rising price of everything from houses to tomatoes.

Many ask why they should shoulder a crisis they say the US and Britain started by invading Iraq. And the UN has been accusing everyone of 'abject denial'. But this tide shows no sign of stopping. Tens of thousands of Iraqis flee Iraq every month. For now, there are no tented camps. Wealthy Iraqis are buying or renting their own homes; poorer ones slip into poorer neighbourhoods. But they're becoming increasingly destitute. It's hard to find work.

'I have two choices,' says Iman, who fled to Damascus with her teenage twins after her husband was assassinated. She's Shi'ite. Her husband was a Sunni. 'I can go back to Iraq, but my brother-in-law will rip my children away from me. Or I can stay here and beg. But my children say it's better for all of us to die than for their mother to be a beggar.' I ask if she would like to go back to Iraq, if she could. 'Don't mention Iraq,' she pleads. 'It made me love my husband, my job, my life. But now I despise it.' I ask her if she has a photograph of her children. She draws a breath and pulls a yellowed snapshot from her purse, its corners creased with time. In the blurred image I see her, a younger woman laughing with ease, hair falling to her shoulders, her arms around her husband, their children in his arms and a Christmas tree. 'As a Muslim you celebrated Christmas?' I ask. She nods and looks away. The past is a foreign country. This was the Baghdad of old, an ancient land of cherished traditions, the capital of capitals in the Middle East. And yes, for now, that Baghdad is gone.

72

The Sacrifice of Small-Town America

James Coomarasamy

It was small-town America which was suffering the greatest number of casualties in the war in Iraq. Nearly half the American troops who had died were from places with fewer than 25,000 inhabitants.
(31 March 2007)

Windthorst is a small Texas town that's getting smaller. 'There used to be around a hundred dairy farms here when I was growing up,' Nubbin Johnston told me. 'Now there are only fifty.' A large man, dressed in denim dungarees, Nubbin quietly dominates his living room, much as his gleaming silver milk truck dominates his driveway. Like most families in this community, originally founded by German Catholic settlers at the end of the nineteenth century, the Johnstons live and breathe the dairy farming business. Their shelves are home to herds of porcelain cows, their floor scattered with antique farming implements. They've even stuck a cow-print border along the top of their walls. For the past few weeks, though, Nubbin and his wife, Angela, have been mourning a far more personal loss than that of the dwindling dairy farms: the loss of their son.

Twenty-one-year-old Gary Johnston died in Iraq at the end of January, the victim of a bomb blast in al-Anbar province. On the day I met his parents and talked to them about his death, Gary's belongings had just arrived in the post from his Marine unit's base. A dozen plain brown paper parcels lay unopened on the kitchen table, sharing space with Tupperware containers brimming with brisket, ham and cheese, the leftovers from Gary's funeral. The food had been donated by local well-wishers, but also by the military, as had the DVD of his funeral ceremony; a small town memorial, on a very large scale. The Johnstons sat me down in front of their computer to watch the edited version, keen for me to see exactly what kind of tribute their son had been paid.

It was one that was clearly rich in both emotion

270

and numbers. Windthorst is a town of fewer than 500 people, but the images from that day show an eleven-mile-long funeral cortège, snaking its way through streets lined with American flags. Such was the demand for seats that the Marines had rigged up a video screen in the local municipal gym where a solemn, packed hall watched a live feed of the service. Even that wasn't enough to accommodate all the mourners.

As Angela viewed the images of her only son being laid to rest, she spoke calmly about the pride she had felt that day, joked about the pall-bearers fumbling as they folded the Stars and Stripes, which had been draped over the coffin, smiled as she pointed out one of Gary's comrades, forced to wear his civilian clothes because he'd forgotten his military cap. Her husband, Nubbin, watched in silence.

Also in the room, some watching, others unable to, was a group of friends and neighbours who'd been touched by Gary's death. Their stories revealed the tight, interwoven fabric of Windthorst so typical of the small American towns which are bearing the brunt in human lives of the war in Iraq. There was Bill and Viney Wolff, who'd arranged their daughter's wedding to coincide with Gary's leave, just the sort of gesture you'd expect in a town where everyone knows everyone else. And there was Gary Hoff, a Vietnam veteran, who remembers other young men from Windthorst dying in that earlier conflict. He was young Gary's boss, when he worked as a farmhand before joining the Marines. 'That boy was like a son to me,' he said, with tears rolling down his face. Words that sound, as I read them, like a cliché, but when

271

uttered by a proud Texan farmer, believe me, don't. There was nothing clichéd either about Kelly McCorcle, a school friend of the Johnstons whose son, Ben, is also a Marine and due to leave shortly for a tour of duty in Iraq. Dabbing at her own tears, she admitted that Gary's death had intensified her anxiety, but she was adamant that it hadn't eroded her resolve or her faith in her son's mission.

In fact, doubt was about the only emotion missing from the room. Everyone there believed that US troops should remain in Iraq: to protect America from terrorists; to honour the dead, such as Gary; to complete the job, even if it's one whose definition is becoming less certain. But Nubbin Johnston was certain of one thing. 'My brother died in vain in Vietnam,' he said, his big frame shaking. 'That won't happen to my son.'

He took a breath, looked at his neighbours, then spoke for them. 'You want to know why small-town America is losing so many of its people in Iraq?' he asked, his voice quivering. 'It's because small-town America still believes in this country, still believes in fighting for the freedom to worship whichever God you believe in. Our young men and women like Gary have been sacrificing their lives for this for over 200 years. This is America.'

It's one side of it, at least. A side that's often forgotten in the opinion polls and the foreign policy debates, but one that continues to sacrifice much, for a war it still supports.

73

No More Heroes

Gavin Esler

*In the closing years of the twentieth century it began
to seem as if the American hero was dead, replaced
by a new culture of whining, litigation and political
correctness. (20 December 1996)*

Twisting across the Great Dismal Swamp in
North Carolina, the road eventually reaches the
Currituck Sound. There is relief in the sea breeze.
It is heavy with salt, but anything is better than the
dead, humid air that in summertime hangs over the
swampland like a curse.

Driving along the spine of the Outer Banks, on
your left behind the sand dunes you can smell the
freshness of the Atlantic. The endless beaches that
greeted the first Europeans in the New World
begin around Cape Cod and end up dribbling into
the soupy water off Florida. Here in the middle,
the giant sandbanks and low scrub are connected
by a series of bridges and defend the rest of the
United States from bad weather in the Atlantic. At
the elbow of the Outer Banks, Cape Hatteras
attracts so many shipwrecks that quaint lighthouses
string the coast like glittering beads on a necklace
of rock and sand, while road signs remind you this
is the principal evacuation highway to escape
hurricanes.

Little towns of wooden holiday homes appear

with folksy names like Duck, Sanderling and Kill Devil Hills. Along the strip of Anywhere USA tourist hotels, fast-food joints and gas stations, there are drive-through liquor stores, known as 'Brew Threws', where you can have your beer loaded without the unspeakable inconvenience of getting out of your car. And then there is a strange piece of sand staked out grandly as a National Memorial. Here at Kitty Hawk in 1903 the American century began with a very American story. To the amusement of locals, Wilbur and Orville Wright moved down from Dayton, Ohio, to test their heavier-than-air machine on the blustery Carolina coast, confident, despite all previous evidence, that they would make it fly. In 1899, Wilbur wrote from his Dayton bicycle shop to the Smithsonian Institution in Washington for information about the new 'science', actually not much more than dreams and hocus-pocus, of aeronautics. Just four years later on 17 December 1903, with the promise of a soft crash landing on sand, Orville took the flyer aloft for twelve seconds, covering a distance of 120 feet at a walking pace. 'They have done it,' a witness said. 'Damned if they ain't flew.'

No nation has ever marketed its heroes so assiduously. Like most British boys I grew up on *Hawkeye*, Superman, *Rawhide*, the Wright Brothers, John Glenn, John Wayne, Clint Eastwood and Neil Armstrong. They were all so magnificent I doubt if I could have separated the real from the fictional, and I still marvel at the way Americans live up to their myths, combining, like Wilbur and Orville, imagination, talent and persistence in the face of conventional wisdom

274

which argues only a nut would try to fly.

All along this coast are testaments to heroism and ruthlessness, from the north in Massachusetts where the Pilgrim Fathers landed, to Jamestown in Virginia where in 1607 the first settlers saw their numbers cut by disease and starvation from 105 to just 32 in one winter, yet they struggled on. Or further south at Cape Canaveral where the space programme, a mere sixty years after the Wright brothers, ensured, as President Kennedy demanded, that the first and only footprints on the moon would be American.

Driving to Kitty Hawk, thinking about American heroes, I catch a preacher on the car radio, a crackly AM station. He is ranting about the decline of American virtues, calling a display of pornographic art 'un-American'. Does any other country use its name this way, as a compliment or, negatively, as the worst criticism? In Tokyo, are inefficient workers regarded as 'un-Japanese'? Do the Parisians criticise unromantic souls as 'un-French'?

The radio preacher is moving rapidly to attack a profound moral decline in American life, quoting Alexis de Tocqueville's observation that 'America is Great because America is Good.' American greatness is under threat because American goodness is being undermined, and the preacher cites the usual suspects: pornography, crime, illegitimacy. But he adds a few others: a decline in self-reliance, a rise in vexatious lawsuits and a lack of personal responsibility.

If he is correct, then the American hero is dead. There is no scientific proof, but in conversations with Americans politically from the left, right and centre, of different races and social backgrounds, from California to New England, I have heard a similar complaint: that Americans' image of themselves as a 'can do' hardy people is disintegrating. That instead of being self-reliant, Americans too often are selfish and self-indulgent. That heroes like the Wright brothers are being replaced by a new national anthem of whining and political correctness.

The American hero of the seventeenth century was a rugged adventurer. In the eighteenth century, a pioneer settler or patriotic anti-British revolutionary. In the nineteenth century he was a cowboy. And now in the late twentieth century the American cultural icon must surely be a therapist. The anecdotal evidence is compelling.

Case One: Alison Wood, a police officer in Palm Beach, Florida, was fired for 'poor attendance and job performance'. She sued, claiming that because she is an alcoholic she is legally disabled and, under the 1990 Americans with Disabilities Act, cannot be fired.

Case Two: Deborah Birdwell of Cookeville, Tennessee, weighs 366 pounds, or 26 stone. She is so fat she cannot fit in ordinary seats, but sued a cinema chain for emotional suffering when they would not let her put a portable chair in a space reserved for wheelchairs.

Case Three: Rhode Island. Bonnie Cook weighs 320 pounds and was refused a hospital job. She sued, claiming her weight was a 'disability'. The court awarded her the job plus $100,000, even though a doctor found her to be 'morbidly obese' with difficulty in walking, lifting, bending, stooping and kneeling.

Case Four: Albuquerque, New Mexico, and the notorious story of an elderly woman, Stella Liebeck, who bought a coffee in McDonald's, stuck it between her legs while in her car and spilled it, causing third-degree burns. Damages were reduced from $2.7 million to a mere $640,000.

Or Case Five: Anaheim, California. Billie Jean Matay takes her three grandchildren to Disneyland and is robbed in the car park. The Disney people helped her to recover in a backstage area but Ms Matay sued. She was 'traumatised' when she saw Disney characters taking off their costumes. Her lawsuit claims the children were exposed 'to the reality that the Disney characters were make-believe'. The shocking truth would appear to be that Mickey Mouse is, gasp, not a real mouse.

In this perverse America, John Wayne is weeping because the Rule of Law has buckled under the Rule of Lawyers. But the litigation explosion and associated collapse of common sense is not just a cause of American anger but also a symptom of a growing culture of whining whose motto is that You Can Get Mad And Get Even at the same time, a culture which, like most things American, is spreading to Britain and beyond. Ordinary Americans, irritated and disgusted by this trend, speak of a decline in national character, fearing that their fellow countrymen covet the role of victim. A study conducted by the Center for National Policy talked to groups of voters from California to Texas and Ohio and concluded anger was one result of this sense of moral drift.

'There is a widespread feeling,' the study asserted, 'that life is not as it should be', that America is 'rudderless' and that people no longer know what America 'stands for'. The sense was of a profound moral malaise, that the 'rules of the American way of life have broken down'. The study found irritation that 'selfishness is now the norm' amid an 'erosion of American ideals, values and beliefs'.

Americans are angry because most aspire to their country's heroic, self-reliant myths and resent the whining culture of victimhood which has seeped from the local courthouse to the White House and a president, Bill Clinton, who notoriously 'feels your pain'. Charles Sykes, in his book *A Nation of Victims*, writes of an FBI agent who embezzled $2,000 and blew it in an afternoon gambling at Atlantic City. He was reinstated at work after a court ruled his gambling addiction was a 'handicap'. Or in Philadelphia a school district employee was fired for consistently turning up late for work. He sued, alleging he was a victim of 'Chronic Lateness Syndrome', the adult equivalent of saying the dog ate your homework. Or there was the convicted murderer who argued he was the victim of Foetal Alcohol Syndrome. Your mother drinks, so you are not responsible if you murder people? Or Washington DC mayor Marion Barry, videotaped smoking crack cocaine—a victim, naturally, of FBI racism.

In this distorted mirror, some behaviour—getting drunk, smoking crack, stealing money—is no longer a mistaken, culpable personal choice. It is a disease and therefore blameless. And the sense of shame formerly attached to the behaviour has been transferred to criticising it. Try suggesting, for example, that a 'morbidly obese' person might lose a few pounds in weight and the full fury of the

278

American culture of the victim descends upon your head.

Victimhood is not just blameless but incurable, since we are all victims now, and consequently no one is responsible for anything. The culture of victimhood therefore devalues those genuinely victimised by racism, real disease or handicap, because if everybody is a victim, then nobody is. And competitive victimhood has entered its most absurd phase: the 1990s designer victim, the angry white male.

The pot-bellied middle-aged white men in combat fatigues who join anti-government militias claim to be 'victims' of a US government threatening to take away their assault rifles. The 1994 Congressional elections, which amounted to an anti-Clinton landslide, were widely interpreted as the revenge of angry white men on Clinton policies stretching from helping minorities to homosexuals in the military. And the central premise of one of the most poisonous books ever published in America, the underground hit *The Turner Diaries*, is precisely this sense of white victimhood. The book proudly boasts that the FBI calls it 'the Bible of the racist right', and begins with the rounding up of gun owners by 'the hated equality police'. It ends with a race war in which white 'heroes' hang black people, Jews and white 'collaborators' from lamp posts, a justifiable race war, the book argues, because whites are 'victims' of a tyrannical government trying to take away their guns.

Caught, in Robert Hughes' phrase, between the obtuse whining of the left-leaning 'politically correct' and these desperate maunderings of

279

the right-wing 'patriotically correct', normal Americans have every reason to fear that their central heroic myth of being a 'can do' hardy people is in trouble.

Here in North Carolina at Kitty Hawk, eighteen-wheel juggernauts and pick-up trucks carry the banner of America's most revered victims: the lost cause, the Confederacy. North Carolina licence plates declare proudly 'First in Flight', but some also show Confederate flags with nostalgic references to the standard-bearer of the lost cause, the Confederate president Jefferson Davis.

'Don't blame me', one popular sticker says, of America's current political problems. 'I voted for Jeff Davis.' It would all be humorous nostalgia except for the new culture of victimhood. The local senator, Jesse Helms, for example, in his 1990 election campaign against a black candidate Harvey Gantt ruthlessly exploited white male anger. Helms' campaign ads showed a white man crunching up a job rejection notice. The voiceover boomed portentously: 'You needed that job. And you were the best qualified. But they had to give it to a minority because of a racial quota. Is that really fair?' The culture of victims reached transcendent absurdity here. The message is that black people, the real victims of generations of racial injustice, are now victimising white folks, as some politicians pander to the sickest delusions of victimhood while simultaneously pleading for a stronger America.

The wind is picking up at Kitty Hawk, and I am trying to pace out the track of the first flight, marvelling that 120 feet would hardly make up the

280

length of one wing of a modern jet airliner. De Tocqueville, as usual, got it right. 'There is in America,' he wrote in 1831, 'so much distinguished talent among the subjects and so little among the heads of government.'

There will always be heroic Wilburs and Orvilles, crazy, admirable people determined to live up to the American myths of pioneer, pilgrim, cowboy and astronaut. But the runway suddenly seems littered with lawyers, therapists and politicians claiming flying should be banned because a morbidly obese person could not possibly squeeze into the cockpit.

America, I feel your pain.

74

Why Live Here?

Simon Winchester

This correspondent, a former geologist, wrote a book saying San Francisco could once again be levelled by a massive earthquake. It was a message some Californians were reluctant to accept.
(3 December 2005)

The first time that I ever saw San Francisco it was dawn, and I was standing on a mountain top thirty miles away, and the city was gleaming white in the rays of the rising sun. I was struck, more than anything, by its sheer fragility. It looked so unlike the great cities of the East—New York, Boston,

Chicago—which were big and battleship grey and seemingly bolted on to the landscape with iron. San Francisco seemed to cling oh-so-delicately on to its hills. It looked, in a word, vulnerable. As we all know it is.

A little less than a century ago it was utterly destroyed in one of the world's most infamous earthquakes, and the geologists who today study the San Andreas fault that runs underneath it predict that the time is more than ripe for a replay of that terrible event. A greater than 60 per cent chance, they say, of a big calamity in the Bay area, some time in the next quarter-century. This is not a message the local residents like to hear.

A week ago I was giving a talk in a bookstore on Market Street and saw a long white envelope on the podium, marked for me. I imagined, optimistically, that it was a cheque. It turned out to be anything but: an anonymous letter, urging me to get out of town. 'You geologists,' it began. 'If you can tell us we have three hours' warning, fine. But if you simply want to tell us that we live somewhere dangerous and that a quake might happen, well, we don't want to hear, thanks very much. Why don't you just go away and let us get on with our lives? We're happy here in California. Life is so darn good.' Denial seems a powerful component of life in seismically active parts of America.

So I am out on the road these days on a quasi-evangelical mission to try to reverse it. And my pitch, or my sermon, goes like this. In mature countries in the old civilisations of Asia, Europe and Africa, the big cities are, by and large, where they ought to be. So London, Paris, Cairo, Beijing, Moscow, all thousands of years old, are all in seismically stable places untroubled by terrible weather. But by the same token these ancient countries are littered with the ruins of cities built where they ought not to have been built: Pompeii, Petra, Ayutthaya in Thailand, Heliopolis.

As tourists we cluster around these ruins in awe. Ruins are part of our cultural inheritance, important for the perspective that they bring, reminders of our impermanence. But America is a country without any ruins. Maybe the odd ghost town in Utah and Nevada, but basically no ruined cities. The country is young enough to have set down its cities wherever it pleases, without ever stopping to ask if the world agrees. And the world does not always agree. Which prompts me to wonder out loud whether—if one can imagine a map of America drawn up, say, two centuries from now—whether there may in fact be a litter of abandoned and ruined cities.

New Orleans, for example. It is a little eccentric to create a city on a swamp, six metres below sea level, between a river and a lake, in a part of the world afflicted by near-constant summer hurricanes. Might this not, one day, be abandoned to the elements? And what of Tucson, Phoenix, Las Vegas, even? There is no water there. And there is no great world tradition of building cities to last in the middle of deserts. So Phoenix may go the way of Petra, though it is a little difficult to imagine its ruins attracting quite so many tourists.

And then what of San Francisco? A heresy, of course, to imagine it ever being abandoned and yet it does lie athwart one of the most dangerous tectonic plate boundaries on the planet. Might it not be possible to suppose that some peoples of the future will wander, amazed, around the stumps of the Golden Gate Bridge, or the shell of the TransAmerica Pyramid, and wonder: why did anyone ever choose to live here?

This is where the audiences start to become restless, and a faintly hostile muttering can be heard. But I try to still them with a soothing balsam. Why not take a leaf, I ask, from the one country that has learned to live with earthquakes for the past 2,000 years, and that, of course, is Japan? And with the sudden realisation that it is, after all, entirely possible to come to terms with earthquakes and survive, everyone in the room begins to nod happily and sagely and promise that, yes, they will mug up on how it's done in Tokyo and Osaka and Kyoto. And so all in the American West will in consequence live happily ever after, earthquakes notwithstanding.

As the man wrote: 'Life here is so darn good. We're happy here. And that is what it's all about.' 'So can I stay?' I asked. 'Sure,' they said. 'Stick around.'

75

Dancing with Martha

Stephen Evans

When our correspondent travelled to Detroit, the city best known for its motor industry and its connection with Motown Records, he met some of the soul singers whose records he had bought back in the 60s and 70s. (1 June 2002)

The perks of the reporter's trade don't come much richer than dancing with the Motown legend Martha Reeves in her own flat. It happened to me when I interviewed her for a radio documentary on the record company. I went to the small apartment where she still lives in ravaged, downtown Detroit on a Saturday morning, a tiny apartment crammed with a piano, pictures, plaques, awards—all the accoutrements of true stardom, all the accoutrements, that is, apart from wealth. She's got a kitchen so small you couldn't swing a microphone in it. Nonetheless, when I arrived she made me a cup of tea because, she said, the British love tea and she loves the British.

Then she sat down to breakfast on the sofa with a tray on her knees. At which point there was one of those awkward moments where I tucked into my breakfast and she immediately closed her eyes, clasped her hands in prayer and said grace as I munched my muffin.

Having ignored my faux pas, though, she talked about Detroit, about music, the car industry; about her youth, about the virulent, violent racism directed at her, like being shot at—about matters large and small.

And after all the talk of the formal interview, Martha Reeves sang for me, just for me, the hymn she sings in the bath (though I hasten to say that she didn't sing it for me in the bath) and she sang a bit of Motown. And then, the icing on the icing, she stood up, put her CD on and pulled me up to dance with her ('Dancing in the Flat' as the song might put it).

Martha Reeves was and is a delight—not a trace of the prima donna, just an articulate, intelligent woman reflecting on the ups and downs of life. The same could be said for the others I interviewed: Gladys Knight with her loud, disarming laugh, more anxious to talk about the diabetes her mother had than the extraordinary life she's lived. Or I remember a marvellous lady called Cal Street who was and is the lead singer of a band called the Velvelettes. She was in her early teens when she started; now she's a hospital administrator in Kalamazoo and still sings with the group, often at a Detroit club called the Roostertail where I caught up with her—again nothing but a relish for life, only a tinge of anger when she mentioned hearing about another group taking their name, the Velvelettes, and living off it on tour in Britain.

What was heart-warming about all these people was their friendliness and lack of bitterness, even though stardom hasn't left them with any great fortune. They were part of a great movement—a musical movement and, in a sense, a political movement. It didn't make them rich financially but it did enrich them as human beings, and for the human enrichment they are grateful while not being obviously bitter about the absence of enduring financial benefit.

These are the people who stayed in Detroit when Motown abandoned it, deserted the grit that produced the pearl. Detroit, it has to be said, took some staying with. The city never really recovered after the riots in 1967—or the rebellion, depending on your point of view. It does its best; there's a new monorail train that runs around the city centre these days—finally, after all those years when the

286

car companies did their best to block public transport.

It's still not a happy town. One of the people I met was Barrett Strong, who sang Motown's first big hit called 'Money', and who wrote the classic 'Heard It Through the Grapevine'. Barrett's trying to make a go of a recording studio in the suburbs, but it's a struggle. An even bigger struggle is his sadness. When I met him, a white friend's son had come home from school and used the word 'nigger'. She, the white mother, had wanted to tear into her son; Barrett, the black man, was more resigned, saying with desperate sadness: 'It's just the way it is.'

But it's still a rough town. Not quite as rough as it was when there were 800 murders in one year, and not quite as rough as when disgruntled car workers would go into the factory and shoot the foreman and be cleared of murder by the jury. But it's still rough enough to keep the streets deserted at night.

In Detroit, they're even aggressive when they play chess. I watched big, macho men, wearing big, macho training shoes and basketball vests, playing chess of all things in the heat and humidity of July. They strutted above the stone chess tables in the riverside park, shouting at their opponents' pieces: 'Get that rook out my way, man.' Or bawling at the opponent's king, bawling and pointing at a chess piece: 'Get your butt in that corner. You're dead, man, you're dead.'

Now, when they play chess like that, you know it's a tough city.

And yet, and yet, y'know . . . Detroit still has some of the funniest, shrewdest, warmest people that I've ever met.

76

Pole to Pole

David Shukman

Our correspondent visited some of the coldest, most inhospitable parts of the earth, reporting on the effects of climate change, talking to scientists about global warming and enjoying hearty meals.
(10 March 2007)

Far from the cries of environmental protestors and the rhetoric of greener-than-thou politicians, there are hardy teams of scientists out seeking the truth of climate change in the least hospitable corners of the planet. It's the coldest places on earth that are experiencing the most rapid warming, and for the past few years I have set myself the task of reporting on exactly what the researchers are discovering. It has been a long and vivid journey. I have endured a blizzard under the midnight sun of Greenland, gazed spellbound at the deep blue of a cavern in the Antarctic ice, and become stuck in notorious Siberia, whose tortured history my own grandfather survived a century before me.

Many of my destinations are hard to find on a map. But one night, at an unmarked spot on the Greenland ice-sheet, I find myself in a tent half buried in snow. I'm with a climate research team funded by the American space agency NASA but

288

there's nothing space age about our shelter—eight of us huddle around one small gas heater. Tonight the temperature falls to minus 17 degrees Celsius, minus 30 if you add the effect of the gale. As steam rises from plates of fried halibut, I eat without pause and want far more. Food is to become an obsession on my polar travels, the cold spawning constant hunger.

Our tiny outpost could not be more remote. Beyond the canvas, past the scientific instruments blasted by the storm, a thousand miles of barren ice stretches towards the North Pole; no lights, no roads, just us. But what happens here matters to us all. Greenland's ice-sheet, two miles thick in places, stores enough water to raise the global sea level by twenty feet and, with the Arctic temperatures rising fast in the past thirty years, there are worrying signs that the melting of the ice is accelerating. That's why this research is so crucial.

It's time for coffee. To make it, our host plunges a shovel into a dustbin and scoops out a load of snow, which he tips into a pot on the stove. This is our water supply; this is no ordinary dinner party. We have to be entirely self-sufficient. The thought unnerves me so I turn down the offer of coffee and reach for the malt whisky instead.

Beside me is the man who founded this research base fifteen years ago. A tall, genial professor, Konrad Steffen has the clear blue eyes, lined face and beard of a veteran of the Arctic. His colleagues say he never feels the cold. Known as 'Koni', his goal is simple: accurate measurement. Not for him the cosy analysis of other people's data. He once, reportedly, stayed awake for several days and nights to monitor exactly how much solar radiation was reflected by the snow. On one expedition a polar bear chased one of his huskies around his tent. On another, the ice he was camped on broke away and started drifting out into the ocean. Koni's only escape was to rev up his snowmobile and, like a stuntman, jump the gap.

The next day the weather is still brutal. Our camera jams, so does the back-up and even a third grinds to a halt. The horizon vanishes in unrelenting white. Our plan was to stay just one night. But the helicopter meant to pick us up can't make it. We're stuck. One of our companions is another ice scientist, Jay Zwally. It was Jay who'd cooked so well the first night, and now, in a surreal bid to lift morale, he feeds us lobster. In a land where the days and nights roll into one, these things count.

The science goes on around us. The discoveries at this camp have revolutionised predictions for climate change. The ice-sheet was always assumed to be almost too cold to move, but research here has revealed a startling reality: that the ice-sheet, which is always creeping downhill towards the coast, actually doubles in speed during the few warm weeks of summer. So if the summers get longer as predicted, and the temperatures rise, the more rapidly the ice will reach the sea and so raise its level—with implications for every coastal city on the planet.

Eventually the sky clears a little. The helicopter is on its way for us. We hear its drumbeat approach but then it retreats. The pilot still can't see clearly. Our faces and spirits drop. Hours later the helicopter does manage to land and then lift us away. Our stay lasted four days and I'm desperate for a shower. The pilot wrinkles his nose. My next destination may be all the way to the other end of the world, but I will be cleaner.

Antarctica is the great white continent, the coldest, least explored terrain on earth. But at the British Antarctic Survey's base at Rothera there is heating and hot water in abundance. I'm in a corner of modern Britain. I can e-mail my wife or pick up a phone connected to a switchboard in Cambridge and there are reassuring sights like jars of pickle and marmalade. To my great relief, we are fed no less than four times a day. I'm not alone in my hunger. Mid-morning coffee is known as 'smoko', a Royal Navy tradition, in which biscuits make way for heartier fare like steak and kidney pudding. As I tuck in, I look up at reminders of a more heroic Antarctic age: photographs of Robert Scott swaddled against the cold, Shackleton's vessel *Endurance* trapped in the ice. But that Antarctica feels alien if you're in central heating.

Step outside, though, and there's a land of brilliant white sixty times the size of Britain, twice the size of Australia. This morning, with the sun high and no wind, I see Antarctica at its most impressive. Ahead there's a towering cliff of the palest blue; the ice turns that colour after years of being compressed. Below it, shimmering like gemstones, are thousands of intricate, shifting icebergs. The air is so clean that islands that seem close enough to touch are in fact a dozen miles away. The only sounds are the occasional crack of ice and cry of a bird.

But the scene is misleading. The weather can turn savage in an instant. On a boat trip, the wind suddenly alters and drives a dense mass of ice towards the jetty, blocking it and nearly preventing us from landing. And up on the ice-sheet, the untouched snow hides the potential death traps of crevasses. As part of our survival training, we are taught how to abseil down into one. It is like descending into an aquarium, a fairy-tale cavern bathed in blue light, countless icicles twinkling. I reach out to touch the crystal walls, incredibly smooth. I hardly know where to look: the luminous frozen pool or the miniature temple lit from within or the tiny frozen bubbles.

The air trapped in the ice is mesmerising and invaluable. It has provided a record of our changing climate and evidence of the rise in greenhouse gases. Few discoveries have proved so important—establishing a link between carbon dioxide and temperature, and showing that over the past 800,000 years the natural variations in climate never saw the gas reach the levels it has today. Analysis of Antarctica's ice is one of the foundation stones of the global debate about the need to reduce carbon emissions. It is eerie to see it this close up.

And then I remember why I am down in the crevasse: to do safety training. The history of Antarctic exploration is littered with grim tales of pioneers falling to their deaths in icy fissures exactly like this one. They wouldn't have noticed the fabulous glow of blue. Or the bubbles so critical to climate science.

I climb above the base to visit the memorials to those who have died at Rothera. The research here has revealed that this part of Antarctica has warmed at an extraordinary rate in the past fifty years, but this understanding has come at a price. Most recently a young biologist, Kirsty Brown, investigating how marine life is threatened by the higher temperatures, was dragged underwater by a leopard seal and drowned. I shudder as I look at her plaque. Antarctica has a dark past, and now my journey is to become darker still.

Nowhere has a more sinister reputation than Siberia, the very name conjuring up images of ice and exile, endless winters and the notorious Gulags. Now I am stuck there, trapped as I was in Greenland, by a blizzard. Yet again my travels to research global warming are halted by the cold. I'm in a research station, a collection of wooden houses and laboratories, near the town of Cherskii, which is so far east that it shares a time zone with New Zealand, eleven hours ahead of London. It's also so far north that it's well inside the Arctic Circle. It will take a long series of flights to get out: 300 miles to Sredno Kolymsk, 800 miles to the regional capital Yakutsk, 4,000 miles to Moscow. I feel tired just thinking about it.

Cherskii sits on the mighty Kolyma river and is not the best place to let the mind wander. Kolyma is a byword for all the worst excesses of the Soviet prison camps, the most distant and the most brutal parts of a nightmare chapter in Russian history. The ships carrying the prisoners passed along the grey waters that I am beside now, and the thought of what the stunted trees once witnessed is grotesque. Now this region may be the scene for another kind of horror, playing a potentially dangerous role in the acceleration of global warming, the thawing permafrost amounting to a climate time bomb, as one scientist puts it.

Frozen for tens of thousands of years, the Siberian soils are now stirring, releasing vast quantities of greenhouse gases. And locked inside this earth are the remains of the millions of animals that once roamed this terrain, including the magnificent woolly mammoths. This makes the land a rich store of carbon and, once warmed, it becomes a potent source of methane and carbon dioxide. The fear is of a vicious cycle of change.

The chief scientist here is the flamboyant Sergei Zimov, a fearless figure whose favourite form of transport is an armoured personnel carrier. I ride with him, effortlessly surfing over tree stumps and mud. Sergei and his colleagues, Russian and American, have pioneered new techniques for measuring the escape of the gases. Some rise from the mud; others bubble up from the lake beds. As I watch, one researcher stumbles on the enormous thigh bone of a mammoth.

Day after day our flight is cancelled. Luckily, I never need worry about the next meal. Sergei's wife, Galya, produces dishes of barbecued sturgeon and stewed moose. And, as the vodka takes hold, I wonder how another David Shukman, my grandfather, fared in Siberia one hundred years before me. I, of course, chose to make this visit; he was ordered here as a conscript in the Russian army and sent to fight the Japanese. While I fret about my delayed flight, I recall that my grandfather was one of the first to ride the Trans-Siberian railway, a hellish month in a goods wagon lined with felt and meagrely supplied with tea and bread. I have a satellite telephone; news of his injury in battle took months to reach home. And he wouldn't have cared about the melting permafrost. In fact he'd have yearned for a little global warming.

77

Massacre at Baramulla

Andrew Whitehead

Of all the world's trouble spots, Kashmir is one of the most enduring. It has bedevilled relations between India and Pakistan ever since the two countries gained independence back in 1947. Within weeks of the end of the British Raj, Indian troops and pro-Pakistani forces were fighting in Kashmir. They still are. (9 August 2003)

The white paint is peeling from the gravestones, the shingle needs weeding, and apart from the nuns, no one comes here any more to place flowers, to say a prayer or pay remembrance. Still, you couldn't want a more tranquil spot for a cemetery; around the small enclosure is a tiny orchard, a few hens scratching away underneath the trees. Butterflies hover in the dappled morning sun. Bulbuls and hoopoes add a splash of colour. And the chorus of birdsong almost drowns out the brook that came to life just hours earlier carrying storm water down towards the River Jhelum.

Look up, and the hills rise steeply in front of you. This is where the Himalayan foothills start to crowd in on the Kashmir valley. They loom a little menacingly, fir trees silhouetted like saw's teeth against the mist. It was down those hills that the raiders came one Monday morning in October 1947. They laid waste to the convent, looted the mission hospital and shot dead the men and women whose graves now lie in the grounds. Just six dead. Not many: neither by the shameful standards of the bloodshed which marred the end of the British Raj, the partition mayhem out of which emerged an independent India and a new Muslim nation of Pakistan; nor in comparison to the recent annals of Kashmir—more than 30,000 dead in fourteen unfinished years of separatist insurgency against Indian rule.

Yet if there was a moment when the Kashmir crisis first erupted, that was it: that autumn day when St Joseph's convent at Baramulla was desecrated. Sister Emilia from Verona, ruddy faced and resolutely cheerful, lived through it. Now in her late nineties, she still lives through it. Still at Baramulla, still having nightmares, still telling her tale of the convent's moment of tragedy and of glory, when the tribesmen attacked. She heard the shots fired, she watched a young Spanish nun bleed to death, her final words: 'I offer myself for the people of Kashmir.' She tended the three infant sons of the British military couple who were also killed. She was herself lined up to be shot, when providence intervened in the form of a convent-educated officer with some authority over the gunmen who ordered them to hold fire. The killings stopped, but for eleven days the survivors of the massacre, more than seventy nuns, priests, patients and refuge seekers, were trapped in a single hospital room.

The attackers were not local: big, black-bearded

beasts, in the words of one of the missionary priests. They had come from the tribal areas of north-west Pakistan, close to the Afghan border; if not sent by Pakistan's government, then making their way with official connivance to claim Kashmir for Pakistan. And also to liberate Kashmir's Muslim majority from the arbitrary rule of their Hindu maharaja, to seek revenge for the massacres of Muslims in other parts of the princely state. And more than anything else, to pursue the age-old goal of tribal *lashkars*, or raiding parties, to carry away any item of value they came across, including, according to much first-hand testimony, Kashmiri women.

Baramulla was the first town of any size in the Kashmir valley the tribesmen came across. Their advance had panicked the maharaja into a belated decision to sign up with India rather than Pakistan—that was on the eve of the attack on the convent. At dawn the following day, the first airlift of Indian troops into Kashmir began. A few hours after the attack on the convent, at a hillock just a short distance away, troops of India's Sikh Regiment fought their first encounter with the pro-Pakistan tribal irregulars. The initial clash in a conflict which has never been close to resolution, which has frustrated every attempt at friendship between India and Pakistan, which has propelled both countries into a nuclear arms race, which has helped the army to power on one side of the partition line and helped fire Hindu nationalism on the other, which has made Kashmir, in the eyes of policymakers in Washington and London, the most likely crucible of nuclear war.

Step away just fifty yards from the calm of the

convent orchard at Baramulla and you are on the main road running through the Kashmir valley. It is one of the most militarised highways I've ever travelled along. There are any number of Indian bases along the road, jeep patrols with commandos at the controls of mounted machine guns, foot patrols stalking along the side of the road. I saw one youngster hauled away from a roadside stall and, if the Indian security forces are still as ruthless as they certainly once were, his friends and family have cause for concern.

The convent remains caught up in a climate of violence. 'There is a long way to go to attain real peace,' said Sister Rosie, the softly spoken South Indian who's now the Mother Superior. She spoke with anguish of a recent mine blast nearby which had claimed several lives. 'We pray every day for peace in Kashmir,' she told me. 'We pray for the people of Kashmir and for other war-torn countries in the world.'

There aren't many Catholics in Kashmir, but those there are regard the victims of the attack on St Joseph's mission back in October 1947 as martyrs. 'The blood of the martyrs will not be spilt in vain,' I was told. 'Some day good will come out of it. One day there will be a solution to the Kashmir problem.' Well, it takes real faith to imagine that the Kashmir conflict could be resolved any time soon. The people of Kashmir, a people not given to fighting, remain caught up in the power politics of the region, just like those men and women whose bones lie beneath the convent orchard at Baramulla.

78

Face to Face with Benazir

Owen Bennett-Jones

*The Pakistani opposition leader Benazir Bhutto was
assassinated after attending an election rally in
Rawalpindi. (29th December 2007)*

It must be eight years ago now: it was in the
cavernous hall of Benazir Bhutto's ancestral home
in Larkana, Sindh, southern Pakistan—her
political base, her vote bank. We'd had dinner,
forty people or so around her huge dining table,
and then she had moved into a larger, more public
room. It was late, but it was packed. She sat in a big
upright chair—on a dais as I remember, a throne
really—and standing in a semicircle around her,
former cabinet ministers and others, courtiers to
whom she had given plum postings when she had
been prime minister, ambassadorships or sinecures
within Pakistan.

In conspiratorial whispers they gossiped and
schemed: they tried to catch her attention or, if
they were out of favour, to avoid it. Some tried to
interest her with bits of political news from
Islamabad or Lahore. Who is pleasing her, they all
worried, and how are they doing it? I remember
thinking: any historian studying the court of
Elizabeth I should get down here immediately; this
surely is how it was.

Beyond the inner semi-circle of senior party

leaders there was a second group, not as close to the leader but of significance to her party machine, many of them Pakistan People's Party members of parliament. To be given a party slot at the elections they had to be big names in their own area, members of known political families with the resources and local powers of patronage to win their parliamentary seats. These were the men labelled in Pakistan 'feudal lords'—which is a perfectly good description. I spoke to one and asked about his set-up. 'Oh, I'm down by the Iranian border,' he replied amiably.

'I've got a million acres. And a million men. But I love London, go every summer to buy a new shotgun at Holland and Holland,' he said, adding with a twinkle in his eye, 'and to see the barmaid at the pub near my cousin's in south London. Oh so charming. "Last orders!" "Two pints of Fosters, please!" Nothing like it.'

Benazir Bhutto was caught between two worlds as well. The Pakistani writer Tariq Ali had it right in a recent article in the *London Review of Books*. While she called her autobiography *Daughter of the East*, his article about her had the headline 'Daughter of the West'. Her latest political comeback was the culmination of years of persuading Washington that, with the people's backing, she could help General Musharraf fight America's war on terror in Pakistan.

On the outer fringes of the throng around Benazir Bhutto that night in Larkana eight years ago were the local villagers who had somehow blagged their way in. They were welcome enough, as long as they stayed in their place. But one had a camera and took a picture. The flash had not even faded away before, with a ferocious, imperious expression, Benazir Bhutto pointed in his general direction.

Her minders, who had obviously been mingling in the crowd for just such an eventuality, wrestled him to the ground, grabbed his camera, ripped out the film and hurled him out of the door into the courtyard. I looked at her surprised, shocked. 'I am sorry,' she said, solicitous of my western sensibilities. 'They are so enthusiastic, but don't you see I had my hair down, no covering, and one of my advisers here was whispering something in my ear. If that picture got into the papers just think what they would say.'

You know what they say about those people who can enter a room and everyone . . . ? Well, she was one of them. I invited her to a party in our house in Islamabad once, never expecting her to turn up. She arrived at eleven, just as everyone was leaving—until she came, that is. Then they all stayed. It went on until four in the morning, with everyone listening to one woman speak.

So . . . Benazir Bhutto was domineering, articulate, brave, charismatic, good fun, quite flirtatious, very cynical and flawed. Tens of millions of Pakistanis, illiterate and impoverished, looked to her with hope, faith, even love. She failed them.

Of course there were extenuating circumstances. When she had power, or at least when she was prime minister, the army was always breathing down her neck and the civil service resented taking orders from a western-educated, secular-minded woman.

But for all that, the evidence that she abused her

office to make money is overwhelming, even if her lawyers, grand masters of delaying tactics, always managed to put off the final legal showdown. She leaves many Swiss bank accounts swollen with dollars from kickbacks.

But whatever the criticisms, it is worth remembering this: Benazir Bhutto seemed indestructible. She survived the execution of her father, she endured imprisonment and came out stronger, she outlived exile and saw off the corruption cases and she survived previous attempts on her life. 'What do you expect me to do,' she said, after an attempt on her life in Karachi last October, 'give in?'

It was never an option. She really did have guts. Which is why even those Pakistanis who despaired of her failings are shocked this weekend, shocked and appalled at her brutal death at the hands of a nameless fanatic.

79

Dolly Makes Changes

Jill McGivering

After several weeks of turmoil, an interim government was installed in Bangladesh. It declared a state of emergency, and promised to crack down on corruption and to hold what it called 'credible' elections as soon as possible. (25 January 2007)

He was a thin scruffy boy, part of a pack. They

swarmed round the car as soon as we pulled up at the lights. I could see his fingers smear the window as he pressed against it, waving his bags of popcorn and shouting at us to buy. We wound down the window to talk to him. His name was Ruhul, he said. He stood squarely, puffing out his chest to hide his nerves. He was ten, he said, although he looked much younger. He sold fifty bags of popcorn a day. And every evening, he had to pay off the local policemen or face jail. Did he think that was fair? He was indignant. Of course it's not, he said. But I have to pay them or I can't work. We left with our back seat piled high with popcorn.

Bangladesh is still one of the world's poorest countries. It's also corrupt and dysfunctional, led for the last fifteen years by two female leaders, first one, then the other. They're locked in a bitter feud so malevolent they refuse to talk, let alone co-operate. When one wins an election, the other boycotts parliament, calling national strikes and protests. Here politicians are associated with corruption and chaos.

But despite its politicians, the economy is booming. It's several years since I last visited Dhaka and I barely recognised it. Where I remember piles of decaying rubbish and crumbling buildings, the central business districts are now flash and efficient. The air used to be black with the clogging fumes of cheap petrol. Now the traffic runs on clean fuel and the air is filled instead with the beat of construction. Gleaming modern buildings are popping up through the dirt like mushrooms, pushing slum dwellers further out.

I went to one of Dhaka's semi-permanent slums to meet Dolly, a neatly dressed, bright-eyed girl of seventeen. She was eager to practise her English, learned, she said, only from books. She led me across a rickety bamboo walkway. Down below, I could see stagnant water. A series of corrugated iron shacks were set along the walkway, tiny tree houses, each home to an entire family.

Somewhere richer, Dolly might lead a girl-guide troop or be head girl. Here she's been sorting out the slum's sanitation problems. A couple of years ago, she said, hygiene here was very poor. So she assembled a group of teenage friends, all girls, and, helped by a charity, they started to make changes. Gradually, pestered by Dolly and her team, local families started to clean up their act. Now they only drink boiled water. They dispose of their rubbish properly, instead of letting it pile up. Before there weren't any toilets. Now everyone uses the new block of latrines. Dolly showed it off proudly. Everyone, she said, helps to keep it clean.

Dolly explained all this in a confident, no-nonsense tone, as if common sense was the most natural thing in the world. Dolly's parents hung behind her, proud but shy. They had very little education but Dolly plans to go to university. She's in no rush to get married, she explained. Plenty of time for all that later.

While Dolly studies, many others will find jobs in the country's booming garment industry. It employs more than two million people nowadays, almost all women. I visited one factory with its owner, Annisul Haq, a handsome former television presenter. On the factory floor, the background tinkle of Bangla pop music was almost drowned out by machinery. About 500 women sat, two to a table, guiding cloth through whizzing sewing machines or stamping out buttonholes. The whole vast area fluttered with blue-and-white striped shirts, which are heading for an American department store.

Mr Haq is fed up with the country's politicians. The disruption caused by the recent strikes hit him hard. He has enough problems already, he said: bad roads, an erratic power supply and a bureaucracy he described as medieval. 'Politicians are the last straw,' he said.

'Back in England,' he went on, 'you probably heard about the state of emergency and thought, oh no, the people are suffering! But now you're here, you can see people welcome it.' He was quite right. Everyone I've met, from rickshaw drivers up, hailed the state of emergency as a happy rest from the chaos caused by politicians. No more political protests, no more national strikes; a chance, at last, to get on with normal daily life.

Personally I hope the people of Bangladesh do, in the end, get the kind of government they deserve. Democratically elected, yes, but also accountable, supporting its people, not a burden on them. They could really do with someone like Dolly, who might clean up the country's institutions with the same drive and vision that created one of the cleanest slums I think I've ever seen.

80

Guns, Goons and Gold

Jonathan Head

The Philippines is known for having one of the liveliest democracies in Asia and one of the most violent and corrupt. Winning political office is seen as the key to maintaining power and wealth in the Philippines, and candidates compete fiercely, often resorting to violence. (19 May 2007)

Everywhere I went in Masbate I felt I was being followed by a girl called Lovely. It was the youthful face of Lovely Abapo, to give her her full name, grinning with braced teeth, that stared out at me from pink posters plastered on every wall and every tree. Just twenty-three years old, she was running for city councillor in the election and had a strong chance of winning, not because of any special talents she had, but because of her name. The Abapos are one of the big landowning families on Masbate. They own extensive ranches around Milagros, centre of the cattle industry on the island, and they've always won elections. In fact Lovely's father, Bing, has just completed his last term as the Milagros town mayor. The constitutional constraints against holding office indefinitely are no barrier to the ambitions of the big families on Masbate, though: this time round Bing ran for deputy mayor instead, and the deputy mayor, who just happened to be his son

306

Bong-Bong, ran for mayor.

If that all sounds like a political pantomime, it's one with a lethal subplot. A handful of families own pretty much everything on Masbate and, to keep it that way, they need to control local government. They're willing to do almost anything to win; and as most of them maintain heavily armed militias, that usually results in shooting. The Abapos know all about that now. On polling day, Boy Abapo, who was Bing's brother, was shot dead in an ambush.

With some apprehension I joined Maloli Espinosa when she went out campaigning in the poor *barrios* of Masbate town. In the van she had two loaded handguns at her feet and a plain-clothes escort armed with M16s and Uzi machine guns. Until last year, Maloli was insulated from all this, living in Manila and working as a top executive in the country's largest broadcasting company. But a sense of duty to her family and, she insists, to the people of Masbate pulled her back to run for Congress in the province.

On the wall of the family hacienda is a large portrait of her father, astride a horse in full cowboy regalia. The Espinosas too are big landowners, some say the biggest on Masbate. The cowboy image is tragically apt. Her father was gunned down after stepping off a plane in 1989, it's presumed by an assassin in the pay of a rival family. At the time he was the most powerful political figure on the island, alternately serving as congressman and governor. His brother Tito was shot dead a few years later, and then his son Moises. I asked Maloli why on earth she would want to put herself in the firing line like this. She

307

told me she trusted God to protect her, although the arsenal of weapons she carries suggests that trust only goes so far.

The local people call it the three Gs—guns, goons and gold, the driving force of politics in much of the Philippines. And Bishop Joel Baylon has had enough of it. He's nailed a covenant, five metres high, on the cathedral wall in Masbate, which he's demanded candidates for political office must sign. It was supposed to bind them to a code of honourable conduct during elections; the ballot, it reads, is the sovereign will of the people, and it's sacred.

The goons, the hired thugs of the big families, seem to agree with the bit about ballots being sacred. They're willing to pay an awful lot for them. A local resident explained it to me like this. A goon will approach the head of a *barangay*, or neighbourhood, which has traditionally voted against his candidate. Bargaining will then ensue over the price for delivering the votes in the neighbourhood; usually that entails a sizeable sum of money for the *barangay* head, and the promise of neighbourhood improvement projects to help everyone else. The bargaining becomes more intense towards the final hours on polling day; that's why, I was told, unlike almost anywhere else in tropical Asia, most people show up in the afternoon, not the morning, to vote. They've been holding out for the best price.

I asked Bishop Baylon if he thought it would ever change. It's a patronage system, he explained. Ordinary people feel a sense of obligation when they receive favours from the big families, even though these favours seem trivial when you consider all the economic development Masbate is being denied because of its feudal politics. It's the third poorest province in the Philippines.

One man told me he would be giving his vote to a candidate because this man had donated 4,000 pesos—about £50—to his brother for a funeral. But your vote is secret, I said, you are free to support anyone you think is the best candidate. He agreed with that but it still wouldn't feel right voting for anyone else, he said. I asked another man whether he was fed up seeing the same old names and faces at election time. He laughed at me. 'Who else but the big families can run?' he asked. 'Who else has enough money?'

81

A President Calls

Damian Grammaticas

The new president of Georgia, Mikhail Saakashvili, was trying to transform his country, once a part of the Soviet Union, into a modern Westernised nation. He vowed to clean up an economy mired in crime and corruption and said he hoped to attract more foreign tourists. (30 October 2004)

There I was—three days into my holiday—and things weren't quite going to plan. I was high in the Caucasus mountains, camping in a wild, untouched forest of beech, walnut and oak trees, next to the ruins of a beautiful old Georgian monastery at

309

Pitareti. It was a lovely spot. But I wasn't in a position to appreciate it. I was lying face down in the grass. A couple of metres to my right, my wife was also staring at the dirt. In front of me, a short, stocky Georgian, a black balaclava over his head so only his eyes were visible, was brandishing an old hunting rifle. A second man, taller and skinnier, also armed and wearing a homemade balaclava, was rummaging through our bags, looking for valuables he could steal.

Every now and again he'd shout at our guides, who had their hands up, and wave his gun threateningly. 'Don't worry, they won't hurt you. Just give them all you have, so there isn't any trouble,' said Reso, the youngest guide, only sixteen years old and remarkably calm in the middle of an armed robbery. Nearby the other three, Georgi, Gia and Rati, were looking glum. A doctor, an engineer and an artist, they'd long shared a passion for trekking through these mountains on horseback. Recently they'd decided to turn their hobby into a serious business. My wife and I were among their first tourists.

I'd been to Georgia several times, reporting on the Rose Revolution that swept Eduard Shevardnadze from power last year. Each visit had whetted my appetite to see more. Squeezed between Russia and Turkey, on the cusp of Christian Europe and Islamic Asia, Georgia is a fascinating place of dramatic, snow-capped mountains, crumbling castles and exuberant, welcoming people. When I'd interviewed the new, young and energetic President Mikhail Saakashvili after the revolution, he'd said his priority was to attract investment and rebuild Georgia's economy, ruined by the collapse of the Soviet Union. He'd sacked half the police for corruption, and Georgia, once known for kidnappings and lawlessness, was changing.

'This is a beautiful country,' Mr Saakashvili had told me. 'We have great food, wine and history. Tourism can help us develop.'

As my wife and I rode up through the mountains, I could see Mr Saakashvili was right. We passed orchards laden with apples and plums, fields where farmers were cutting their hay by hand with scythes, loading it into horse-drawn carts. We galloped through meadows of wildflowers, and climbed to the top of mountain ridges that gave stunning views. We camped by lakes and then by the old monastery at Pitareti.

When the robbers appeared from the woods, we'd all thought it was a joke. They looked so amateur and shabby, with museum pieces for weapons. Then one of them had fired a shot. The crack echoed around the valley. He cocked the hammer on his ancient rifle again, and pointed it at Georgi, shouting: 'Do what I say!' Another bang. This time he'd fired into the air. They made off with money, mobile phones and watches. Georgi, Gia and Rati were distraught. 'We're so sorry,' they said. 'We will sort this out.' In the next village they made a telephone call to a friend in Tbilisi. It turned out the friend was Georgia's deputy minister for security. A few minutes later the phone rang. Georgi turned to me. 'It's for you,' he said. On the line was a voice I recognised.

'Hello,' it boomed, 'this is Mikhail Saakashvili. I have just heard what happened. I am terribly sorry.' 'Mr Saakashvili,' I said, thinking, crikey,

311

what do you say to a president when you've just been robbed? 'It's very kind of you to call. Don't worry, we're fine, we were having a fantastic holiday.' 'Fine?' he replied. 'It's not fine. We need more tourists like you. I promise we will catch these people.'

In the old Georgia that might have been the end of the affair. In Mr Saakashvili's new Georgia, things are changing. Policemen started arriving, each one bigger and more scary-looking than the last, brandishing their Kalashnikovs. Statements were carefully written down. Roadblocks were put up. A tough-looking man from the Interior Ministry appeared to oversee the investigation. Within two days one robber had been caught.

Every Georgian, it seemed, was desperate to make amends to us. The head of the local government invited us to a banquet, the table groaning with tasty cheese, salad and meats. He made us drink glass after glass of vodka, toasting our bravery, wishing us better fortune and hoping the incident wouldn't colour our view of Georgia.

And that was just the start. Feast after feast was laid on by local officials, by our guides, even by the police, anxious we didn't leave with a bad impression of their country. In the end we couldn't face another mouthful. It was a relief to get back to the mountains and to our riding.

The police chief has promised to find the second bandit. And our guides have invited us back for another holiday in the Caucasus. I'd like to return. And if I do, my real worry will not be robbers in the hills, but whether I can cope with the mountains of food and wine that Georgians in their generosity shower on any visitor.

82

A Murder in Osh

Natalia Antelava

*There were demands for Kyrgyzstan to carry out a
thorough and impartial investigation into the murder
of an independent journalist called Alisher Saipov.
The twenty-six-year-old was shot dead by an
unidentified gunman in the Kyrgyz town of Osh, near
the border with Uzbekistan. He was one of the most
outspoken journalists in the region, well known for
his criticism of Islam Karimov, the president of
Uzbekistan. (3 November 2007)*

Behind every international story that you read,
every radio report that you hear or television piece
that you watch, there is likely to be a person we,
the reporters, never tell you about. Often it's the
first person we meet when we fly into a foreign
country. Someone who explains to us the nuts and
bolts of the story we have come to cover, who fills
us in on the situation and puts us in touch with
vital contacts. This person is a local journalist.

And after we, the global media, exhaust our
short attention span and leave, our local colleagues
stay behind. They have to live the story that we tell
in passing. Their main sources are people in the
streets and they are, more often than not, the first
ones to get the word out.

In many ways, they are the real journalists. And the best I have ever known was Alisher Saipov. Twenty-six years old, slim, boyish and restless, Alisher had dedicated his entire life to telling the story of a place that many people know little about: Uzbekistan—Central Asia's most populous country and home to one of the world's most oppressive regimes. An ethnic Uzbek himself, Alisher grew up just across the border from Uzbekistan, in the Kyrgyz town of Osh. And that, he used to say, gave him a degree of freedom and the responsibility to speak up for those who did not have a voice.

'Freedom is a precious commodity, and it should not be wasted,' he told me once. He did not waste a second of it. For Alisher, journalism wasn't just a job, it was a tool, an instrument to push for what he saw as desperately needed change. Methodical, passionate and thorough, he dug deeper than anyone else into the reality of Islam Karimov's Uzbekistan. He wrote endlessly about torture in Uzbek prisons, about the total clampdown on dissent, about the economic collapse of what was once Central Asia's richest nation and about the rise of Islamic radicalism, driven—he always said— by the government's persecution of Muslims in Uzbekistan.

With his sound recorder, a camera strapped around his shoulder and a cheeky smile stretched across his face, he was constantly on the move, investigating, writing, planning and dreaming. His contacts ranged from Islamic radicals to politicians, from refugees to secret service officers. Whether it was a man on the run, or the man who was after him, Alisher always seemed to have the phone number. He went where others would not go, and asked questions no one dared to raise. He was—we used to joke—the king of scoops, the master of making headlines.

I first met Alisher in the aftermath of a bloody crackdown in the Uzbek city of Andijan in 2005, where government troops opened fire on demonstrators, killing hundreds of civilians. Hundreds more fled across the border, into southern Kyrgyzstan. Alisher's investigations revealed that the Uzbek security services were kidnapping some of these refugees, taking them back to Uzbek jails. He was the first person to warn that President Islam Karimov's hand had stretched far beyond his country's borders.

Just over two weeks ago, bursting with pride and excitement, he showed me his new project, an Uzbek-language newspaper. Published in Kyrgyzstan and smuggled across the border by traders and merchants, it was the only Uzbek-language publication that challenged the authorities. The paper was becoming increasingly popular ahead of the December presidential election, in which President Karimov will seek re-election. And with its popularity, Alisher's name too was gaining prominence. He was beginning to feature heavily on Uzbek state-controlled television, portrayed as a terrorist, a dangerous man with a hidden agenda of overthrowing the Uzbek state. The last time I saw him he told me that there were even rumours that the Uzbek government had put a price on his head.

We talked for hours that evening. About his paper, about the upcoming election and about reports of a fresh wave of repression. But more than anything else, we talked about his new family—his young wife and newborn baby daughter. 'Being a dad,' he said to me, 'is like discovering a whole new world.' He only got three months to enjoy being a father. On 24 October, at seven in the evening, as he walked out from his office in the centre of Osh, a gunman fired three bullets into his head and chest.

His murder was an execution. And it sent a chilling message not just to his friends, but to all of his colleagues around the world who live and work in dangerous places; to all of those who give their communities a voice, who are trying to promote freedom in countries where it does not exist; to all of those whose names you may not know but without whom we could never tell you the full story.

83

My Secret Police File

Oana Lungescu

In 1989, Romanians toppled one of Europe's most repressive Communist dictatorships in a bloody revolution. In 2007, they were preparing to join the European Union but still struggling to cast off the legacy of the past. (4 December 2004)

The man from the secret police had a face that was instantly forgettable. It was early 1983 and I had agreed to meet him on a street corner in the centre of the Romanian capital, Bucharest, to discuss a translation job. But when he took out a key from his pocket and opened a big metal door, I became scared. As we stepped into a small room with a desk and two armchairs, I realised this was a side entrance to the Bucharest police headquarters. He was the officer in charge of my case for the dreaded Securitate. And he had an offer to make: a passport for me to emigrate, in order to join my mother abroad, and cancer drugs for my father. In exchange, I would have to inform on Romanians living abroad. He called me in every Monday for several weeks until one day I broke down in tears and told him I just couldn't do it. A few months later, my father died. I eventually got my passport in 1985.

It was customary for the Securitate to try to recruit those who wanted to leave the country, so my case was nothing special. Still, every time I went back to Bucharest, I avoided that street corner. But fifteen years after the fall of Romania's Communist dictator Nicolae Ceauşescu, I felt ready at last. So, in September, I applied to see my secret police file. This became possible only three years ago, under a law passed by a centre-right coalition. The former Communists, now the ruling Social Democrats, have shown little interest in uncovering Romania's murky past.

So far, only 12,000 people have asked for their files. 'I would like to see mine,' a friend confessed, 'but I'm also afraid of what I might find there.' In the western city of Timisoara I met Alexandra Razvan, a lawyer who had joined the anti-Communist protests in the late 1980s. Reading her file, she discovered that a colleague at law school

317

had also been an assiduous informer. I remembered him too. A friendly, bearded young man, I had often interviewed him for the BBC Romanian Service after 1989, when he became an MP for the ruling party.

For Radu Filipescu, an engineer who spent three years in prison for distributing leaflets against Ceausescu, the discovery of his file brought back bittersweet memories. 'They had recorded every conversation I'd had with my father when he came to visit me in prison,' Radu told me, 'and I was very happy to read them again, so many years after my father died.'

Like Radu and Alexandra, I too made my way to the ugly brown building that houses the parliamentary committee for the study of the Securitate archives. The historian Claudiu Secasiu, a member of the committee and an old friend, had news for me: they were still looking for my personal file. 'It's like a lottery,' Claudiu said, 'it can take months or years, because we don't actually control the archives, which are stacked on more than seven miles of shelves. They are still overseen by the four information services that succeeded the Securitate.'

But Claudiu had managed to find something. Two huge files, with the same title on their cardboard covers: 'Operation Ether'. This was the code-name for the Securitate's surveillance of foreign broadcasters and as I leafed through the yellowing pages, I recognised the microphone name I still use when broadcasting in Romanian: Ana Maria Bota. There were transcripts of interviews I had done for the BBC in the late 1980s with or about Romanian dissident writers. 'Must be referred to the National Council for Socialist Culture,' someone had scrawled in the margins. I had always suspected that some of our most loyal listeners were in the Securitate. But there was much more about other people, including writers I knew. Personal letters, some photocopied, others in the original. 'Sometimes,' Claudiu explained, 'the Securitate kept the letters, so you'd have to go into their archives to read your own mail!' The smell of the paper, the sheer amount of it, the range of handwriting and typewriters, the army of people involved in all this bureaucracy of fear— suddenly I felt overwhelmed and I began to cry.

Still, I was glad to be there and I will be back if my own file is found. Before I left Bucharest, I went looking for that metal door. It's very rusty now, clearly unopened for many years. But around the corner the flag of the European Union flies next to the Romanian one. To prepare for Romania's planned admission to the EU in 2007, that part of the police headquarters has become the National Institute for Public Administration.

I wonder what my case officer is doing now.

84

Return to St Kilda

Julian May

In August 1930, the residents of a group of islands off the north-west coast of Scotland packed up and left for good. St Kilda now has World Heritage status, but with the departure of the St Kildans a way of life that had existed for thousands of years vanished overnight. (27 August 2005)

I stood in the doorway of number 16, the last house in the single street that curves around the bay. Behind me, the hill rose almost vertically to its summit where a sheer cliff drops 400 metres to the sea. In front of me, waves pounded the shore of boulders. Beyond them a ship wallowed. Prehistoric-looking brown sheep bleated curiously at me.

In Rachel MacDonald's roofless cottage I understood why this place, rather than some enclave in Central Asia or a clearing in an antipodean jungle, was for years known as the most remote settlement in the entire British empire, but St Kilda is not so far away, just 100 miles or so west of the nearest point of the Scottish mainland.

Seventy-five years ago, at the end of August 1930, the last thirty-six islanders banked up their turf fires, opened their Bibles at Exodus, put some oats on the table, then left for ever, bringing to an end a habitation and a way of life that stretched back at least 2,000 years. And standing in Rachel MacDonald's ruined home, I understood both why they left this harsh, beautiful place and their sadness at doing so.

St Kilda is an archipelago of sea-stacks, skerries and four islands of which only one, Hirta, was permanently inhabited. It was remote in ways other than geographical ones. The people, who never numbered more than a couple of hundred, spoke not English but a distinctive form of Gaelic.

Their economy, their whole culture, revolved round seabirds: the fulmars, gannets and puffins. They ate them and exchanged their feathers and precious oil for goods such as tea and sugar from the mainland. The birds were harvested by cragsmen lowered on homemade ropes down the dizzying cliffs.

In the Victorian era, at the height of Britain's imperial adventure, this self-sufficient life held a strange fascination. St Kilda became a fashionable tourist destination and steamers regularly dropped anchor in Village Bay. But the visitors could not comprehend the St Kildans they gawped at. There is an astonishing recording in the BBC's archives of an islander saying that her mother, in payment for a bale of tweed which had taken all winter to weave, was given an orange. She didn't know what it was.

There had been worse traumas: St Kilda's graveyard is one of the most heart-rending places I have seen. It is full of tiny hummocks where infants are buried. Newborn babies were all anointed where the cord had been cut, with a concoction of fulmar oil, dung and earth, and eight out of ten of them died of neonatal tetanus. The minister finally put a stop to this in 1891 and after that the babies lived. Add to this grief, emigration and harsh religion and it's no wonder that the St Kildans lost heart. By the 1920s there were no longer enough people to do all the work. In 1930 they planted no crops and petitioned the government to take them off the island.

So is today's St Kilda still deserted? Not a bit of it. Recently Norman Gilles, now eighty and one of three surviving St Kildans, returned for a visit. He

321

could be forgiven for thinking there were almost as many people there as when all the St Kildans left and perhaps they should've held on. Because after the evacuation the army built a radar tracking station. It is still there, though these days it's run by a private firm. Military buildings from the 1950s are wedged between the village street and the church.

St Kilda is now owned by the National Trust for Scotland. There are two National Trust wardens and in the summer volunteer work parties come to maintain the buildings. There's a resident archaeologist.

Britain's largest colony of puffins breeds here, those small black-and-white seabirds with bright stripy bills. But this year there were live chicks in only a quarter of their nests. Puffins live on sand eels and, because of changing sea temperatures, these have vanished.

That ship wallowing in the bay was a small cruise liner. Weather permitting, smaller boats make frequent crossings to the mainland. A century on, St Kilda has become a chic destination once again. Neil Mitchell, one of the wardens, told me there were 15,000 visitors last year. Recently he found the first piece of litter: a plastic water bottle wedged between the stones of a wall.

85

Sunday on the Isle of Lewis

Michael Buchanan

A quiet Sunday used to be guaranteed on the Scottish Isle of Lewis. The Sabbath had long been observed as a day of rest by the islanders, but times were changing. (17 June 2006)

I come from a small island of approximately 1,200 people in the Outer Hebrides of Scotland. Barra is five hours by ferry from the Scottish mainland. It's at the southern end of a string of islands jutting out of the Atlantic Ocean off the north-west coast of the United Kingdom. To me it's a stunning little paradise of white sandy beaches, small sheltered bays and stupendous views, but I accept that I might not be the most objective of commentators.

Its small population meant that when I lived there, the local school could only educate me until I was sixteen years old. In order to gain the necessary qualifications to get into university, I had to go to the largest of the islands, Lewis, to the Nicolson Institute, the main school in the town of Stornoway.

The Niccy, as we called it, was a culture shock. Firstly, the number of pupils there was greater than the entire population of Barra. And secondly, the overwhelming majority of them were Protestant, mainly Free Church of Scotland. Now that in itself didn't matter, though I'm a Catholic from a Catholic-dominated island. It did, however, mean that my Sundays changed.

While previously I'd have gone to mass in the morning before going out to play football in the afternoon and maybe visit some friends in the evening, in Stornoway, Sunday—or the Sabbath— was a day of rest. That didn't simply mean that the shops were closed. It meant that bars and restaurants didn't open, that children's playgrounds were padlocked shut, and that being seen outside was frowned upon. It meant there was no way on or off the island on Sunday, as neither planes nor ferries moved. It meant that Lewis was off-limits for anything other than going to church. And every Sunday that's what people did. They put on their best suits, usually black for the men and merely dark for the hat-wearing women, and went to church twice a day. There they'd hear a strict interpretation of the Bible, often including the justification for the quiet Sabbath: the fourth commandment, which states that Sunday should be a day of rest.

At first, this was difficult to take. Bright, warm Sundays were wasted watching rubbish on television or worse still doing homework. The sense of being locked up was stifling at times, leading to petty arguments with the other two guys who shared my lodgings. But within months I began to appreciate the change in pace, the knowledge that for one day a week I didn't have to do anything, and well before my two-year stint in Lewis was up, I'd grown to respect the deeply held beliefs of the islanders.

So when after almost a decade away from the island I drove towards Stornoway one Sunday morning recently, everything looked very familiar. The occupiers of the few cars on the roads were wearing recognisable, church-attending attire. I checked in to my guest house and asked where I could get some lunch. To my surprise the landlady said there were two places I could go. The restaurant, a bright bistro-style eatery, was not only open, it was quite busy. Though tourists appeared to be in the majority, the melodic accents of some other diners showed that many local families had come out for some Sunday lunch as well.

After a sandwich and salad, I headed out for a walk, the sunshine glistening off the calm blue waters of the port. Though virtually every shop was closed, Stornoway was no longer the quiet retreat I remembered. A petrol station and grocery store opened for several hours and though the car ferry stays firmly tied to the pier, there are now three flights to the mainland on Sundays. There were far more cars on the roads, far more people walking in the nearby woods.

For dinner that night, I went to a café bar that's recently opened. I had to wait half an hour for a table, they were that busy. One of the teenage waitresses told me that around half the clientele were locals. When I asked what her parents thought of her working on a Sunday, she said it wasn't an issue.

A friend who's lived through all the changes says that though the number of people who attend church remains higher in Lewis than in most of the UK, it has clearly declined and that the pressures of the 24/7 society are becoming as evident in the Outer Hebrides as they are in London or New York. With that thought, I went to see Andrew

Coghill, a minister in the Church of Scotland and a leading member of the Lord's Day Observance Society, a pressure group that aims to keep Sunday holy. He agreed that changes were afoot, but vowed to continue to resist efforts at secularisation. 'There is something very special about the Hebridean Sabbath,' he said in a quiet, calm voice, 'and if that is lost it would be a tragedy.' As I left him, the stillness of the morning was broken only by the sound of the singing birds.

86

The Power of Evangelism

Justin Webb

Religious belief always has been an important part of American life, but a lively, sometimes bitter, debate was under way about whether religion had seeped into parts of the nation which should remain secular. (7 May 2005)

From the air, Mississippi has the colour and texture of fresh broccoli. At a distance the trees look tightly coiled; rich green in the sunlight, purple patches in the shade. Mississippi is home to millions of trees and not many millions of people. It is a verdant, sweaty place. As your plane comes down to land there are glints all around of sunlight on still water, meandering rivers, reservoirs and swamps, where the line between the still brown liquid and the vegetation is blurred. The state is

326

mostly rural and poor, shacks and mobile homes nestling under the canopy of the forest, rusting pick-up trucks bouncing down dirt roads.

And churches, everywhere churches: pristine Catholic cathedrals with long pointy towers—cool and confident-looking with wide lawns and copious car parks; Baptist houses of worship, with those vaguely threatening messages on billboards outside: 'Jesus is coming—where are you going?' And in the denser undergrowth, the deeper heart of the state, tiny little brick buildings—some not much bigger than a garage. There are more churches per head of population in Mississippi than in any other state, and historically, you could argue, more racial prejudice, more un-Christian behaviour.

I came to Mississippi assuming, in a European secular sort of way, that holy scripture—which once led Mississippi whites down the road of bigotry, was unlikely to be the state's saviour today. On the radio the so-called family Christian station was explaining why God invented women and the devil invented feminism. So far, so predictable. But a visit to Mississippi in 2005 provides a reminder that while religion has motivated all manner of charlatans and creeps in American life and still does, it is also the primary motivation for many of those who genuinely do good and are not collecting money or condemning other people's vice. In a nation without anything but the most basic social services, without a national health service, many of those picking up the pieces are religious, often fundamentalist Christians. To be sure, the president has encouraged this trend; but in Mississippi I didn't get the impression that they needed much encouragement from far-off Washington.

I went to a prison housing the most dangerous young offenders, considered so beyond the pale that they are being tried as adults. The American penal system is brutal—the sentences are long and the conditions harsh. I had been invited to this place by Dr John Perkins, a renowned black prison visitor, a man who brings Bibles and talks to the kids about the lives they might one day lead. I assumed we would be treated with icy courtesy by the whites who run the place. But I got it all wrong. We'd been inside for two minutes when a request, an order, came that we were to lunch with the sheriff, the man in charge. He was a redneck straight out of central casting, huge and menacing. Then suddenly, as giggly as a schoolgirl, he hugged Dr Perkins and thanked Jesus Christ for the food. Over lunch he told their story, of a meeting at a prayer breakfast which led to an invitation for Dr Perkins to visit the jail. A couple of highly motivated evangelical Christians have built a personal relationship unthinkable in even the recent past and are now significantly improving the lives of mainly black sixteen- and seventeen-year-old murderers and rapists, people the rest of the nation is happy to lock up and forget.

This was surprise enough, but there was more to come. We were introduced to Cynthia Cockerne, an elderly frail white woman who has been running the rudimentary prison education effort. She was a person of quite extraordinary cheery religious fervour, in almost every sentence referring to the Lord. She and Dr Perkins did their stuff with the kids, and when we said our goodbyes Dr Perkins walked out with me and announced casually: 'That woman is a saint, and to think that her great-uncle killed my brother.' It was a racist killing, unpunished as they all were in those days in these parts, which this elderly couple had only realised linked them when they chatted recently about places where they had lived and events they had witnessed. They are reconciled now and working hard to make life better in modern Mississippi.

I think the so-called Christian right has overplayed its political hand in George Bush's America, but the power of evangelism at the grass roots is still huge. The televangelists and the religious fire-and-brimstone politicians come and go, but Dr Perkins, Mrs Cockerne and the sheriff are a mighty engine and they'll still be hard at work long after Mr Bush has gone.

87

The Jungarian Gate

Ian MacWilliam

The borderland between China and the Central Asian republic of Kazakhstan is an area seldom visited by outsiders. But this long frontier, nearly a thousand miles from north to south, used to be one of the most heavily guarded Cold War borders, separating the Soviet Union from Communist China. Before that it had seen the comings and goings of countless tribes and peoples passing back and forth across the vast Central Asian steppe. (7 June 2007)

The Jungarian Gate isn't a gate at all. This little-known geographical feature is a narrow gap in the mountains which divide the vast Eurasian steppe in two. The steppe is an ocean of grassland which stretches from Turkey to Mongolia. Cutting through the middle, along the modern Kazakh-Chinese border, are three mountain ranges: the Altai, the Jungar Alatau and the Tien Shan. They've blocked the movement of the nomadic Turks and Mongols who have always roamed freely across this grassy sea. The Jungarian Gate is the most important of the gaps which penetrate the mountainous ridge. Through this narrow gateway a few miles wide, nomadic tribes, Silk Road merchants, outlaws and invaders have passed through the centuries.

I set off from Kazakhstan's largest city, Almaty, to visit the Jungarian Gate, travelling north by buses and taxis until the blue haze of the Jungar Alatau mountains resolved itself into snow-capped peaks and ridges. I was following in the footsteps of Stephen Graham, a remarkable English journalist who walked alone through this borderland in 1916, sleeping by the roadside and chatting with nomadic Kazakhs and Russian settlers as he went. His lyrical account of his travels is full of vivid descriptions of the endless blue skies, the rolling golden grasslands and the wildflowers which carpet the foothills during the lovely Central Asian spring: crimson poppies, delphiniums, purple larkspur, cranesbill, grass of Parnassus and Siberian iris.

I took a rough road into the foothills to the secluded valley of Lepsinsk, an area settled by Russian Cossacks from Siberia in the late nineteenth century. This once-thriving town has dwindled now to a quiet village. I stayed in the log house of Sabir, a local Tatar who wants the valley to become a destination for ecologically minded tourists to hike in the hills and watch the wild birds, to see honey being made and wonder at the emerald green waters of the high mountain lake of Jasi Kul.

Sabir's brother, Rashid, had just moved back from Almaty to help him in the tourism business. After a divorce and some restless years in the big city, Rashid told me he needed to come home to his roots, to a life close to nature and the wide skies. But enticing tourists to Lepsinsk hasn't been easy. The valley lies only twenty miles from the Chinese border. 'The border guards still have a Soviet mentality,' Sabir told me. 'They don't like to give permits to foreign visitors to come here.'

The 'Yellow Peril', as the Kazakhs see it, is still a lively concern here on the border. But if the Soviets feared Communist China, the Central Asians today fear capitalist China. The Kazakhs are keenly aware of their 1.3 billion neighbours to the east. Chinese businessmen are already active in the big city markets and here they still remember those earlier invaders who came from China through the Jungarian Gate.

From Lepsinsk, I found a taxi to continue my journey due east. Six camels appeared suddenly on the road, huge two-humped Bactrians which looked down their noses at our little taxi. Behind came a dozen horses and a flock of goats and fat-tailed sheep, then four mounted men dressed in thick sheepskins and big hats. 'We spent the winter there under the mountains,' the leader told me,

331

'but now we're taking our animals to the spring pastures.'

The taxi driver looked towards the mountain ridge. 'I was born over there in a yurt—you know, a tent—fifty years ago,' he said.

We juddered further along the potholed road. The wind became stronger and colder. A constant wind blows here out of China, known as the Yevgeh. Fearful tales tell of people freezing to death from its effects.

At last a notch appeared in the blue mountains ahead, the Jungarian Gate. We came suddenly to a deep ravine where a river crossed and the road plunged down into snowdrifts. Two horses were tied up near a concrete bunker, their rumps turned to the wind. A wild-looking Kazakh in a huge fur hat poked his head out, leapt on to one of the horses and thundered off across the plain to round up some distant cattle. Genghis Khan and Tamerlane had once done much the same. In their youth, both world conquerors lived as outlaws in the steppe until they became two of the most powerful and bloodthirsty men in history. But that was in an earlier age when the nomads of the steppe were still a force to be reckoned with, bursting forth from time to time to change the course of history.

I looked into the distance, through the mountain gap where the first glimmer of China was just visible. And who knows, with the rise of China and the revival of trade along the old Silk Road, perhaps the Jungarian Gate will come into its own once more, a vital transit point on the high road from China to Europe.

88

From Sussex to the Wakhan

Alastair Leithead

Foreign troops were continuing to battle a Taliban determined to regain control of Afghanistan. One corner of the country untouched by the violence was the Wakhan corridor in the north-east, a region sandwiched between Tajikistan, Pakistan and China. Up there in the mountains, a British doctor was trying to educate local people in health matters.
(8 September 2007)

Slowly but sure-footedly the yak picked its way up along the narrow mountain track, snorting with every step under the weight of the bags strapped to its sides. On its back, slumped, sleeping among carpets and blankets, lay a small, blonde two-year-old girl, soothed by the rhythmic swaying of the yak and the lilting song of the man with the deeply weathered face who led it by a rope, step by step up the steep side of the mountain.

We had left behind the rushing sound of river rapids in the valley bottom as we climbed higher and higher through thinning air. Towering above us, a sharp, sculptured peak with its blue glaciers glistening in the sun, 7,000 metres above sea level. On this side, the Hindu Kush mountains, just a couple of days' walk to Pakistan; on the other, the Pamirs, the home of the Kyrgyz nomads, with passes into Tajikistan and China. We were on a day trip up to a high meadow with the Duncan family from England. Mum, Dad and four children, a kite, three yaks and a lunch of mutton and rice laid out on a vast picnic space of Afghan carpets. A family holiday in the hills and a long, long way from the fighting, the kidnapping and the killing that dominates most of the reporting from Afghanistan.

It's a two-day drive from the nearest airstrip to reach this remote part of the country. The memorably named Wakhi people of the Wakhan corridor are desperately poor. Surviving one year to the next depends on what happens in the next couple of weeks as they bring in the harvest and hope winter doesn't come early. If it does, the crops are ruined and they have to survive on wild plants foraged from the hillsides, or making bread from animal fodder which contains poisons that can paralyse or cause brain damage. So everyone is busy in the fields, cutting the crops and laying them out to be threshed under the hooves of donkeys roped together, chased and whipped to trample the crop in a circle to separate the wheat from the chaff.

In the small mud homes the women dressed in bright red and purple fabrics, unusually for Afghanistan with their faces uncovered, sieve the grains down even further to be stored in sacks. But even with a good harvest there isn't enough and families are hungry by the spring. Before help came, a third of the children born here died before the age of two, and many women die in childbirth. But there is one thing the Wakhi people have that's almost unique in Afghanistan: peace. This finger of land poking out into China is a strange,

334

neglected Afghan backwater. It's too far away for the Taliban to stir up trouble or for bandits to find anything of value to steal.

And it's a backwater that the Duncans have called home for four years now. The winters are long and a perishing minus 25 degrees Celsius, when the steep valley sides limit the day's sunshine to five hours or less and merely surviving takes up most of the time. Dr Alex Duncan comes from the English county of Sussex, but he and his wife Eleanor now live the most sparse existence doing their bit to stop children dying and to teach people who have never been to a clinic how to look after themselves. They have no running water, a pit-latrine in the garden, and wind turbines and solar panels which save enough power during the day to light their one-room mud and wood-beamed house at night. Lessons at home start early for the children, who are eight, six, three and two. Dinner is usually flatbread and a bit of salad from the garden, local yoghurt, or, when the opportunity arises, a bit of meat and rice. A few luxuries brought in by lorry once a year keep them going, but they have no beds: the living room becomes the dining room becomes the bedroom, and each night the family cuddles up under a pile of blankets and duvets.

It seems a crazy way to live with a young family, but, thanks to the Duncans, who live modestly and have taken the trouble to understand cultural quirks and taboos, fewer local children are now dying. Billions of pounds in aid money are thrown at Afghanistan every year, but so little of it reaches the parts that need it most. The government is still struggling to govern. This country's problems will take decades to resolve, but really getting to know the place and its people seems a good way of making an impact.

And who knows, it could one day bring the kind of peace and stability that allows yak-riding holidays in the Afghan hills.

89

Rescued in the Caucasus

Jonathan Fryer

Sometimes it's only when things go disastrously wrong that a foreign correspondent gets to know what a country and its people are really like.
(2 December 2006)

Outside the historical museum in Sisian, in southern Armenia, a small flock of sheep, carved in stone, seems to be grazing under the trees. These are not postmodern artworks, like the concrete cows in the fields around Milton Keynes, but old Christian gravestones, rescued from derelict churches in the surrounding province. In the grey light of dawn, there is something quite sinister about them. But then, Sisian as a whole is a pretty gloomy place scarred, like so many towns in Armenia, with empty industrial plants and abandoned storage yards which closed when the Soviet Union fell apart.

It was therefore quite a relief to be heading out of town and up into the mountains to visit a famous monastery. The landscape is majestically wild: barren and inhospitable. Some of the roads are in a shocking state of disrepair. But I'd started feeling queasy even before the bone-shaking ride. I hadn't slept the night before, in the box-like but friendly guest house in Sisian. And I hadn't been able to face breakfast: I was finding it difficult to breathe, and all energy had drained away from me. I must have been allergic to the mattress stuffed with lambswool, I concluded. But by the time the driver stopped outside an old caravanserai, or travellers' inn, at a mountain pass nearly 3,000 metres up, I'd lost the ability to stand. I lay down on a stone bench, but when I tried to get up again, I simply rolled on to the ground.

'I am taking you to hospital,' the driver declared. 'Oh, I'm sure that's not necessary,' I mumbled, in that very British way of not wanting to make a fuss. Wisely, he ignored me. And down the other side of the pass we drove, towards Lake Sevan. By the time we reached the little town of Martuni, I was barely lucid. But I was *compos mentis* enough to make out the sign over the door of the decaying block we entered: 'Martuni Mental Hospital'. There was no one in the corridors, with their cracked and stained walls. But an Armenian companion managed to locate a doctor, and I was steered into the local equivalent of the accident and emergency department. A mask was slapped on to my face and hooked up to an oxygen tank that looked like a Second World War bombshell. Needles were inserted into the veins of both hands, as steroids and other medication were pumped into me to counter what was assumed to be an asthma crisis.

A few hours later an ambulance arrived, all the way from the capital, Yerevan, over a hundred miles away, to transfer me to a modern facility there. The entire Martuni Mental Hospital staff turned out to watch me being hoisted into the vehicle, still attached to two drips and with an oxygen feed in both nostrils. I was a little disconcerted to discover that the tiny, wizened old man who'd been standing to one side was the ambulance driver. Once behind the wheel, however, he was a demon of racetrack skill and aggressiveness. Lights flashing, sirens wailing, we careened at breakneck speed through the countryside. Any car that didn't instantly swerve out of the way was greeted with a choice Armenian insult over the vehicle's loudspeakers from the demon driver, such as: 'Do you think with your head, or with what?'

The two paramedics in the back with me—one male, one female—each held on to one of my hands. They kept up a non-stop commentary which stretched their basic English and my schoolboy Russian. I realised later that they'd been instructed not to let me lose consciousness. But at the time my mind struggled to follow, let alone appreciate, the string of bawdy jokes they regaled me with. At one moment, when I did seem to be drifting off, the male paramedic dramatically slid open a side window of the ambulance, letting in an icy blast of air. 'Look,' he said, in the tone of an enthusiastic tour guide, 'Lake Sevan! One of the prides of Armenia!' And indeed there it was, beautiful in the setting sun, a huge expanse of water with swirling skies above it. 'You'll be all right,' the woman paramedic said, patting my head. 'She wants to marry you,' her companion announced, to guffaws from the demon driver. 'Rubbish ambulance,' her voluble colleague continued. 'Russian. You have Mercedes ambulance in England, yes?'

To be honest, I didn't notice what make of ambulance it was that took me to the hospital when I was flown back to London two days later, to be diagnosed with and treated for pernicious pneumonia in both lungs. I then enjoyed all the benefits of modern drugs and intensive medical care. But I will never forget that it was the quick thinking and extraordinary human warmth of strangers in one of the remotest parts of the Caucasus which saved my life.

90

Hospital in Kabul

Emma Jane Kirby

*After years of civil war, rebuilding was proceeding at a snail's pace in Afghanistan; and hospitals were in a desperate state, with many doctors and nurses having left the country to seek work abroad. Nilab Mobarez, a surgeon who had left Afghanistan thirteen years earlier to work in a clinic in Paris, went back to Kabul to visit the hospital where she used to work.
(6 April 2002)*

A thick, oppressive dust hangs perpetually over Kabul and a film of dirt has crept into every street and smothered every building. But when Nilab suggested we should check out her old hospital, I was naively hoping that the word 'clinic', especially 'chest clinic', would have to offer some sort of reprieve or exemption from the grime of the city outside—although of course, the dust had got there long before us.

There was no electricity in the hospital, so even at midday the corridors were suffused in a dingy, dusky light. Women in dirty burkhas huddled side by side on the stone floors groaning lethargically, and outside the intensive-care ward an old man with an unravelled turban had built a tiny campfire and was stirring a muddy, brown stew with a piece of wood. 'That's the hospital kitchen,' said Nilab in a voice heavy with irony. 'And the women are crying because they can't afford the prices, which means their families in the wards here won't get fed today.'

A filthy curtain separated the intensive-care ward from the rest of the hospital, and inside, four rusty iron beds had been crammed into a tiny space. The air was heavy with the maddening dust and each patient was wheezing erratically, fighting with every breath against its clogging, stifling weight. I felt as if I was trapped inside someone's asthma attack.

Abdul, a young doctor who had qualified under the Taliban, was listening to an elderly man's chest. The old man was coughing pathetically and staring at us with dull eyes. 'He's had a heart attack,' explained Abdul. 'He needs oxygen urgently, but'—he shifted uncomfortably—'we don't have any oxygen so we're going to try to move his bed nearer the window.'

Nilab began to quiz Abdul about his training

340

and about the other patients in the ward. Again he looked embarrassed. 'This boy,' he said, pointing to a listless child lying on an uncovered mattress, 'has rheumatic fever. He also has stomach pains— maybe appendicitis—but I don't know what to do for him. Under the Taliban, medical students weren't allowed to take part in dissection classes, so I've only ever taken out an appendix from a plastic doll.'

Until this moment, Nilab had seemed to have taken everything in her stride. Now she became visibly angry and demanded to be taken to the operating theatre. Abdul walked with us, head down, muttering: 'I'm sorry. Really, I'm so sorry.'

The operating theatre looked as if it had taken a direct hit, although in twenty-three years of war, no bomb had ever touched this hospital. The sheet of dust that covers the whole of Kabul had taken on a different quality in here, clinging to the sticky residues of iodine and cleaning fluid until it had become a thick black soot. Everything was broken; wires hung from the walls, the glass from the operating lamp crunched under our feet and tiles lay in pieces on the floor, persuaded off the walls by a persistent damp which made the room smell sour and fusty. On the filthy pillow of the operating table, a few needles were wrapped in a dirty piece of green rag. Someone had marked the rag with the ludicrous lie 'Sterile'.

It was the first time I'd seen Nilab cry. 'How has this happened?' she asked me. 'This isn't an operating theatre; this is just a place to catch infections.' She turned over a packet of bandages in her hand which were marked 'Use by June '97' and moved to a long cupboard in front of us. 'Each

341

time I operated, I would take my white coat from in here,' she said. She grasped the cupboard handle and the door promptly fell off.

A team of nurses and doctors in off-white coats had gathered at the door of the operating theatre and their eyes were searching Nilab with anticipation. In her well-tailored Chanel suit and with her thirteen years of experience doctoring in a plush Western hospital, Nilab was, for them, the fairy godmother who could turn all of this around. But I knew that the bootload of medical supplies that were sitting in our car couldn't even scratch the surface of this hospital's problems. I watched her take a notebook from her handbag and begin a list. 'No.1,' she wrote in a determined hand. 'Buy trowel and cement and stick tiles back on wall.'

I left Nilab writing and wandered downstairs to the hospital pharmacy. Three men in anoraks were sitting on broken wooden crates sharing a mug of tea. One of them got up when he saw me and offered me his box, wiping away the dust with his sleeve. I asked him if he was the chemist and he bowed proudly and said yes, he was, and yes, this was the Kabul Chest Hospital pharmacy.

There was of course nothing in it. Rows and rows of empty cupboards gaped hungrily and a few glass bottles with no stoppers collected dust, for want of anything better to do. The pharmacist answered my questions politely and informatively and without a single trace of self-pity. 'Yes, madame, it is very difficult for us, because as you see, we don't really have any medicines. Oh yes, madame, you're absolutely right, it's very hard to turn away the people who come here, but as we don't have so much as an aspirin to offer them, it's

342

probably better for them just to rest at home.'

I thanked the pharmacist for his interview and turned to go, switching off my tape recorder. 'Please, madame,' he said, without breaking his tone, 'I wondered whether I might ask you one question.' I was surprised but nodded curiously. 'I wonder,' he said quietly, looking at me with expectant eyes, 'I wonder if you could tell me: is anyone coming to help us?'

91

American Healthcare

Justin Webb

The question of healthcare was increasingly being debated in the United States, a country in which nine million children were not covered by health insurance and where more and more adults simply couldn't afford it. (27 January 2007)

It was the summer of 1981. Mrs Thatcher was only two years into her first term, Ronald Reagan only months into his. I was starting out as well: writing stories for the *Beaver* newspaper at the London School of Economics about students throwing eggs at government ministers and the iniquities of low-cost coach travel to Greece. I had arrived in London from a boarding school in the West Country and a black-and-white world had suddenly burst into colour.

My room-mate in our hall of residence was a

cheerful American with lively eyes and a vague resemblance to Bruce Springsteen, a resemblance of which he was enormously proud. Bo Nora was exotic: my friends at school had been called Patrick or Adrian and mostly hailed from Somerset. Bo came from Chicago and studied at the University of California; he was at the LSE for only a few months.

Bo and I never felt the slightest bit mortal. I remember us listening to a programme on the local London radio station where people with emotional problems would call in for counselling. We laughed. We had no problems. I said goodbye to Bo on Great Portland Street tube station and we stayed in touch for a few years. And then life took over and Bo Nora became a memory. I moved to Northern Ireland, back to London, to Brussels and here to America.

A few months ago, twenty-five years after that central London goodbye, I tracked Bo down. I found his e-mail address and sent him a message. His reply talked of marriage and career and children and then came these words: 'After several years of increasing physical difficulties, I saw a doctor in 1991 and was diagnosed with multiple sclerosis. I retired due to further disability and incapacity. Presently, I am spastic quadriplegic.'

I went to see Bo the other day in his home on the outskirts of Chicago; we had supper, Bo's eyes flashing with recognition as we talked about London and university and people we'd known. His wife fed him. Bo is not a bitter person—funny how happiness is wired into some people whatever life brings—but one subject genuinely pained him. Bo has health insurance, I presume provided by the law firm he worked for when he was diagnosed. This is good news for Bo, bad news for the insurance company. Bo is expensive and the insurers don't want him, and they make it obvious. Every year Bo gets a letter asking him if he is still ill. Someone has to fill in a form for him: yes, I am quadriplegic; no, no miracle appears to have happened.

He told me recently he had to have a minor procedure associated with the condition; the bill was $78,000 dollars—£40,000. In the end he paid only a small part of it himself, but of the various entities that chipped in—the state, the insurer, the hospital—you can bet that no one wanted to and everyone would have got out of it if they could. Americans who fall ill are cut no slack: a society which expects everyone to pay their way expects it of them as well. As a jolly man selling life insurance pointed out to me the other day, most personal bankruptcies in the United States are the result of illness.

The story of American healthcare is one of huge expenditure for little obvious benefit. By head of population, America spends twice the amount Britain does on health. But life expectancy here is lower and infant mortality is higher, way higher in some ethnic groups. Most of the money seems to go on overheads and on profits for the many private companies providing care: the hospital groups, the drug manufacturers and above all the insurance companies who write letters to Bo enquiring about his MS and write incessantly to all their other customers as well—endlessly negotiating, fussing, harassing.

As the costs spiral upwards and private

employers ditch their healthcare schemes to stave off bankruptcy, increasing numbers of Americans have reduced their health insurance to the barest minimum and when something goes wrong they are dependent on the back-up provided by the state. So in a nation where socialised medicine is a phrase to be spat out contemptuously, Americans are on course by the year 2050 to spend every cent the government takes in tax on health-related claims. Nothing left even for the tiniest war.

For the time being Bo Nora will go on getting his annual letter, but all of America is cottoning on to what Bo has known for years: there must be a better way of looking after sick Americans. If Iraq is eventually resolved, the issue waiting next in line for the president, or more likely for his successors, is restoring health to American healthcare.

92

A Desert Exorcism

Frank Gardner

One of the most secretive rituals in the Arab world is the zar, the ceremonial exorcism of evil spirits from the body. When someone is believed to be suffering from a curse, the tribe gathers to summon a jinn, or genie as it is known in the West, to drive out the bad spirit. (3 May 1997)

When the offer came to attend a Bedouin exorcism I had mixed feelings. The last time I went to one of

346

these things a hyperventilating Sudanese woman threw an axe through the air, and it missed my head by centimetres. This time, I was assured, there would be no such violence. Yet my guide and cameraman strongly advised against going. We were deep in the Wahiba Sands, Oman's largest desert of dunes, and despite his university education and Western habits he shared his fears that desert spirits, once summoned, cannot be controlled.

Tonight we would visit a neighbouring tribe. Three of their women were suffering from a mysterious affliction. They wouldn't talk, they wouldn't eat, said the tribesmen squatting beside me. Only by calling on the *jinn* to enter the women's bodies could they be cured, I was told.

So off we set, jolting across a moonlit desert in a jeep that creaked and wheezed with old age and poor maintenance. I gripped the door frame as we side-slipped through deep sand, then swerved to avoid the thorn bushes that loomed ghost-like from the night. How the Bedu ever find their way through the desert at night is a mystery to me. To my cosseted, urban mind, each bush looked identical to the last. This was surely a desert without landmarks.

But I was in good hands. The engine coughed, the brakes squealed and we drew up at a large, plywood hut surrounded by miles of empty desert. A dozen pick-up trucks were parked haphazardly outside, as if abandoned in a hurry. Khaled, the driver, beckoned me inside and involuntarily I found myself taking a deep breath.

Adjusting my eyes to the sudden darkness, I tripped over almost at once. A turbaned form

347

shifted and grunted below me as I looked round the room. In the dim light of a paraffin lamp I made out forty or so seated human figures, the men in mauve robes lining the walls, the women covered completely in loose, patterned veils in a corner. The air was thick with the smoke of frankincense that coiled upwards from the incense-burners and at first it was hard to breathe.

Against a wooden pillar sat a huddled figure, as stiff and as lifeless as a mummy, its head bent back, its eyes staring up. Only when the drumming began did it give any indication of life. The figure emitted a croak, then started to sing in a thin, constricted voice. 'This man,' whispered the Bedu beside me, 'is a very big man. He is the sheikh of all our tribe.' The sheikh had a face like the Turin shroud, but it was the drums that caught my attention. Massive and booming, they lay balanced across three men's knees as they beat out a synchronised rhythm, summoning the *jinn*.

The entrancing, mesmerising beat filled the room like a living thing while everyone sat deathly still. I flinched. As if at some hidden signal, a shape detached itself from the women's corner and hurled itself, screaming, across the bare earth floor. With pulsing, regular convulsions this amorphous form bobbed and swayed while the drums beat faster. Another figure joined it, then another, the three women rocking violently from side to side on their knees. Now, I was told, the *jinn* had entered their bodies and taken over their minds and their movements. They knew nothing of their actions and afterwards they would only remember entering the hut, nothing more.

The drummers were chanting now, their voices

rising and falling in a strange, unfamiliar chorus. A woman stood up behind one of the trembling forms and held her veil above her while she moved. It was a special shawl which is brought out only for an exorcism. In the half-light of the paraffin lamp, in the choking, smoky atmosphere, I could have sworn that the cloth was moving by itself, as if possessed by some demonic force. I edged away from the circle, suddenly keen to distance myself. Abruptly the drumming stopped. With a gasp of expelled air, the woman who had first leapt to her feet collapsed across the knees of the sheikh, her frail body exhausted, the *jinn* departed. With a shock, I saw that she was old and withered, yet when the spirit gripped her body she had flung herself about like a teenager at a rave.

People coughed, someone lit a cigarette and a murmur of conversation dispelled the lingering sense of magic that filled that room. Outside, through the open door of the hut, the full moon shone like daylight, painting the desert with an unnatural silver wash. A man appeared at the doorway, his loose robes flapping in the soft breeze; then he was gone.

The ceremony was over: it was time to depart. I rose stiffly, my joints creaking after squatting cross-legged for so long. Curious eyes followed me to the door, as if surprised that a stranger had been allowed to witness this secret ritual. As we drove back to the camp I stuck my head out of the window, filling my face with fresh air, tying to make sense of what I had seen. Khaled turned to me, his face serene. 'The women are cured,' he said. 'The *jinn* have done their work.'

93

Starting from Scratch Again

Peter Biles

Somalia, in the Horn of Africa, was thrown into renewed turmoil following the eviction from Mogadishu of the Islamist forces who'd controlled the capital for the previous six months. Somalia had been without a functioning government for sixteen years and was living up to its reputation as a 'failed state'. (6 January 2007)

Mogadishu International Airport hasn't been used much over the last ten years, but let's just imagine what it's like flying in. The plane approaches from the south, descending quickly over the Indian Ocean. The end of the runway juts out towards the sea and it's hard to get a glimpse of much more than the large red sand dunes and the turquoise-coloured water breaking on the rocks. At first glance, it can look like a tropical paradise. But Mogadishu has never been for the faint-hearted. Since 1991, when an ageing dictator by the name of General Mohamed Siad Barre was overthrown, Somalia has been one of the most dangerous places on earth.

A few months after Siad Barre fled, I was in Mogadishu talking to a friend—a Somali doctor, Hussein Mursal, who worked for a British relief agency. Clan fighting had broken out in the city. Members of Mursal's own family had been shot and wounded when looters came to the house to pillage. I asked Mursal how long he thought the conflict might last. Would it be weeks or months? 'Oh no,' he said, 'they're going to be locked into this for years to come.' He was right, of course.

This past fortnight, I've thought a lot about Somalia, as the news has filtered out. First, when it was confirmed that Ethiopian troops were inside the country, in support of Somalia's fledgling transitional government. Then with the announcement that the Union of Islamic Courts and its militia had abandoned Mogadishu with even more haste than Siad Barre did sixteen years ago this month. These past few days the Islamists have been on the run, boxed in against the Kenyan border in the south, pursued by the Ethiopians with their tanks and airpower, blocked by an American warship offshore and probably monitored from above by American satellites. This could be the end of the Islamists, or more ominously it could herald the start of a Taliban-style guerrilla war.

It's become a cliché to say that 'the troubles in Somalia threaten to spill over into the rest of the Horn of Africa'. But Ethiopia has quietly meddled in Somalia for years and now the visible presence of the Ethiopians is both provocative and dangerous. Foreign forces are not welcome. The Ethiopians know this, but they're also deeply fearful of an Islamist threat from within Somalia, and they're determined to crush it. And so far, the Ethiopians are pretty pleased with themselves. As a darling of the West, Ethiopia's prime minister, Meles Zenawi, has been able to get away with brutally putting down internal dissent in his own country and now moving thousands of troops into Somalia. A warmonger he may be, but Meles is on the side of Bush and Blair in the 'war on terror' and he is the most important leader in a rough neighbourhood.

So the Ethiopians are trying to fill the power vacuum in Mogadishu, for while the Somali government has international recognition, it has little power. Somalia's warlords will no doubt see this as a new window of opportunity, for they haven't gone away. In fact, some of them are members of the transitional government, including Hussein Aidid. He came to Somalia as an American Marine in 1993. When the Americans left, following the ill-fated 'Black Hawk Down' episode in which eighteen US soldiers were killed after the shooting down of two of their helicopters, Hussein Aidid stayed on and became a powerful faction leader. It was his father, the late General Mohamed Farah Aidid, who controlled large parts of Mogadishu in the early 90s and whom the United States tried, in vain, to capture.

I met General Aidid when he was at the height of his power. I always found him a little deranged and out of touch with reality. But he was certainly a man to be feared. I remember walking across the road one afternoon from the house where I was staying. Just as you might lean across the garden fence to talk to your neighbour, I wandered into the driveway opposite for a chat with some of Aidid's fighters. Astonishingly, they were busy welding a missile pod from a MiG fighter jet on to the back of a jeep, one of the so-called 'technicals'. Within minutes, they'd loaded it with rockets and test-fired a couple of them, which fizzed over the nearby rooftops and disappeared out to sea.

I mention all this because what strikes me most about the recent events in Somalia is how little anything has changed. In 1991, hopes of a brighter future faded quicker than the slogans that were daubed on the streets to celebrate the overthrow of the old dictatorship. Now, as then, Somalia is starting from scratch.

94

We Too Lived Here

Monica Whitlock

There is a city in Central Asia so secret that few have seen it. Kampyr-tepe in southern Uzbekistan was built by Alexander the Great several hundred years before the birth of Christ. But after falling into decline, it has been uninhabited for more than a thousand years. Since it was rediscovered a generation ago, it has been closed to the public because it stands in a sensitive and tightly guarded military zone, right on the Afghan border.
(17 April 2004)

The city perched on a high shelf of land cut into clay walls that dropped sheer into the plains below. Caught in the light of a winter afternoon, an entire city spread as far as we could see, the dun-coloured dust touched with gold. It was here that Alexander raised his capital more than 2,000 years ago—the furthest conquest, then, of the Greeks in Asia.

From our vantage point, we could see why. Far below, beneath a swirl of starlings, we could see the plains melt into those of Afghanistan, Alexander's route here from Persia. At our feet spread the whole of the south. There was not a sound but the birds flocking and turning across the precipice, wheeling and turning back.

The small houses were in the nearest part of the city. Square rooms opened on to a grid of narrow passages, criss-crossing to make streets. Stacks of pots and plates sat outside, as though the people of Kampyr-tepe had left the washing-up one evening after dinner; great round platters and bowls, made of the same ochre dust as the plain. At first we were amazed. Why had they not been taken off to some museum, dated, labelled—or stolen even? But the more we looked, we realised there were just so many that they were ordinary, simply part of the land. When two boys, hard and tough as men, drove their handful of sheep through the city, they did not waste a glance on the pots. Why would they? Foreigners, though, now that was interesting and they spent the rest of the day following shyly and smiling.

Kampyr-tepe was a fortified city in Alexander's time, and remains a military base to this day for a reason as old as the land: its special position at this crossing between Central and South Asia. It is patrolled by the army of modern Uzbekistan. Special permission to visit can only be granted by the government in Tashkent. The way in is through a military checkpoint, at the time specified. Turn up late and the soldiers will bar the way and you will never see Kampyr-tepe, just the plain around pitted with pillboxes and fenced with barbed wire.

The deep south of Central Asia has a special stillness and a scent of new bread from the intense sun beating on the straw that, mixed with mud, is the building material used a thousand years ago and now. It wears its past casually. Kampyr-tepe is just one of its treasures. There are sights here, in this quiet and private place, that almost anywhere in the world would have busloads of visitors trooping to and fro.

'You see that big pit there,' said an old farmer, Hamrah Baba, 'when I was a boy, we used to lower each other down there in turns, hanging on a rope. We did not think it was special. Then these men came from Tashkent and found all sorts of things. They found gold and those chessmen.' The gold was thirty-five kilos of solid gold jewellery, set with turquoises. The chess pieces may be the oldest on earth. The pit where Hamrah Baba used to play is in the citadel of Dalverzin-tepe, the capital of the Kushan empire, once one of the richest on the planet.

There are secrets buried with the past, long-dead secrets, and recent political secrets. One night in Soviet times, archaeologists got a call at their dig at a sunken palace right on the Afghan frontier by the River Amu, which some people call the Oxus. It was an urgent order from Moscow. 'Move fast,' they said. 'Get the stuff out. Now.' They dug as fast as they could, grabbing from the ground a frieze of marble musicians and a hoard of daggers, relics of an army that had once passed that way. They were right to feel that something was up. It was the winter of 1979 and a few days later, Soviet tanks rolled into Afghanistan, across the palace, crunching what was left.

355

Long before the Arabs came here with their new religion of Islam, Buddhist monks lived in Central Asia, the conduit through which Buddhism travelled from India to the East. The giant Buddha statues at Bamiyan in Afghanistan lay on the same road. They have been destroyed, but a wonderful sleeping Buddha, sixteen metres long, still lies peacefully in Tajikistan.

Near Kampyr-tepe we were invited to the site of a Buddhist lamasery, where the mendicant monks lived underground in a labyrinth to protect them from the terrible heat and cold of the plain. One could almost feel their soft steps in their sunken corridors, imagine them rinsing their begged rice at the stone bowl that still stands in their kitchen. They left no gardens, no orchards, no grand palaces. What they left was something simpler.

'They left some very special papers,' said our guide excitedly. 'We found them in sealed jars.'

'What did they say?' I asked.

'Oh, they said that we too lived here.'

Correspondents

PAUL ADAMS: BBC Diplomatic and Defence correspondent, formerly in Jerusalem.

NATALIA ANTELAVA: BBC correspondent in Central Asia.

BRIAN BARRON: Works throughout the world as a BBC News correspondent.

MARTIN BELL: Former BBC News correspondent and former MP.

OWEN BENNETT-JONES: A presenter for BBC World Service and former Islamabad correspondent.

PETER BILES: BBC correspondent in Africa.

MALCOLM BILLINGS: BBC World Service presenter and specialist in reporting archaeology.

ELIZABETH BLUNT: BBC correspondent in Africa.

CHRIS BOWLBY: BBC Current Affairs programme-maker and former correspondent in Europe.

MICHAEL BUCHANAN: BBC television and radio reporter.

KEVIN CONNOLLY: BBC correspondent in the United States, formerly based in Europe.

JAMES COOMARASAMY: BBC correspondent in the United States.

PETER DAY: BBC Business Editor and programme presenter.

LYSE DOUCET: BBC World Service presenter and correspondent.

MARK DOYLE: Africa specialist at BBC World Service, formerly a correspondent based in Ivory Coast.

DAVID EDMONDS: author and BBC World Service producer.

GAVIN ESLER: BBC television presenter and former Washington correspondent.

STEPHEN EVANS: presenter of programmes on BBC World Service and former North America Business correspondent.

CHRISTIAN FRASER: BBC correspondent based in Rome.

JONATHAN FRYER: author and broadcaster specialising in international affairs.

IMOGEN FOULKES: BBC correspondent in Switzerland.

FRANK GARDNER: BBC Security correspondent, formerly based in the Middle East.

MISHA GLENNY: author and former BBC correspondent in Central Europe.

CARRIE GRACIE: BBC television presenter and former Beijing correspondent.

DAMIAN GRAMMATICAS: BBC correspondent in Delhi, formerly in Moscow.

RICHARD HAMILTON: former BBC correspondent in Morocco.

ANDREW HARDING: BBC correspondent in South East Asia.

FRANCES HARRISON: BBC correspondent, formerly in Tehran.

PASCALE HARTER: former correspondent in Africa, now based in Spain.

CHARLES HAVILAND: BBC correspondent in Kathmandu.

HUMPHREY HAWKSLEY: author and BBC correspondent.

JONATHAN HEAD: BBC correspondent based in Bangkok.

CHRIS HOGG: BBC correspondent in Tokyo.

WILLIAM HORSLEY: former BBC correspondent in

358

Europe.

JAMES INGHAM: BBC correspondent in Caracas.

ALAN JOHNSTON: presenter of *From Our Own Correspondent* on the BBC World Service and former correspondent in Gaza.

FERGAL KEANE: BBC special correspondent.

BRIDGET KENDALL: BBC Diplomatic correspondent, formerly in Moscow.

EMMA JANE KIRBY: BBC correspondent, now based in Paris.

DANIEL LAK: BBC correspondent, formerly based in Nepal.

JOHN LAURENSON: Paris-based writer and broadcaster on international affairs.

BILL LAW: BBC Current Affairs programme-maker and reporter.

ALASTAIR LAWSON: BBC Asia specialist and former correspondent in Bangladesh.

ALASTAIR LEITHEAD: BBC correspondent in Kabul.

ARTYOM LISS: Moscow-based BBC producer.

ALLAN LITTLE: BBC correspondent, formerly in Paris.

SUE LLOYD-ROBERTS: BBC television programme-maker and reporter.

OANA LUNGESCU: BBC correspondent based in Brussels.

IAN MacWILLIAM: former BBC correspondent in Central Asia.

MARK MARDELL: BBC Europe Editor.

JULIAN MAY: BBC programme-maker.

JILL McGIVERING: BBC correspondent, formerly based in Delhi.

CHRIS MORRIS: BBC correspondent in Delhi.

JIM MUIR: BBC correspondent in the Middle East.

ADAM MYNOTT: BBC correspondent in East Africa.

ANDREW NORTH: former BBC correspondent in Baghdad.

HUGH O'SHAUGHNESSY: author and specialist in South American affairs.

MARTIN PLAUT: BBC Africa Editor.

MATTHEW PRICE: BBC correspondent in New York, formerly in the Middle East.

STEVE ROSENBERG: BBC correspondent in Berlin, formerly in Moscow.

WILL ROSS: BBC correspondent in Africa.

DANIEL SCHWEIMLER: BBC correspondent in South America, based in Buenos Aires.

DAVID SHUKMAN: BBC Environment correspondent.

JOHN SIMPSON: BBC World Affairs Editor.

NICK SQUIRES: Sydney-based journalist and writer.

JOHN SWEENEY: BBC television presenter and reporter.

HUGH SYKES: BBC radio and television correspondent.

NICK THORPE: BBC correspondent in Central Europe.

MARK TULLY: BBC presenter and former Delhi correspondent.

JUSTIN WEBB: BBC North America Editor.

HAMILTON WENDE: Johannesburg-based author and journalist.

TIM WHEWELL: BBC programme-maker, presenter and reporter.

ANDREW WHITEHEAD: former BBC correspondent in Delhi.

MONICA WHITLOCK: former BBC correspondent in Central Asia.

MARK WHITTAKER: BBC World Service presenter and reporter.

DAVID WILLEY: BBC correspondent in Rome.

DAVID WILLIS: BBC correspondent based in Los Angeles.

SIMON WINCHESTER: author and geologist now based in the United States.

RUPERT WINGFIELD-HAYES: BBC correspondent in Moscow, formerly in Beijing.

CAROLINE WYATT: BBC Defence correspondent, formerly based in Paris.